A
LIFE
OF
ONE'S
OWN

Also by Joanna Biggs

All Day Long: A Portrait of Britain at Work

A LIFE OF ONE'S OWN

NINE WOMEN WRITERS BEGIN AGAIN

JOANNA BIGGS

ecco
An Imprint of HarperCollins Publishers

Earlier versions of "Sylvia" and "Simone" appeared
in the *London Review of Books* (December 20, 2018,
and April 16, 2020, respectively).

A LIFE OF ONE'S OWN. Copyright © 2023 by Joanna Biggs.
All rights reserved. Printed in the United States of America.
No part of this book may be used or reproduced in any manner
whatsoever without written permission except in the case of brief
quotations embodied in critical articles and reviews. For information,
address HarperCollins Publishers, 195 Broadway, New York, NY 10007.

HarperCollins books may be purchased for educational,
business, or sales promotional use. For information,
please email the Special Markets Department at
SPsales@harpercollins.com.

Ecco® and HarperCollins® are trademarks of HarperCollins Publishers.

Originally published in Great Britain in 2023 by Weidenfeld & Nicolson,
an imprint of The Orion Publishing Group Ltd.

FIRST U.S. EDITION

Library of Congress Cataloging-in-Publication Data has been applied for.

ISBN 978-0-06-307310-4

23 24 25 26 27 LBC 5 4 3 2 1

For Devika, Frances, Lidija, Melanie,
Sam, and Željka, with love

Contents

Mary

Around the time I realized I didn't want to be married anymore, I started visiting Mary Wollstonecraft's grave. I'd known it was there, behind King's Cross railway station, for at least a decade. I had read her proto-feminist tract from 1792, *A Vindication of the Rights of Woman*, at university and I knew St. Pancras Churchyard was where Wollstonecraft's daughter, also Mary, had taken the married poet Percy Bysshe Shelley when they were falling in love. When I thought about the place, I thought of death and sex and possibility. I first visited at thirty-four, newly separated, on a cold gray day with a lover, daffodils rising around the squat cubic pillar: "MARY WOLLSTONECRAFT GODWIN," the stone reads, "Author of A Vindication of the Rights of Woman, Born 27th April 1759, Died 10th September 1797." I didn't tell him why I wanted to go there. I had a sense that Wollstonecraft would understand, and I often felt so lost that I didn't want to talk to real people, people I wanted to love me rather than pity me, people I didn't want to scare. I was often scared. I was frequently surprised by my emotions, the things I suddenly needed to do or say that surged up out of nowhere.

Unexpected events had brought me graveside: when I was

thirty-two, my fifty-seven-year-old mother was diagnosed with Alzheimer's. It wasn't genetic; no one knew why she got it. We would, the doctors said, have three to nine more years with her. Everything wobbled. This knowledge raised questions against every part of my life: was this worth it? And this? And *this*? I was heading for children in the suburbs with the husband I'd met at nineteen, but this life, the one that so many people want, I doubted was right for me. I was trying to find my way as a writer, but jumping from genre to genre, not working out what I most wanted to say, and not taking myself seriously enough to discover it, even. Who do you tell when you start to feel these things? Everything seemed immovable. Everything seemed impossible. And yet I knew I had to change my life.

There was a string of discussions with my husband, threading from morning argument to online chat to text to phone to therapy session to dinner, where we floated ideas about open marriage and relationship breaks and moving countries and changing careers and dirty weekends. But we couldn't agree on what was important, and I began to peel my life away from his. We decided that we could see other people. We were as honest and kind and open as we could manage while we did this, which sometimes wasn't much. The spring I began visiting Wollstonecraft's grave, he moved out, dismantling our bed by taking the mattress and leaving me with the frame. I took off my wedding ring—a gold band with half a line of "Morning Song" by Sylvia Plath etched inside—and for weeks afterward, my thumb would involuntarily reach across my palm for the warm bright circle that had gone. I didn't throw the ring into the long grass, like women do in the movies, but a feeling began bubbling up nevertheless, from my stomach to my throat: it could fling my arms out. I was free.

At first, I took my freedom as a seventeen-year-old might: hard and fast and negronied and wild. I was thirty-four and I wanted so much out of this new phase of my life: intense sexual attraction; soulmate-feeling love that would force my life into new shapes; work that felt joyous like play but meaningful like religion; friendships with women that were fusional and sisterly; talk with everyone and anyone about what was worth living for; books that felt like mountains to climb; attempts at writing fiction and poetry and memoir. I wanted to create a life I would be proud of, that I could stand behind. I didn't want to be ten years down the wrong path before I discovered once more that it was wrong.

While I was a girl, waiting for my life to begin, my mother gave me books: *The Mill on the Floss* when I was ill; *Ballet Shoes* when I demanded dance lessons; *A Little Princess* when I felt overlooked. How could I find the books I needed now? I had so many questions: could you be a feminist and be in love? Did the search for independence mean I would never be at home with anyone, anywhere? Was domesticity a trap? What was worth living for if you lost faith in the traditional goals of a woman's life? What was worth living for at all—what degree of unhappiness, lostness, chaos was bearable? Could I even do this without my mother beside me? Or approach any of these questions if she wasn't already fading from my life? And if I wanted to write about all this, how could I do it? What forms would I need? What genre could I be most truthful in? How would this not be seen as a problem of privilege, a childish demand for definition, narcissistic self-involvement when the world was burning? Wouldn't I be better off giving away all I have and putting down my books, my movies, my headphones, and my pen? When would I get sick of myself?

The questions felt urgent as well as overwhelming. At times I couldn't face the page—printed or blank—at all. I needed to remind myself that starting out on my own again halfway through life is possible, has been possible for others—and that this sort of life can have beauty in it. And so I went back to the writers I'd loved when I was younger—the poetry of Sylvia Plath, the thought of Simone de Beauvoir and Mary Wollstonecraft, the novels of Virginia Woolf and George Eliot. I read other writers—Elena Ferrante, Zora Neale Hurston, Toni Morrison—for the first time. I watched them try to answer some of the questions I had. This book bears the traces of their struggles as well as my own—and some of the things we all found that help. Not all of the solutions they (and I) found worked, and even when they did, they didn't work all of the time: if I'd thought life was a puzzle I could solve once and for all when I was younger, I couldn't believe that any longer. But the answers might come in time if I could only stay with the questions, as the lover who came with me to Wollstonecraft's grave would keep reminding me.

"I am then going to be the first of a new genus," Mary Wollstonecraft wrote to her younger sister Everina at the age of twenty-eight, having quit her job as a governess and made her way to London to write. Like so many of the women I turned to, Wollstonecraft was forced to make her life for herself, which she did over and over, which is why I thought to begin with her. "I tremble at the attempt yet if I fail—I *only* suffer—and should

I succeed, my dear Girls will ever in sickness have a home—and a refuge where for a few months in the year, they may forget the cares that disturb the rest." Wollstonecraft wasn't exactly boasting—she barely knew what sort of writer she was yet; she knew it was risky—but she was breaking a path. Wollstonecraft's life, then and now, is an argument and a provocation. She never thought that the book that made her famous, *A Vindication of the Rights of Woman*, was her best work, or even that it was particularly well written, but she knew that her life was different from most women's lives, and that this was special in itself. "This project has *long* floated in my mind," she ended her letter to Everina. "You know I am not born to tread in the beaten track—the peculiar bent of my nature pushes me on."

Mary Wollstonecraft was born in the spring of 1757 in Spitalfields, East London, the eldest girl in what became an unhappy family of seven. Her father, Edward John, was finishing a weaving apprenticeship; her mother, Elizabeth, was born in County Donegal and doted on her firstborn son as an escape from her marriage. (Neglected wives make the best mothers, Wollstonecraft would later argue.) Wollstonecraft remembers sleeping outside her parents' bedroom door as a girl so that she could intercede when her father went to hit her mother; she told her closest friend, Jane Arden, of his "violent temper." When Mary was six, her father inherited and moved the family to the North of England to become a gentleman farmer, losing nearly all the money in the attempt. When the Wollstonecrafts returned to London, Mary's liveliness drew the attention of a clergyman and his wife, who lent her Shakespeare and Milton, and it was through them that she met the first love of her life, Frances, or Fanny, Blood.

Meeting eighteen-year-old Fanny left an "indelible impression" on the sixteen-year-old Mary, William Godwin said in his posthumous account of his wife's life. Fanny sang, drew, and played. She was a little mother (as Mary was) to her siblings, although her own health was suffering. She wrote better letters than Mary, who, "abashed" at her spelling, rushed to catch up in order to write back more stylishly. "To live with this friend is the height of my ambition," Mary wrote to Jane. "She has a masculine understanding, and sound judgment, yet she has every feminine virtue."

Wollstonecraft escaped her family at twenty-three, taking a position she wasn't suited to as a companion to a lady in Bath. "I am particularly sick of genteel life," she wrote to Jane. There are no Austenesque ball scenes in Wollstonecraft's writing, but I like to think of her rolling her eyes at the edge of the cotillion. She felt pulled back home while her mother was dying in 1782 (the maternal last words—"A little patience, and all will be over!"—often turn up in her writing) and if she wasn't already de facto head of the family, this made her its matriarch. Soon after, Mary's youngest sister, Bess, gave birth to a girl. "Her mind is in a most unsettled state," Mary wrote to Everina from Bess's bedside. Something had to be done. "I can't stay and see this continual misery," Mary wrote, "and to leave her to bear it by herself without any one to comfort her is still more distressing—I would do anything to rescue her from her present situation." Mary began planning Bess's liberation: she would leave her husband (who "cannot behave properly," Mary said), and together the three sisters would set up a school in the North London village of Newington Green. "I am convinced this is the only expedient to save Bess." The legal consequences were severe: Bess's daughter belonged to her father by rights, and would have to be left behind. Mary wavered—normally happy to be single, now "I almost wish for a husband—For I want some body to support me"—but they did leave, changing coaches midway through the journey so as not to be followed, with Bess biting her wedding ring all the way. "The getting her out of his power is delightful," Mary wrote once they were safe. "I knew," she added, "I should be the *shameful incendiary* in this shocking affair of a woman's leaving her bed-fellow." The infant left behind, called Elizabeth after Wollstonecraft's mother, died before her first birthday. We know her father paid for a fine funeral. We know that later in life, Bess broke with her sister, and they were not reconciled by the time of Mary's death.

Mary did set up a school with her sisters, and she even roped in Fanny. They taught out of rooms in Islington and then in Newington Green (there is still a school there now, with a plaque remembering Mary). While living there, she went to hear the sermons of Richard Price, the republican minister of the Newington Green Unitarian Chapel, who had an international reputation as a radical. He had supported the Americans against his own country in the War of Independence, becoming friends with Thomas Jefferson, George Washington, and Benjamin Franklin, and he would go on to praise the French Revolution from the pulpit, sparking the pamphlet war in which Mary would make her name. The Wollstonecrafts' school was thriving, and Mary had even written a book, *Thoughts on the Education of Daughters*, but Fanny's health was failing: she left London for Lisbon, where her fiancé was living, hoping the warmer weather would help. "I much fear that he values her not for the qualities that render her dear to my heart," Mary wrote to Fanny's brother about the fiancé. "Her tenderness and delicacy is not even conceived by a man who would be satisfied with the *fondness* of common (I mean the general run) of women." I wonder if any man could be good enough for the women Mary herself loved.

Fanny didn't get better. On hearing she was close to death (and heavily pregnant), Mary left the school to go to Portugal and care for her friend. Fanny died in November 1785, days after giving birth to a boy. Six months later, Mary was grieving still, writing that Fanny had been "my best earthly comfort—and my poor heart still throbs with *selfish* anguish—it is formed for friendship and confidance—yet how often is it wounded—" The school in Newington Green foundered and Mary took a job as a governess to the family of Lord and Lady Kingsborough in Cork, where she was deeply valued. The children would run to Mary instead of to their own mother, and years later, the eldest girl still felt an "unbounded admiration" for her former governess. In Ireland, Mary spent her evenings writing a novel based on her experiences in Lisbon, and working out how to refuse Lady Kingsborough's poplin hand-me-downs. "I think now I hear her infantine lisp," Mary wrote to William Everina. "You cannot conceive my dear Girl the dissipated lives the women of quality lead." She was dismissed after a year, and returned to London. On her arrival, she went to the publisher Joseph Johnson, who had brought out her *Thoughts on the Education of Daughters*, and offered him her intellectual abilities. She could translate from French; review books for his journal, the *Analytical Review*; and write more of her own books. Johnson "assures me that if I exert my talents in writing I may support myself in a comfortable way," she wrote to Everina, continuing: "I am then to be the first of a new genus." She was twenty-eight.

Joseph Johnson was in his late forties, a long-term bachelor who may have been gay. (None of that stopped people saying he and Mary were married; she saw him "as the only person I am *intimate* with—I never had a father, or a brother—you have been both to me, ever since I knew you.") His success was built on his editions of the then popular poet William Cowper, but he was known for his radicalism: he also published *The Interesting Narrative of the Life of Olaudah Equiano* and illustrations by William Blake as well as translations of Condorcet, Madame Roland, Goethe, Schiller, and Herder. Johnson put Wollstonecraft up in a small house in Blackfriars, and she began reviewing for him (if he did "not like the manner in which I reviewed Dr. Johnson's sermon on his wife, be it known unto you—I will not do it any other way") and working on a book of stories for children. "Whenever I am tired of solitude," Mary wrote to Everina, "I go to Mr. Johnson's, and there I meet the kind of company *I* find most pleasure in." Over boiled cod and rice pudding, she might talk to Johnson's closest friend, Henry Fuseli, the painter—hung over the dining table was *The Nightmare* (1781), in which an incubus squats on a swooning woman's stomach—as well as dissenters she was in sympathy with such as Joseph Priestley or visiting radical superstars like Thomas Paine. It was at a dinner for Paine that Mary first met William Godwin: "The interview was not fortunate," Godwin remembered. Mary talked so much that he "heard her very frequently when I wished to hear Paine" and a year after the dinner they had made only a "very small degree of progress toward a cordial acquaintance." Women couldn't go to university, but at Johnson's table Mary could try out her voice, argue her views, and make friends. The dinners were a proving ground.

When Price gave a sermon arguing that the uprising in Paris in 1789 was the fulfillment of a prophecy, Edmund Burke, the leading conservative politician, attacked him in *Reflections on the Revolutions in France*. Mary was incensed and wrote her first political tract, *A Vindication of the Rights of Men*, in defense of her friend. She saw off Burke's arguments point by point. I wish to "shew you to yourself," she wrote, "stripped of the gorgeous drapery of which you enwrapped your tyrannic principles." Wollstonecraft stood against conservative thinking, against slavery, against England thinking itself a model nation, and for women being treated like human beings. From that publication she gained a fan, William Roscoe, a Liverpool merchant who commissioned the first portrait of her. (Godwin by contrast was "displeased" with the book, pointing out grammatical mistakes.) She wrote to Roscoe that better than her portrait is "a more faithful sketch—a book I am now writing, in which *I* myself, for I cannot *yet* attain to Homer's dignity, shall certainly appear, head and heart." The book was *A Vindication of the Rights of Woman*.

The *Vindication* was written in six weeks. On January 3, 1792, the day she gave the last sheet to the printer, Wollstonecraft wrote to Roscoe: "I am dissatisfied with myself for not having done justice to the subject.—Do not suspect me of false modesty—I mean to say that had I allowed myself more time I could have written a better book, in every sense of the word." Wollstonecraft isn't in fact being coy: her book isn't well made. Her main arguments about education are at the back, the middle is a sarcastic roasting of male conduct book writers in the style of her attack on Burke, and the parts about marriage and friendship are scattered throughout when they would have more impact in one place. There is a moralizing, bossy tone, noticeably when Wollstonecraft writes about the sorts of women she doesn't like (flirts and rich women: take a deep breath). It ends with a plea to men, in a faux-religious style that doesn't play to her strengths as a writer. In this, her book is like many landmark feminist books—*The Second Sex, The Feminine Mystique*—that are part essay, part argument, part memoir, held together by some force, it seems, attributable solely to their writers. It's as if these books, to be written at all, have to be brought into being by autodidacts who don't for sure know what they're doing—just that they have to do it.

On my first reading of the *Vindication* as a twenty-year-old undergraduate, I looked up the antique words and wrote down their definitions (to vindicate was to "argue by evidence or argument"). I followed Wollstonecraft's case for female education. I knew she'd been a teacher, and saw how reasonable her main argument was: that you had to educate women, because they have influence as mothers over infant men. I took these notes eighteen months into an undergraduate degree in English and French in the library of an Oxford college that had only admitted women twenty-one years before. I'd arrived from an ordinary school, had scraped by in my first-year exams, and barely felt I belonged. The idea that I could think of myself as an intellectual as Mary did was laughable. Yet halfway into my second year, I discovered early women's writing. I was amazed that there was so much of it—from proto-novelists such as Eliza Haywood, aristocratic poets like Lady Mary Wortley Montagu, and precursors of the Romantics like Anna Laetitia Barbauld— and I was angry, often, at the way they'd been forgotten—or, even worse, pushed out of the canon. Wollstonecraft stood out, as she'd never been forgotten, was patently unforgettable. I longed to keep up with her, even if I had to do it with the shorter *OED* at my elbow. I didn't see myself in her at the time. It wasn't clear to me when I was younger how hard she had pushed herself.

Later in her life, Wollstonecraft would defend her unlettered style to her more lettered husband:

> I am compelled to think that there is something in my writings more valuable than in the productions of some people on whom you bestow warm elogiums—I mean more mind—denominate it as you will—more of the observations of my own senses, more of the combining of my own imagination—the effusions of my own feelings and passions than the cold workings of the brain on the materials procured by the senses and imagination of other writers.

I wish I had been able to marshal these types of arguments while I was at university. I remember one miserable lesson about Racine, just me and a male student who'd been to Eton. I was baffled by the tutor's questions. We would notice some sort of pattern or effect in the lines of verse—a character saying "Ô désespoir! Ô crime! Ô déplorable race!"—and the tutor would ask us what that effect was called. Silence. And then the other student would speak up. "Anaphora," he said. "Chiasmus." "Zeugma." I had no idea what he was talking about; I'd never heard these words before. I was relieved when the hour was over. When I asked him afterward how he knew those terms, he said he'd been given a handout at school and he invited me to his room so that I could borrow and photocopy it. I must still have it somewhere. I remember feeling a tinge of anger—I could see the patterns in Racine's verse, I just didn't know what they were called—but mostly I felt ashamed. I learned the terms on the photocopy by heart.

Mary knew instinctively that what she offered was something more than technical accuracy, an unshakable structure, or an even tone. Godwin eventually saw this too. "When tried by the hoary and long-established laws of literary composition, *A Vindication of the Rights of Woman* can scarcely maintain its claim to be placed in the first class of human productions," he wrote after her death. "But when we consider the importance of the doctrines, and the eminence of genius it displays, it seems not very improbable that it will be read as long as the English language endures." Reading it again, older now, and having read many more of the feminist books that Wollstonecraft's short one is the ancient foremother of, I can see what he means.

There are funny autobiographical sketches, where Mary is having a moment of sublimity at a too-gorgeous sunset only to be interrupted by a fashionable lady asking for her gown to be admired. There is indelible phrasemaking, such as the moment when Mary counters the Margaret Thatcher fallacy—the idea that a woman in power is good in itself—by saying that "it is not empire, but equality" that women should contend for. She asked for things that are commonplace now but were unusual then: for women to be MPs, for girls and boys to be educated together, for friendship to be seen as the source and foundation of romantic love. She linked the way women were understood as property under patriarchy to the way enslaved people were treated, and demanded the abolition of both systems. She was also responding to an indisputably world-historical moment, with all the passion and hurry that implies. Specifically, she addressed Talleyrand, who had written a pamphlet in support of women's education, but generally, she applied herself to the ideas about women's status and worth coming out of the brand-new French republic. In 1791, France gave equal rights to Black citizens, made nonreligious marriage and divorce possible, and emancipated the Jews. What would England give its women? (Wollstonecraft was right that the moment couldn't wait: Olympe de Gouges, who wrote the *Declaration of the Rights of Woman* in October 1791 and ironically dedicated it to Marie-Antoinette, was guillotined within two years of publication.)

And though I love the *Vindication* for its eccentricities, I also love it for its philosophy. It is philosophically substantial, even two centuries later. Wollstonecraft understood how political the personal was, and that between people was where the revolution of manners she called for could be effected. "A man has been termed a microcosm," she wrote, "and every family might also be called a state." The implications of this deceptively simple idea would echo down the centuries: what role should a woman occupy at home, and how does that affect what she is encouraged to do in the wider world? Every woman in this book struggles with that idea: from Plath's worry that becoming a mother would mean she could no longer write poetry to Woolf's insecurity about her education coming from her father's library rather than an ancient university. Much of Wollstonecraft's own thought had risen out of her close reading of Rousseau, particularly her engagement with *Émile*, his imaginary working-through of an ideal enlightenment education for a boy. I didn't find as an undergraduate, and still don't, that her argument for women's education, which is that women should be educated in order to be better wives and mothers, or in order to be able to cope when men leave them, to be feminist. But now I can see that Wollstonecraft was one of the first to make the point that feminists have repeated in various formulations for two hundred years—though I hope not forever. If woman "has reason," Mary says, then "she was not created merely to be the solace of man." And so it follows that "the sexual should not destroy the human character." That is to say, that women should above all be thought human, not other.

With so much of Wollstonecraft's attention taken up by revolutionary France, perhaps it was inevitable that she would go there. She wrote to Everina that she and Johnson, along with Fuseli and his wife, were planning a six-week trip: "I shall be introduced to many people, my book has been translated and praised in some popular prints; and Fuseli, of course, is well known." She didn't say that she had fallen in love with Fuseli. The painter was forty-seven and the proto-feminist twenty-nine. Mary hadn't been without admirers—she met a clergyman she liked on the boat to Ireland; an MP who visited Lord Kingsborough seemed taken with her too—but marriage didn't appeal. She joked with Roscoe (not just a fan but another admirer, surely) that she could get married in Paris, then get divorced when her "truant heart" demanded it: "I am still a Spinster on the wing." But to Fuseli, she wrote that she'd never met anyone who had his "grandeur of soul," a grandeur she thought essential to her happiness, and she was scared of falling "a sacrifice to a passion which may have a mixture of dross in it . . . If I thought my passion criminal, I would conquer it, or die in the attempt." Mary suggested she live in a *ménage à trois* with Fuseli and his wife. He turned the idea down, the plan to go to Paris dissolved, and Mary left London on her own.

She arrived in the Marais in December 1792, when Louis XVI was on trial for high treason. On the morning he would mount his defense, the king "passed by my window," Mary wrote to Johnson. "I can scarcely tell you why, but an association of ideas made the tears flow insensibly from my eyes, when I saw Louis sitting with more dignity than I expected from his character, in a hackney coach, going to meet death." Mary was spooked: she wished for the cat she left in London, and couldn't blow out her candle that night. The easy radicalism she had adopted in England came under pressure. Though she waited until her French was better before calling on francophone contacts, she began to meet other expatriates in Paris, such as Helen Maria Williams, the British poet Wordsworth would praise. In spring 1793, she was invited to the house of Thomas Christie, a Scottish essayist who had co-founded the *Analytical Review* with Johnson. There she met Gilbert Imlay, an American, and fell deeply in love.

Imlay was born in New Jersey and had fought in the War of Independence; he was writing a novel, *The Emigrants*, and made money in Paris by acting as a go-between for Europeans who wanted to buy land in the US and the Americans who wanted to sell it to them. It is as if all Mary's intensity throughout her life so far—the letters to Jane Arden, her devotion to Fanny Blood, her passion for Fuseli—crests in the affair with this one man, whom she disliked on their first meeting and decided to avoid.

Imlay said he thought marriage corrupt; he talked about the women he'd had affairs with; he described his travels through the rugged west of America. After the disappointment with Fuseli, she offered up her heart ecstatically, carelessly: "Whilst you love me," Mary told him, making a man she'd known for months the architect and guardian of her happiness, "I cannot again fall into the miserable state, which rendered life a burthen almost too heavy to be borne." And yet she also noticed she couldn't make him stay: "Of late, we are always separating—Crack!—crack!—and away you go."

When my husband and I agreed we could see other people, he created a Tinder profile, using a photo I'd taken of him against a clear blue sky on the balcony of one of our last apartments together. He wanted to fall in love again and have children: pretty quickly he found someone who wanted that too. I met someone at a party who intrigued me, another writer visiting from another city, and I began spending more time with him; in front of paintings, at Wollstonecraft's grave, on long walks, at the movies, talking for hours in and out of bed. After being married for so long, it was strange and wonderful to fall in love again: I felt illuminated, sexually free, emotionally rich, intellectually alive. I liked myself again. But I fought my feelings for him, reasoning it was too soon after my husband, that sentiments this strong were somehow wrong in themselves, that he would be gone back to his own city soon and so I must give him up no matter what I felt. When he was gone, though, I saw I had found that untamable thing, a mysterious recognition, everything the poets mean by love. I wrote him email after email, sending thoughts and feelings and provocations, trying out ideas for my new life, which I hoped would include him.

Sometimes I must have sounded like Wollstonecraft writing to Imlay.

Mary moved to Neuilly, a leafy village on the edge of Paris, and began writing a history of the revolution; throughout that summer of 1793, she and Imlay would meet at the gates, *les barrières*, in the Paris city wall. (Bring your "barrier-face," she would tell him when the affair began to turn cold, and she wanted to go back to the start.) "I do not want to be loved like a goddess; but I wish to be necessary to you," she wrote. Perhaps there was something in her conception of herself that made her think she could handle a flirt like Imlay. "Women who have gone to great lengths to raise themselves above the ordinary level of their sex," Mary's biographer Claire Tomalin comments, "are likely to believe, for a while at any rate, that they will be loved the more ardently and faithfully for their pains." Mary perhaps believed she was owed a great love, and Imlay was made to fit. "By tickling minnows," as Virginia Woolf put it in a short essay about Wollstonecraft, Imlay "had hooked a dolphin." By the end of the year, Mary was pregnant.

Françoise Imlay (always Fanny, after Fanny Blood) was born at Le Havre in May 1794, and Mary wrote home that "I feel great pleasure in being a mother," and boasted that she hadn't "clogged her soul by promising obedience" in marriage. Imlay stayed away a lot; in one letter, Mary tells him of tears coming to her eyes at picking up the carving knife to slice the meat herself, because it brought back memories of him being at home with her. As she becomes disillusioned by degrees with Imlay, whose letters don't arrive as expected, she is falling in love with their daughter. At three months, she talks of Fanny getting into her "heart and imagination"; at four months, she notices with pleasure that the baby "does not promise to be a beauty; but appears *wonderfully* intelligent"; at six months, she tells Imlay that though she loved being pregnant and breastfeeding (nursing your own child was radical in itself then), those sensations "do not deserve to be compared to the emotions I feel, when she stops to smile upon me, or laughs outright on meeting me unexpectedly in the street, or after a short absence."

Imlay's return keeps being delayed, and Wollstonecraft uses her intellect to protest, arguing against the commercial forces that keep him from "observing with me how her mind unfolds." Isn't the point, as Imlay once claimed, to live in the present moment? Hasn't Mary already shown that she can earn enough by her writing to keep them? "Stay, for God's sake," she writes, "let me not be always vainly looking for you, till I grow sick at heart." Still he does not come, and her letters reach a pitch of emotion when she starts to suspect he's met someone else. "I do not choose to be a secondary object," she spits; she already knew that men were "systematic tyrants"; "my head turns giddy when I think that all the confidence I have had in the affection of others is come to this—I did not expect this blow from you." She starts signing off with the threat that this letter could be the last he receives from her.

In April 1795, she decided to join him in London if he would not come to her. "I have been so unhappy this winter," Mary wrote. "I find it as difficult to acquire fresh hopes, as to regain tranquillity." Fanny was nearly a year old, and Imlay had set up home for them in Soho. She attempted to seduce him; he recoiled. (He had been seeing someone, an actress.) She took the losses—of her imagined domestic idyll, of requited love, of a fond father for her daughter—hard, and planned to take a huge dose of laudanum, which Imlay discovered just in time. I find it unbearable that Mary, like Plath, would think that dying is better for her own child than living, but neither Mary nor Sylvia were well when they thought that, I tell myself.

Imlay suggested that Mary go away for the summer—he had some business that needed attention in Scandinavia. A shipment of silver had gone missing, and he could do with someone going there in person to investigate. She could take Fanny, and a maid. The letters Mary wrote to him while waiting in Hull for good sailing weather show that she had not yet recovered: she looks at the sea "hardly daring to own to myself the secret wish, that it might become our tombs"; she is scared to sleep because Imlay appears in her dreams with "different casts of countenance"; she mocks the idea that she'll revive at all: "Now I am going toward the north in search of sunbeams!—Will any ever warm this desolated heart? All nature seems to frown—or rather mourn with me." But she had an infant on her hip, a business venture to rescue that may also bring back her errant lover, and from the letters she wrote home, she'll mold a book that will unwittingly create a future for herself, even when she was not entirely sure she wanted one.

Letters Written During a Short Residence in Sweden, Norway and Denmark wasn't the book that made her name, but it was the one that caused her readers to love her. When her daughter Mary Wollstonecraft Godwin eloped with Percy Shelley, they took the *Letters* with them on their honeymoon and read passages out loud to each other. Coleridge admired it, and may have based a poem on one of its passages. And it changed Godwin's mind about her. "If ever there was a book calculated to make a man in love with its author, this appears to me to be the book," he wrote. "She speaks of her sorrows, in a way that fills us with melancholy, and dissolves us in tenderness, at the same time that she displays a genius which commands all our admiration." She knew that the book relied on the force of her personality: she admitted that she tried to correct "this fault, if it be one" but that cutting out anything written in the first person made the prose "stiff and affected" and so she decided to let herself "flow unrestrained." (When I found it hard to write this book, embarrassed at revealing the parts of myself I'm not so proud of, I tried to let Mary encourage me.) Alongside the finished publication, the letters she actually sent to Imlay have also survived. At first she was baffled and hurt and accusing ("Will you not come to us in Switzerland? Ah, why do you not love us with more sentiment?") but then she began to glimpse the hard-won knowledge that can come out of a depression. "Love is a want of my heart," she wrote to Imlay from Gothenburg.

I have examined myself lately with more care than formerly, and find, that to deaden is not to calm the mind—Aiming at tranquility, I have almost destroyed all the energy of my soul—almost rooted out what renders it estimable—Yes, I have damped that enthusiasm of character, which converts the grossest materials into a fuel, that imperceptibly feeds hopes, which aspire above common enjoyment. Despair, since the birth of my child, has rendered me stupid—soul and body seemed to be fading away before the withering touch of disappointment.

If she avoids sad feelings, all feeling goes. And she is starting to suspect that her feelings are what lend her work power. "We reason deeply, when we forcibly feel," as Wollstonecraft puts it in Letter 19, when she is explaining the reason she keeps returning to the theme of women's oppression. She feels it strongly, so she tries to work out why. She had been steeped in the Enlightenment philosophy of Rousseau, Locke, and Kant, but now she argues that emotion might be worth more than reason. Or if that is putting it too strongly, she argues that emotion comes first, and needn't be suppressed when putting together an argument. Because your feelings also give the information you need to live your life well.

In Mary's private notes to Imlay, there are two desires: to recover from her despair and to reconcile with the lover who was in some part responsible for it. It's as if she wants to show him both how much he hurt her and how brave she is in healing from the injury. This seeps into the published book, infusing a simple account of rowing in a boat off the coast of Norway with an existential quality:

The young woman whom I mentioned to you, proposed rowing me across the water, amongst the rocks; but as she was pregnant, I insisted on taking one of the oars, and learning to row. It was not difficult; and I do not know a pleasanter exercise. I soon became expert, and my train of thinking kept time, as it were, with the oars, or I suffered the boat to be carried along by the current,

indulging a pleasing forgetfulness, or fallacious hopes.—
How fallacious! Yet, without hope, what is to sustain life,
but the fear of annihilation—the only thing of which I
have ever felt a dread—I cannot bear to think of being
no more—of losing myself—though existence is often
but a painful consciousness of misery; nay, it appears to
me impossible that I should cease to exist, or that this
active, restless spirit, equally alive to joy and sorrow,
should only be organised dust—ready to fly abroad the
moment spring snaps, or the spark goes out, which kept
it together. Surely something resides in this heart that is
not perishable—and life is more than a dream.

Sometimes, to take up my oar, once more, when the sea
was calm, I was amused by disturbing the innumerable
young star fish which floated just below the surface. I
had never observed them before, for they have not a hard
shell, like those I have seen at the sea shore. They looked
like thickened water, with a white edge; and four purple
circles, of different forms, were in the middle, over an
incredible number of fibres, or white lines. Touching
them, the cloudy substance would turn or close, first on
one side, then on the other, very gracefully; but when I
took one of them up in the ladle with which I heaved the
water out of the boat, it appeared only a colorless jelly.

Reading this passage, I can see why Godwin fell in love. Wollstonecraft's practicality in teaching herself to row becomes an
opportunity for her thoughts, meandering as if floating too, to
approach the question of whether souls exist (a not inconsequen-
tial one, if you are religious, as Wollstonecraft was, and you have

contemplated suicide, as Wollstonecraft had). She does think that some part, an emotional part, of us can never die: this part is like a fish that is only a colorless jelly when you try to catch it, but impossibly complex and elegant as it moves through water. Here there is detail, adventure, emotion, and thought all combined together, with no one element dominating or canceling out another. And it is vivid too: I can almost see Mary leaning over the boat to watch the jellyfish, and her curious look as she ladles up a sea monster.

Another reason the book is so vivid is that it is somehow more modern than it ought to be: interested in her own imagination, she lets herself think things more grounded people wouldn't. Sailing down another part of the Norwegian coast, she imagines a time when no part of the world will be left uninhabited. "Imagination went still farther, and pictured the state of man when the earth could no longer support him. Where was he to fly to from universal famine? Do not smile: I really became distressed for these fellow creatures, yet unborn." (We are those fellow creatures, now.) She also argues for a living wage and for trade not to be unrestrained, because "from the manner commerce is at present carried on, little can be advanced in favor of a pursuit that wears out the most sacred principles of humanity and rectitude." Perhaps she is teasing Imlay, but is she not also right?

She spends a portion of Letter 18 defending Queen Matilda of Denmark. Matilda had effectively ruled the country when her husband succeeded to the throne at seventeen, and it became apparent that his paranoia and hallucinations made him unfit to rule. The royal physician, Struensee, subdued the king with drugs, and fell in love with the lonely queen. Struensee and

Matilda became de facto monarchs, and in fact introduced a progressive regime, before being beheaded and forced into exile, respectively. "Poor Matilda! Thou has haunted me ever since my arrival," Wollstonecraft writes. "She probably ran into an error common to innovators, in wishing to do immediately what can only be done by time"—an error Mary understood herself. "I wish to see women neither heroines nor brutes," she argued in the *Vindication*, "but reasonable creatures." Wollstonecraft can see the woman in the myth—and well might she be sympathetic to someone who loved where society said she ought not to, but who nevertheless tried to do the right thing in her public life. "Poor Jackie!" we might have said in the 1960s; "Poor Diana!" in the 1980s. "Poor Britney! Poor Lindsay! Poor Amy!" we might say now.

As summer faded into autumn, so did Mary's hopes that Imlay would meet her in Hamburg and they, reunited, would go together to Switzerland. She wrote letter after letter documenting her anguish, sorrow, comfortlessness, misery, depressed spirits, trembling heart, finally asking from Dover if he'd "formed some new attachment" and saying that "if you wish it, I will cut this Gordian knot" tying him to her and Fanny. In London, she questioned the cook and found she had been supplanted, and reached another crisis point. On October 10, she wrote to Imlay to ask him to send Fanny to a friend in Paris, to give the maid her clothes, and pay the cook her wages.

> I shall make no comments on your conduct: or any appeal to the world. Let my wrongs sleep with me! Soon, very soon, shall I be at peace. When you receive this, my burning head will be cold.

I would encounter a thousand deaths, rather than a night like the last. Your treatment has thrown my mind into a state of chaos; yet I am serene. I go to find comfort, and my only fear is, that my poor body will be insulted by an endeavour to recall my hated existence. But I shall plunge into the Thames where there is the least chance of my being snatched from the death I seek.

God bless you! May you never know by experience what you have made me endure. Should your sensibility ever awake, remorse will find its way to your heart; and, in the midst of business and sensual pleasure, I shall appear before you, the victim of your deviation from rectitude.

Wollstonecraft went to Battersea Bridge, but finding it too public, hired a boat to row her to Putney Bridge, where she soaked her clothes in the rain and jumped. Fishermen found her, unconscious, and brought her to a pub to revive her. "If I am condemned to live longer," she wrote in her next letter to Imlay, "it is a living death." She doesn't want his money, his house, his sympathy. "I never wanted but your heart."

For Godwin, the baffling thing about the affair with Imlay was how long it lasted, even though it had been clear, perhaps from the beginning, that he wasn't a person Mary could trust with her own heart: "Why did she thus obstinately cling to an ill-starred unhappy passion?" For Woolf, Imlay can't wholly be blamed because, "thus distracted, thus puzzling even to herself," Mary could not always "follow the rapidity of her changes and the alternate reason and unreason of her moods." (It is interesting to me that Woolf finds her way to some understanding of Imlay, when condemning him is a much more common reaction.)

The difficulty for me in watching Mary's relationship collapse is seeing her self-regard buckle so completely that she attempts suicide twice in a year. But when, like Plath's Lady Lazarus, the worms have been picked off her like sticky pearls, Mary does find whatever she needed to find to begin again. She will make a book out of the letters she sent him so as to "protect and provide for my child." My own heart lifts most when her anger shades into defiance, and she tells him: "You may render me unhappy; but cannot make me contemptible in my own eyes." As well as the Scandinavian letters (it's a form of revenge in itself to make herself so lovable to the world at large), Wollstonecraft was working on a play, drawn from the recent events in her life. It was to be a comedy.

Back in London, she took up with old friends again. Mary Hays, who had written her a fan letter when the *Vindication* had come out three years before, brought her back into the orbit of William Godwin. While she was away, he had made his reputation with a political tract, *An Enquiry Concerning Political Justice*, and a novel, *Caleb Williams*, and now the forty-year-old bachelor was coming out of his study more often, spending time with the playwright Elizabeth Inchbald and a twenty-something aspiring novelist, Amelia Alderson. (Less successfully, he had attempted to seduce a friend's wife—Godwin was famously against marriage—a few years before. The bemused friend took him back once he'd stopped hitting on his spouse.) Mary went to visit him in St. Pancras, which was more daring at the time than it sounds now, and they began seeing a lot of each other.

In July 1796, she slipped a note into the last volume of Rousseau's novel of forbidden love, *La Nouvelle Héloïse*, asking that when Godwin wrote to her "in *verse,* not to choose the easiest task, my perfections, but to dwell on your feelings—that is to say, give me a bird's-eye view of your heart." She wants to hear how he feels about her: is it because she's afraid, after Imlay, to reveal how she feels? "Your sapient Philosophership," she called him teasingly; jealously she told him she didn't want to see him the evening after he'd dined with "Mrs. Perfection," as she called Inchbald. When he finally declared his love in mid-August, and they tried to have sex but didn't quite manage (he may have been a virgin), he retreated and Mary faltered, telling him in a letter that if she could have clicked her heels and been instantly in France or Italy with her daughter, she would have gone. "For six and thirty hours," he wrote back, "I longed inexpressibly to have you in my arms. Why did I not come to you? I am a fool. I feared still that I might be deceiving myself as to your feelings, & that I was feeding my mind with groundless presumptions." He says that she mustn't let her feelings "tyrannise" over her: "I see nothing in you but what I respect and adore." A few days later, she sends him a letter with a fable in it, of a sycamore tree that blooms in an unseasonably warm February, and then is hit by frost. "Whether the buds recovered, and expanded, when the spring actually arrived—The Fable sayeth not"—Godwin writes back angrily: the fable is well told, but does she mean to tell him off because Mary Hays visited him yesterday? "I needed soothing and you threaten me." Godwin's inexperience and lack of confidence meets with Mary's insecurity and hastiness, and I worry whether they will ever find equilibrium. I shouldn't have; they seem nevertheless to have become lovers. "I have seldom seen so much live fire running about my features as this morning when recollections—very dear; called forth the blush of pleasure, as

I adjusted my hair," she wrote to him. "I wish I had been a spectator of the live fire you speak of," he wrote back. Godwin would write "chez elle" in his diary when he went to visit her, and "chez moi" when she stayed with him. She was pregnant before too long.

It is such a relief to have Mary find someone who loved her and could also meet her on an intellectual level, that I hadn't thought about how she felt about him. Apparently at least one friend thought that Mary had truly loved Imlay, and Godwin was just who was around at the time. Tomalin thinks it "quite possible that Mary decided to woo him for a husband in cool—if not quite cold—blood." Mary had spent many pages of the *Vindication* arguing that friendship was the best part of love. She also seems to have found a way to love Godwin through his writing. Reading his essays, she told him, she reminded herself "every now and then, that the writer *loved* me.—Voluptuous is often expressive of a meaning I do not now intend to give. I would describe one of those moments, when the senses are exactly tuned by the rising tenderness of the heart, and according reason entices you to live in the present moment, regardless of the past or future—It is not rapture.—It is a sublime tranquillity. I have felt it in your arms." Thought is crowned with earned emotion.

In their private correspondence, which Godwin edited and made available soon after Mary's death, we see a couple struggling with their feelings as well as their political views. They kept their relationship a secret until Mary became pregnant and decided, despite all their arguments in print against it, to get married. The wedding took place on a Wednesday at the end of March 1797, at St. Pancras Church, but they didn't intend to set up home together, or stop seeing their friends apart from one another. "The wound my unsuspecting heart formerly received is not healed," she wrote to a friend. "I found my evenings solitary; and I wished, while fulfilling the duty of a mother, to have some person with similar pursuits, bound to me by affection; and beside, I earnestly desired to resign a name which seemed to disgrace me." When news got out, literary London was not kind. Several of their friends dropped them in protest at the subterfuge, and others teased them. Fuseli wrote to a friend: had he heard that the "assertrix of female rights" and the "*balancier* of political justice" had got married?

Mary began work on a novel she called *The Wrongs of Woman*, a series of nested stories about all the worst things that could happen to a woman in the eighteenth century. It is initially narrated by Maria, who has been put in an asylum by her husband after she discovered his adultery and left him. Maria falls in love with a fellow inmate after she borrows his copies of Rousseau and is charmed by the notes left in the margins—Maria's jailer is charmed in turn by the lovers, who aren't as crazy as the world says they are. All three gather and tell their stories: there is war, travel to America, drunkenness, rape by an employer, a court case where Maria defends herself, poverty, and madness. "Was not the world a vast prison and women born slaves?" Maria asks. *The Wrongs of Woman* was left unfinished at her death and is sometimes seen as a sequel to the *Vindication*, though she also left a series of "Hints" to that sequel, the most intriguing of which are a couple of sentences that seem to come out of the Scandinavian letters. "Though I allow reason in this world is the mother of wisdom—yet some flights of the imagination seem to reach what wisdom cannot teach," she holds in one. "A writer of genius makes us feel—an inferior one reason," she says in another.

After the wedding, Godwin took a trip to see friends, the Wedgwoods, in Stoke-on-Trent, partly hoping that his absence would make Mary's heart grow fonder. (He promised three-year-old Fanny, who had given him the nickname "Man," as if he were Adam in her little life, that he would bring back a mug from the potteries for her. He found one with an "F" on it.) Godwin's gambit worked. "I wish you, from my soul, to be riveted in my heart; but I do not desire to have you always at my elbow—though at this moment I did not care if you were," she wrote after he had been gone three days. Relaxed now, he took a detour, was later home than Mary expected, and received a dressing-down. Godwin also received visits from "Miss Pinkerton" while Mary was heavily pregnant, which she thought "*wrong*." Together they wrote a note to her: "Miss Pinkerton, I forbear to make any comments on your incomprehensible conduct; but unless you can determine to behave with propriety, you must excuse me for expressing a wish not to see you at our house," they wrote, and signed the note "Mary Godwin."

On August 30, Mary's labor began, and she asked Godwin for a "news paper—I wish I had a novel, or some book of sheer amusement, to excite curiosity, and while away the time—Have you anything of the kind?" She was expecting to be down for dinner; her midwife (Mary insisted on having a woman by her side for the delivery, unusual for the time) had said that the baby would be born that day. "I am in the most natural state, and she can promise me a safe delivery—But that I must have a little patience—"

Those sentences, echoing her own mother's last words, are

the final trace of Mary's writing we have. Godwin tells us that a daughter, Mary Wollstonecraft Godwin, was born that day, but that the placenta didn't come away. A famous doctor was called, and spent several hours removing the last pieces from Mary's womb by hand. She fainted, she revived, fainted again, revived again, and told Godwin that she didn't choose to leave him. At this announcement he let his guard drop and went out to see friends. When he got back, he discovered that Mary had taken a turn for the worse. The last days of Wollstonecraft's life as she died of blood poisoning, probably from the attempt to remove the placenta, went from the sublime to the ridiculous and back again: when the doctor didn't think it a good idea for Mary to breastfeed her baby, puppies were brought in and jokes were made; when nothing seemed to be working, another doctor simply prescribed wine, to be given "rather freely." The last conversation she and Godwin had was about her children. She died at twenty to eight on the morning of September 10, 1797. In his diary, Godwin underlined the time three times. She was thirty-eight, the age I am as I write this.

In the heat of his grief, just weeks after Mary died, Godwin sat with her papers and began work on a memoir of his wife. In his study hung the portrait she had been sitting for while pregnant with their daughter. Made by John Opie, who was once thought to be in love with Mary too, her firm peach lips, blushing cheek, and oyster-white blouse are combined with a clear hazel gaze. Over her hair, which is shining almost blond in places, is a black cap perhaps meant to recall the one worn by Marianne, the mythical heroine of the French Revolution. She looks beautiful; like Godwin I keep her image in my study (mine is a postcard; Godwin's oil is now in the National Portrait Gallery in London, hanging next to Godwin and opposite their daughter Mary, gathered in a room as they couldn't be in life). Out of the openness and modernity of their relationship, Godwin wrote an extraordinary short account of her life, both fond and frank. He was honest about her suicide attempts and affairs gone wrong, as well as about the weaknesses of her writing. He edited her unfinished work for publication, and put her letters with Imlay and himself into the public domain too. Fanny and Mary had been taken care of by their friend Maria Reveley immediately after their mother's death, but Godwin would be their father.

The shock that met Godwin's honest attempt to memorialize Wollstonecraft hardened into scandal, one that affected women writers more generally, particularly feminist ones. For years Wollstonecraft was to be remembered for her life rather than for her work—even the sympathetic American feminist Margaret Fuller would say that she "was a woman whose existence better proved the need of some new interpretation of woman's rights than anything she wrote." Her story was also used as evidence that feminists can't be trusted to have sex, as they enjoy having children out of wedlock. (The work of her friend Mary Hays, who died at the age of eighty-six, was ridiculed for years because its author was said to chase after men who didn't want her.) Women could no longer live like Mary. They ought to be perfect, decorous and patient, virgins before marriage, like the heroines of Jane Austen's novels, which began to appear fourteen years after Wollstonecraft died. (Austen is thought to have known Mary's life story, and perhaps there are traces of how Austen felt about privileging feeling over reason in her portrait of Marianne in *Sense and Sensibility*.) The moment that produced someone like Mary Wollstonecraft was over.

In 1855, when George Eliot mentioned Wollstonecraft's *Vindication* in a review of Margaret Fuller's *Woman in the Nineteenth Century*, the book had been out of print since 1796. "There is in some quarters a vague prejudice against the *Rights of Woman* as in some way or other a reprehensible book, but readers who go to it with this impression will be surprised to find it eminently serious, severely moral, and withal rather heavy." Eliot had gone to it, and quotes it at length, particularly on the question of whether an intellectual woman makes a wayward wife. (Eliot thinks not: "A really cultured woman, like a really cultured man, will be ready to yield in trifles.") Wollstonecraft, Eliot says, "is nothing if not rational; she has no erudition, and her grave pages are lit up by no ray of fancy." I wonder if Eliot had read the Scandinavian letters (also out of print), which dance with fancy. Like Woolf, who concludes that Mary is "alive and active, she argues and experiments, we hear her voice and trace her influence even now among the living," Eliot detects "under the brave bearing of a strong and truthful nature, the beating of a loving woman's heart, which teaches her not to undervalue the smallest offices of domestic care or kindliness." Woolf's Mary is carrying out experiments in living; Eliot's Mary responds to ordinary kindness because she knows how difficult life can be. They each see themselves in her. Mary is of use to both because she was one of the first of her—their—genus, both origin and accompaniment.

*

In London, I used to live fifteen minutes' walk from Newington Green, where Mary went to church and set up her first school. In late 2020, a statue to Wollstonecraft was put up on the green, across from a playground. Like a giant drop of mercury escaped from a thermometer, Maggi Hambling's sculpture imagined a woman rising up from a dense silver swirl that shimmered in the autumn light. The lover with whom I had visited Wollstonecraft's grave was long gone and I persuaded Željka—a beloved post-divorce friend who had just become my flatmate when her own decade-long relationship had finished—to come with me to see it the day it was unveiled: there had been a minor fuss on the internet, because people seemed to think that the sculpture showed Wollstonecraft naked, when it actually shows a female archetype. Men and women were gathering around the muddy plinth, hanging out and talking. "It's Frankenstein's grandmother," we heard someone say (her daughter Mary became a writer herself, producing *Frankenstein* after a night telling ghost stories with Shelley and Byron in 1816). "She has an Afro," another said. "I think she has a penis," we heard. Željka and I were disappointed with the quotation from the *Vindication* that had been chosen for the plinth, "I do not wish women to have power over men, but over themselves," which seemed a little unambitious. I liked that it was silver, which meant you couldn't miss it from any part of the green; I liked that if you stood by the statue, you could see the school she founded and the unitarian chapel that inspired the *Vindication*. But the misunderstandings and misreadings amused me. I shook my head, I tutted. Mary was alive somehow, annoying a lockdown-tired nation, provoking it to come out and stand in a muddy park that was essentially a roundabout for double-decker buses. I had admired her at twenty, but at thirty-eight I thought of her as someone who reminded me to listen to my feelings, even if they scared me. The statue was like a Rorschach test for the state of feminism (as ever, not good) but it wasn't some impeccable eternal flame to the mother of feminism. It was chaotic and untamable and fun, thank God.

George

Mary Wollstonecraft died at thirty-eight, but George Eliot was born at the age of thirty-eight. Jane Austen assisted at the birth: the year Mary Ann Evans was beginning to write fiction, after several years in London editing a magazine and writing essays, she looked at all of Austen's novels again, starting with the last, *Persuasion.* She read them out loud during the evenings she spent with George Henry Lewes, whom she'd recently asked to critique Austen—"the greatest artist that has ever written," he wrote—for the magazine she worked for, the *Westminster Review.* Lewes was rapidly becoming essential to her: to her happiness, to her sense of herself as a writer, to her confidence. For years, Evans had put aside her first attempt at fiction, a descriptive passage about the Staffordshire villages she knew as a girl, along with the hope that she could write imaginatively. She doubted she could write dialogue and construct the sort of conflict that drives a plot. But ought she not to try? Lewes argued. It could be a failure, or it could be an instant *chef d'oeuvre.* A title for a story about a sad clergyman came to her while dozing in the morning. She wrote successful dialogue for it, but still wondered if she could summon up pathos. Say Lewes went into town on purpose later in the week, and she tried to write a funeral scene?

When Evans read it to him when he came home, they both cried, and at the end he went up to kiss her. George Eliot had been born. (The name gave cover, but also comfort. At the very beginning of her career Lewes would be there with her, in the first name "George"—but so would Austen, in the surname "Eliot," also that of the heroine of *Persuasion*, Anne Elliot, whom everyone in that book thinks (wrongly) too old to catch and keep happiness.) At the end of that year, 1857, Eliot wrote in her journal: "Few women, I fear, have had such reason as I have to think the long sad years of youth were worth living for the sake of middle age."

At thirty-eight, Eliot had love, a growing sense of herself, and a book of stories ready for the printer. The bounty was unexpected. She had waited so long for her future, losing hope she could write a novel and "desponding," as she put it, about everything else in her life. She had borne depressions, headaches, the non-return of love, losing her faith, the death of her parents; she had survived a patchy, self-propelled education, a sense she'd never fit in, and the crushing, unpaid, and anonymous editorial work behind an important magazine in literary London. I didn't know any of this when I first read Eliot: she seemed secure, plump and staid at the center of the canon, writer of enormously long books, serious books, including *Middlemarch*, the only one for "grown-ups" as Woolf declared on Eliot's centenary in 1919. She's one of the five totemic writers F. R. Leavis argued in 1948 who made up the "great tradition," for God's sake. When I picked up a beige edition of *Middlemarch* for a pound during my penultimate year at school, I wanted admission to that world of morality and ideas, the one I was reaching for in the small, halting steps I took toward applying to Oxford.

Neither of my parents had studied longer than they had to: my dad began as a print apprentice and my mother worked in offices and department stores before she had me. Reading was always part of my life with my mum: while she breastfed my little brother, she quelled my jealousy by reading Mr. Men books to me, curled up soft at her side; at primary school, she remembered (though I do not, and think it embarrassing now) that I was deputized to read aloud to the class when the teacher couldn't. She herself could often be found reading in bed in the mornings, something by Ian Rankin or Marian Keyes. But I'd lost the habit as I grew up, and by my early teens I might pick up a teen horror or romance, but I didn't read with any conviction. The first adult book that reminded me of how I'd read as a child was Thomas Hardy's *Tess of the D'Urbervilles*, which I read at sixteen, late into the night, scared that Angel might reject Tess after reading her letter confessing her past. In thinking and writing about *Tess*, I started liking books again. I remember at seventeen sitting on the edge of my parents' bed and working up the courage to call the Oxford admissions office for a prospectus, worried that if I spoke wrongly, a mark would be set against my name. I decided open days were uncool (or was it that I was intimidated?), and when my mother decided we would go and look at Oxford anyway, I was embarrassed into silence when she simply walked us through the gate of the college I'd applied for and asked if we could take a look around. And then when they let us in, she smiled and said hello to the dons walking around the quad, as if she belonged there too.

When I got an interview, my mother shifted into high gear: she made a travel plan so that I wouldn't be too much alone in advance of the morning appointment, involving a night in a motel near Oxford; there were outfits to clean and press to give me options; she thought about nightwear and snacks in case the food was bad and an extra jumper in case the rooms were cold and a duffel bag—the blue and pink one, probably—that would be big enough for everything I needed. I submitted, with spots of rebellion. My thoughts were more about what I would be asked: I knew the dons would give me a poem to discuss with them, and so I went over how to identify a sonnet and a ballad, and I thought about what I ought to be reading at the time in case they asked me. I chose *Middlemarch*, for all the reasons I'd bought it earlier that year. But the strange thing was that in the effort to appear strong and studious and serious, Eliot failed me. My mother and I reached the motel, with its logo of a swan coming in to land, in the early evening of that dark day in December. I don't remember what we ate, we must have eaten something, but I do remember telling her about Dorothea, who was going to marry this awful dried-up old scholar called Casaubon, and then taking the novel with me for a long bath in the plastic-paneled tub, reading with the fever of a soap-opera addict. I came out hot and pink and relaxed with good news to tell her: Will Ladislaw had turned up beside Dorothea in a gallery in Rome. When the long-anticipated moment came and the interviewing tutors asked what I was reading, I said, as if fresh out of the motel bath and talking only to my mother, that I hoped Dorothea got with Will.

I had expected one thing from Eliot, and she had given me another. I was still reading my beige *Middlemarch* when I heard I'd got a place at Oxford—the heavy letter, Mum guessed, was good news, as bad would fit on a single sheet—and I didn't know yet that Will and Dorothea would be able to overcome the vicious codicil to Casaubon's will, requiring Dorothea to give up her inheritance should she marry Will after her husband's death. It was a Dorothea-like impulse that caused me to pick up the most imposing book I could think of but I was met instead with the hot pleasure of greedy page-turning. Like finding your great love at thirty-seven, or discovering that you are a fiction writer at thirty-eight, there is some guilt, along with delight and shock, in the change of fortune. Whenever I go to Eliot, then at seventeen and now at thirty-eight, I am surprised again. I had the sense when I first read *Middlemarch* that I was missing things, that I would need to read it again when I was older and had lived some more. Now that I have lived more, the novel's irony comes through, and it seems funnier than it did. (One idea in particular brought a smile to my divorcée's face while reading: the funny ha-ha, funny wry, funny touching notion that problems in love can be improved by marrying.)

Middlemarch was written by one of the most happily married unmarried women writers we have. *Persuasion* is my favorite Austen novel—and perhaps Eliot's too, as she read it again in 1874—because its heroine expects so little from life, but still comes to a happy end. I often reread it at Christmas, roping in a friend to experience it too; it gives me hope that even if I make a wrong judgment for the seemingly right reasons, there might also be second chances for me, if I can see them and make use of them. And what Eliot's life shows me, over and over again, is that no one but her, someone who'd found herself when she'd all but given up on herself, could have produced the books she did. The books that were there when I needed them.

*

Mary Ann Evans was born in November 1819, the last of three children for Christiana Pearson and Robert Evans, who looked after land and estates in the same way as Caleb Garth does in *Middlemarch*. Griff House, where she lived as a child, was on the estate of Arbury Hall, in the very center of England, and before she was sent to school Eliot roamed the lawns, the flower-filled gardens, the orchards, the open green land. There's a passage in *The Mill on the Floss* where the narrator says that "we could never have loved the earth so well if we had had no childhood in it—if it were not the earth where the same flowers come up again every spring that we used to gather with our tiny fingers as we sat lisping to ourselves on the grass." I think one of the things Eliot is saying is that being in and with nature is our first education: picking daisies for chains, finding worms in the mud, gently approaching dogs that might bite.

Evans attended formal school too, in the nearby town of Nuneaton, excelling in languages, painting, and music, and reading Milton, Scott, and Bunyan. But she was severe, priding herself on her ability to renounce pleasure. When her mother fell ill, Mary Ann left school to care for her, and when she died, Mary Ann stayed at home to run the house for her father. She was eighteen: uncompromising in her religion (she refused to go to the theater on her first trip to London); lonely (she and her friends gave themselves fashionable flower names—Ivy, Veronica, and Clematis—and wrote long letters to each other); intellectually intense (she spent six months working on a chart of ecclesiastical history). When her father moved the family to the city of Coventry, and she came into contact with the writers and thinkers—Herbert Spencer, Harriet Martineau, Ralph Waldo Emerson—who gathered at Rosehill, the home of Charles and Cara Bray, a long fuse was lit.

It was in Coventry that Mary Ann would lose her faith and gather the courage to leave for London and a writing life. It was her reading, particularly Charles Hennell's *Inquiry Concerning the Origin of Christianity*, that made her, at twenty-three, stop accompanying her father to church. Ministers who tried to lure back the prodigal found that she had already read (and dismissed) the books they thought would convince her. Her father, her older sister Chrissey, and middle brother Isaac tried too. "I could not without vile hypocrisy," Evans writes in the one letter to her father on the subject that survives, "profess to join in worship which I wholly disapprove. This and *this alone* I will not do even for your sake—anything else however painful I would cheerfully brave to give you a moment's joy." Seven years later, when her father died, it was as if a dam broke, the water threatening to sweep away "a part of my moral nature." The night he died, Evans told friends she was scared of "becoming earthly sensual and devilish for want of that purifying restraining influence"—she could not know yet that the effect would be liberating. It allowed her to see what she wanted, now that her inherited, commanding duty had fallen away. That summer, she left England for Paris, Nice, Milan, Chamonix, and eventually Geneva, scaring the other tourists by crying all the way. By Lake Geneva, among the Shelleyean peaks, she decided that her life must change. "I am determined to sell everything I possess except a portmanteau and carpet-bag and the necessary contents and be a stranger and a foreigner on the earth for ever more," she wrote to her Coventry friends. When John

Chapman, whom she'd met at Rosehill, bought the *Westminster Review*—the radical quarterly founded by Jeremy Bentham and once edited by J. S. Mill—and needed someone to run it for him, Evans moved to London at the age of thirty-one to be his assistant editor.

Evans lived on the £200 a year her father left her, a good middle-class income of about £50,000 today, and worked for free, as she could afford it. An assistant at 142 Strand, where the *Westminster Review* offices were, remembered Evans in the office late with her hair let down, easy chair turned to the fire with her feet dangling over one arm and a proof in her hand. One of the first issues of the relaunched *Westminster Review* carried (unsigned) essays on "Representative Reform," "Shellfish: Their Ways and Works," "The Relation Between Employers and Employed," "Mary Stuart," and "Political Questions and Parties in France": she could put her wide-ranging intellectual interests to use. She also began to write for the magazine—which they did pay her for—on Carlyle, Ruskin, Heine, and Wollstonecraft, among other subjects. An unmarried woman newly arrived in literary London was noticed: Chapman, her boss, was married with two children, and his mistress lived with them too, but he still found himself falling in love with Evans; Herbert Spencer, who worked at the *Economist* on the other side of the Strand as well as writing for the *Review*, used his press comps to take her to the theater; in a bookshop in the Burlington Arcade, she bumped—literally—into George Henry Lewes, who was, with Thornton Hunt, a co-founder of the radical weekly the *Leader* and another of her writers. "A miniature Mirabeau," was her first impression of the man she would marry in all but the conventional sense.

But Lewes was already married, with three children, and Evans was devoted to Spencer. The summer of her first year at the *Westminster Review*, she took her proofs to Broadstairs on the Kent coast, and wrote to Spencer to say he should join her there. Spencer came in early July to see the promised wildflowers, sunsets over the fields of barley, and the sea studded with sails and it was here, in a holiday mood of "delicious, voluptuous laziness," that Evans seems to have confessed her love. "Just that which I feared might take place, did take place," Spencer wrote to a friend after Eliot's death. "Her feelings became involved and mine did not. The lack of physical attraction was fatal." (Spencer would die a bachelor at eighty-four.) There is an extraordinary letter Evans wrote after she'd been rejected, which she gave to Spencer for his journey back to London: Eliot's biographers don't much like its tone and what she says of herself in it, but it is one of the moments I feel close to Eliot, as aren't we all susceptible to running ourselves down after we're rejected? When I am broken up with, I discovered while dating after my divorce, I agree entirely with my breaker-upper, that I am unworthy of love and he was never more right than in his rejection of me. Eliot begs Spencer not to abandon her completely: "I could gather courage to work and make life valuable, if only I had you near me," she writes. "I would be good and cheerful and never annoy you." She dared to ask for her love to be returned, and now, humbled, she says she'll settle for what she had before, and be happy about it. (For years, Evans had suspected she was unlovable.)

It's hard to see her prostrating herself like this, in the sort of letter that you can—I have—want to write directly after a breakup. But even with the humiliation there are flashes of insight into the sort of person she is and of her very own brand of bravery, the one that lured Spencer to the coast in the first place. "Those who have known me best have always said, that if ever I loved any one thoroughly my whole life must turn upon that feeling, and I find they said truly," she writes, not knowing yet how true that will turn out to be. "I suppose no woman ever before wrote such a letter as this," she concludes, "but I am not ashamed of it, for I am conscious that in the light of reason and true refinement I am worthy of your respect and tenderness, whatever gross men or vulgar-minded women might think of me." This sort of imperviousness to *soi-disant* correctness made her suffer in Victorian society, but it is also the quality that makes Eliot's life attractive to us now. So many of the characters in her fiction maintain, and what's more, cherish, their own point of view against the dumb groupthink of their communities. Even as Evans loses herself for love at the age of thirty-three, a corner of her mind holds on to the idea that she is worthy, always was, and always will be. "I suppose no woman ever before," she writes, with a glint.

Back in London, she saw more of Lewes. His marriage, it turned out, wasn't what it at first seemed: he and his wife, Agnes Jervis, had been together for a decade, but they had on principle decided not to stop each other from getting involved with other people too. When Agnes became deeply attached to George's co-editor on the *Leader*, Thornton Hunt (who was also married), the arrangement broke down. It had seemed right to Lewes to put his own name on the birth certificate of Agnes and Thornton's first child, but when the second came, it was clear that his marriage was dead. He was trapped. Filing for divorce was impossible because in allowing his name to be used on the birth certificate, he had already condoned Agnes's adultery, which was the only ground for divorce in mid-nineteenth-century England. The conditions of divorce in the UK only changed in 2022, and you can now say that the collapse of the partnership was no one's fault. When I filled out the form to legally end my marriage in 2015, I could choose from "unreasonable behaviour," "desertion," "living apart" (for two years with agreement or five without), and "adultery." Not wanting to manufacture a complaint where there was none, we agreed on adultery and documented one of my husband's Tinder dates (though I didn't name the third party, and maybe I never even knew her name; I'm weirdly grateful to her nevertheless). Even as I felt thankful we could divorce this way at all—Lewes couldn't have—the subterfuge was absurd. We were trying to divorce gently. I queued in the post office myself to send the form to the court; I texted my husband about the arrival of the decree nisi, then of the absolute. We had one argument about money, but we never had to stand before a judge. One of the arguments for the right to a legal abortion goes: no one wants love to come to this, but when it does, all pain should be kept to a minimum. I feel that way about divorce too. It is historically exceptional that I could take this decision at all, and live it out in the way I have. I am lucky, I know it. Neither of my grandmothers had this freedom.

Just over eight months later, my divorce was official. An unprepossessing sheet of white copy paper arrived in a brown envelope, announcing that on February 16, 2016, my marriage was thereby dissolved. The next day I relinquished the keys to my marital home, and moved into Melanie's spare bedroom while I looked for somewhere new. I'd met Melanie at a party in 2003, when we were both in Paris on our years abroad, and we'd bonded over twice-a-week movies and *vin chaud* at pavement cafés. I'd been with my husband the whole time I knew her, while she had been dating until she met her partner Dan. And it was Dan who met me at their front door in South London. He had made me a neon star-sprinkled sign: "Welcome Jo (& Congratulations on New Freedoms)!" I loved the sign. It was just what I wanted my new life to feel like: improvised, free, fun, and entirely my own.

Lewes was established in London literary life, with a reputation as "sensual," but slowly, over about three years—via Evans's attempts to get him to write about Lamarck and Comte, his unscheduled visits to the *Review*'s offices, their trips to the opera together, and the sharing of confidences—Evans tells her friends in Coventry that he has "won my regard after having a good deal of my vituperation. Like a few other people in the world, he is much better than he seems—a man of heart and conscience wearing a mask of flippancy." When Lewes became ill early in 1854, Evans wrote his pieces for him, a sign that they now saw their lives—literary and otherwise—as shared, or as Evans would put it later in her diary, doubled.

There are so many terms for a marriage that isn't quite one—a *mariage blanc* is sexless, an open marriage thinks hard about the idea of fidelity, a Boston marriage was a way of two women living together before marriage equality—but where are the terms for a partnership that is truer than a legally enforced one? They are rare, I know, which is perhaps why there is no word. I want to call Evans and Lewes's arrangement a *mariage rose* or a *mariage chaud*. In the summer of 1854, they traveled to Germany together—Lewes was working on a biography of Goethe—in a move that was understood as an elopement, not least by Evans. Having arrived at St. Katherine Docks by the Tower of London "about half an hour earlier than a sensible person would have," she had "20 minutes of terrible fear" while she waited. "But before long I saw his welcome face looking for me over his porter's shoulder, and all was well." They were carried away at sunset, and stayed out on deck to see the crescent moon melt into the blushed dawn of their new life.

They had told almost no one in England, and fifteen years later, the "strong woman of the *Westminster Review*" going off with a "gallant" was still being gossiped about. When not seen as a fool she was thought a homewrecker: her brother Isaac broke with her, and many of her friends would too. Chapman wondered what he was supposed to say when people asked. "I have nothing to deny or conceal," Evans wrote from Weimar. "I have counted the cost of the step that I have taken and am prepared to bear, without irritation or bitterness, renunciation by all my friends. I am not mistaken in the person to whom I have attached myself." And they would be happy for more than twenty years, happier than most marriages, and happier perhaps because they weren't yoked together by law—it was as if the choice they made every day to be together, despite the gossip, the excommunication, the cost (as Lewes still supported Agnes financially), made their not-marriage more than a marriage. She told her new London friend Barbara Bodichon—who herself was born out of wedlock—that she and Lewes had a satisfying sex life and used contraception so as not to have more children. She saw Lewes's sons with Agnes as "our boys," and over time all three young men became deeply attached to Evans.

And it would be Lewes's judicious yet unstinting support of Evans that allowed her the conditions to begin writing creatively.

During the summer of 1856, she wrote "Silly Novels by Lady Novelists." Her attack on "the frothy, the prosy, the pious, or the pedantic" run-of-the-mill women's fiction was also a way of trash-talking the competition. But she also reminded the reader (and herself) that women have written novels that rank "among the very finest," and that they don't need to "confound" philosophers because they can "delight" them. The summer she was writing the essay, she was also thinking about Antigone, who defied the rules of society for fraternal love, and Mary Wollstonecraft, who disdained marriage when she fell in love with Imlay. In the evenings, we know already, Austen was her light reading.

When Evans and Lewes went to Ilfracombe on the North Devon coast, she recorded in her journal a growing feeling. She wanted to know the names of things, but also to start naming things herself, to "escape from all vagueness and inaccuracy into the daylight of distinct, vivid ideas." In this wish, she makes me think of an April sunset I saw with my two-year-old nephew. I was bowled over, but so was he, naming all the colors he knew, all the ones he could pick out in the sky: orange, red, pink, blue, yellow, look! an aeroplane. ("But what is it that light cannot transfigure into beauty?" Evans says of a view of Ilfracombe that summer.) My nephew's desire to name and capture what he saw was outpaced by the vocabulary he had to describe it. All my brother and my sister-in-law and I could do was be astonished with him, and encourage him in the attempt. And this seems to have been Lewes's instinct too the first time Evans read out her attempts at fiction to him.

The funeral scene that caused Lewes to kiss her became part

of "The Sad Fortunes of Reverend Amos Barton," which was accepted by John Blackwood for his magazine in 1857 as the first of the *Scenes of Clerical Life*. She soon began on a novel, *Adam Bede*. In adopting "George Eliot" as a male pseudonym, she could leave behind the assumptions that came along with her sex, her beginnings in the Midlands, her critical writing, her scandalous private life, and allow people to imagine she was a harmless Cambridge-educated clergyman named after an English king. The freshly minted identity made "a new era in my life." Barbara was the first of her friends to recognize who'd really written *Adam Bede*, and when Eliot asked her not to give away the secret—"you have sense enough to know how important the *incognito* has been"—she was perhaps also hinting at what the disguise offered someone who had long wanted to write fiction, but had had trouble believing in her own abilities before London, the *Review*, and most of all, Lewes. As Eliot continued to write, Lewes developed other ways of cushioning her from the world. Bad reviews never made it into the house; publishers wrote to him not her; many times he met first readings with kisses rather than editorial suggestions; headaches and backaches were soothed away; the appearance of a new novel was often toasted from Berlin, or Prague, or Florence; even living in sin with him brought the benefit of not having to receive visits and hear gossip. But Eliot's confidence nevertheless wavered. The year *The Mill on the Floss* came out Eliot wrote to Barbara, seeming to count her blessings: "In fact we have no sorrows just now, except my constant inward 'worrit' of unbelief in any future of good work on my part. Everything I do seems poor and trivial in the doing, and when it is quite gone from me and seems no longer my own—then I rejoice in it and think it fine. That is the history of my life." And of many of our lives too.

I was first given a copy of *The Mill on the Floss* by my mother. I was fourteen or fifteen, sick in bed with tonsillitis, and had been for days. I'd probably asked for magazines, but she brought me the book she'd read, and liked, at school. For me, this was no recommendation. The book was so long, and the pages so thin, and the print so small. On the cover was a painting of a girl with black, curly, almost puffy hair, pale skin, and hot pink lips; I longed to look lightly sunkissed with my thick hair cut to an eyelash-skimming length, like the women in the magazines I'd requested. I was ungrateful then, but looking back now, I see how often Mum put things in my path that I didn't know I needed, and left them there. She also did this with *Jane Eyre*. And New York City, I now see. And *Swan Lake*. And coffee, and eating with chopsticks, and not taking a nap in my clothes. She didn't nag or cajole because it wasn't like brushing my teeth or learning my times tables. She often didn't like these things herself, she wasn't passing on a passion, and she was never disappointed if I didn't immediately fall for whatever it was she thought I ought to know about. I can't report back to her that I've only just read *The Mill on the Floss*, more than two decades after she gave it to me. I can't tell if she'd laugh or tease me, or both, but I doubt she'd be angry. She wasn't like some crazed suitor who claims they can't love you if you haven't listened to *Brighten the Corners*, like my first real boyfriend. I don't even know if she'd be pleased that I read the exact edition she gave me, whose pages I still find thin and crowded. But I do wish I could talk with her about Maggie Tulliver. When I read a book

I know a friend loves, I'm often thinking as I read: is it this part they love best? This character? But with *Mill*, it's easy. Maggie is the most lovable thing about it. Maggie is who Mum needed me to see.

Maggie is a key. She is where misunderstood women understand themselves. In *Memoirs of a Dutiful Daughter*, Simone de Beauvoir remembers Maggie as a salve. "I recognized myself in her," Beauvoir wrote. "She too was dark, loved nature, and books and life, was too headstrong to be able to observe the conventions of her respectable surroundings and yet was very sensitive to the criticism of a brother she adored." Seeing herself in Maggie also offered Simone a way out: "Henceforward I saw my isolation not as proof of infamy but as a sign of my uniqueness." Maggie unlocks something—Simone reports tears—and she ultimately dispels shame. Eliot said she'd used the "remotest areas" of her past for the novel; Lewes reports that she wept her way through the writing of the final scene.

Maggie is only made up but she helps her readers see something, change something. In 2001, Joan Didion defended her friend Elizabeth Hardwick's book of essays about women writers and women characters, *Seduction and Betrayal*, from the *New York Times* reviewer's objection that Hardwick had muddled up real and imaginary women. "That the women we invent have changed the course of our lives as surely as the women we are," Didion snapped back in her introduction to the essay collection, "is in many ways the point of this passionate book." This isn't just a psychoanalytic point, but also a practical one. Women's lives in particular have been curtailed by law, by custom, by inhibition too, and it takes the effort of imagining another sort of life before anyone can believe in it and live it.

It is almost a political point: it was said that slavery was natural, even though it was clearly unjust, until it changed. It is said now that addressing the climate crisis is too costly, in all the different ways costs are calculated. It feels to me that the groundwork for those bigger shifts happens in tinier ways, in the attempt to imagine, say, a girl who acts according to her own feelings, even if she risks being misunderstood by those who love her.

In draft, the novel was known as *Sister Tulliver*. Maggie is younger sister to Tom Tulliver, trailing behind him on forbidden trips to the pond or effortlessly outshining him at the lessons her parents don't think it worth paying for a girl to attend. Her hair is wild, her clothes won't stay neat, but she'll share her jam puff and apologize first. When her father loses the Dorlcote Mill, his inheritance and their livelihood, following an ill-judged court case he began, the Tullivers retrench, working and saving to reclaim what was once theirs. Maggie helps her mother keep house and makes a virtue of her loneliness by turning it into renunciation. Her suspicion is that she feels too much. Even in the holding back, "her own life was still a drama for her, in which she demanded of herself that her part should be played with intensity." She is drawn to Philip Wakem, the son of the family who gained possession of Dorlcote Mill after the court case, not believing that she could have any effect on him when there were "elegant, wealthy young ladies" in the world. The day Philip confesses his love is also the day Tom finds out his sister has been meeting his enemy in a tall-pined clearing. She is forced to choose between love and her family, and picks her family.

Years later, the patriarch dead, Tom is able to buy back the mill, which means Maggie can go into society. There she meets Philip again but also captures the attention of Stephen Guest, whom everyone thinks is weeks away from proposing to her cousin Lucy. Maggie is dark and unruly as Lucy is immaculate and blond. In a strange scene, more impressionist than realist, Stephen and Maggie end up in a boat together, rowing down the river, passing where they were supposed to stop, literally getting carried away. Stephen wants to elope; Maggie is tempted too. "Why should not Lucy—why should not Philip suffer?" Maggie thinks, in Eliot's free indirect style. "*She* had had to suffer through many years of her life; and who had renounced anything for her?" I can admire Maggie's renunciations but these moments of selfishness are when I can feel along with Maggie, the moments when the effort to be good falters, and she says (as I have said at times), why not me? It feels deeply characteristic of Eliot—we know how she had struggled—that the inward debate ends not in Maggie choosing escape but in her deciding that she can't cause anyone to suffer the way she has suffered, particularly not her cousin and her first love. "I will not begin any future," she tells Stephen, "even for you, with a deliberate consent to what ought not to have been."

Returning home and confessing is the path that costs her most. Elopement with Stephen would eventually have conferred respectability; marriage to Philip would have had a Romeo-and-Juliet-like poetic justice to it. As it is, the village places the blame on Maggie. She is a "designing bold girl" who stole her cousin's fiancé, and it is to be hoped that she leaves—goes to America, or anywhere—and not "taint" their air any longer. "Life stretched before her as one act of penitence, and all she craved, as she dwelt on her future lot, was something to guarantee her from more falling: her own weakness haunted her like a vision of hideous possibilities, that made no peace conceivable except such as lay in the sense of a sure refuge." There are moments in life where you shock yourself by what you want and what you've done, and they stop you from being able to trust yourself. You may not even be on the wrong path, but your ease in your own reactions has gone. You feel tired, crouched, mistrustful. That's where Maggie gets to, but it's not an entirely unhopeful place after all.

It is only the reader who really sees what Maggie has been through. And as she attempts to rebuild her life, with only her mother by her side, she finds that she's trying to appeal to people who couldn't understand her in any case. Philip and Lucy find ways to let her know that they know who she is, and comprehend what she's done, but her society is full of people who are "incapable of a conscientious struggle such as yours" and so "will be likely to shrink from you; because they will not believe in your struggle." It will be up to Maggie to make allowances for them. While reading *The Mill on the Floss* I made lots of guesses as to why Mum liked this book, and wanted me to read it: perhaps she's reminding me that it's OK to be clever and clumsy, that doing the right thing will be a struggle, that my brothers may judge (or despair of) me but that I can always lean on them, perhaps more reliably than a partner. I get angry she didn't leave me more advice. I wish she'd written a letter for me to open on the day of her funeral like a mother in a weepie, full of things she wanted me to know as I go on in life without her. But she wasn't that sort of person, and there are days I think she was right not to engage in such crystal-ball sentimentality. What if she'd written me a letter full of love for the children and partner I don't have? She couldn't know how I would change; I didn't know myself. So I have to guess what she would say to me now, and what she was trying to say in the gift of *The Mill on the Floss*. Or decide for myself.

One of those ideas is that reading *The Mill on the Floss* isn't about things my mother wanted to tell me, but about understanding something about her. My grandmother, my mother's mother, died while I was reading the novel, as painlessly and quickly as can be from two strokes in the space of a week, at ninety-two. And in the months that followed, as my father went through my grandmother's house, traces of my mother's life surfaced. He found her school reports, where the word "satisfactory" rather than "excellent" appeared over and over; the later ones bearing the traces of a long absence from school due to pneumonia. (She'd fallen sick just as she'd got interested, and missed too much of the syllabus to do herself justice in her exams.) I don't think she would have let me get away with reports like hers. In the line-a-day diaries my grandmother kept, otherwise about doctor's appointments and clothes bought, my mother made appearances: not home from a night out until 4 a.m., she was also relying on my grandmother to pay the taxi fare. When the car pulled up, my grandmother had paid £2. "Furious," she wrote. In a briefcase full of birth, death, and marriage certificates of people I'd never heard of but yet was related to, whole lives pressed into three sheets of paper, Dad found some letters sixteen-year-old Mum had written home from her French exchange in Paris. She wrote of a man following her around the club saying he loved her, the pink suede belt she'd bought and wasn't sure whether she would give to her sister as a present or keep for herself, the stupid photos she and her friends had posed for in the garden at Versailles, and the DJ playing "Hot Love" by T. Rex, "esp. for me, 'cos I love it!!"

I can enjoy this Mum, but she's not the one I knew. There are so many things we didn't get round to talking about together. She first took me to Paris, but I didn't ask her when she first went to Paris herself. I didn't think to ask. As these fragments of her past floated down into the present, without her or my grandmother to make sense of them, I felt like one of the many people in *The Mill on the Floss* who judge Maggie from the outside. But then the novel also offers a solution to my problem. To the reader who wants it, Maggie's story shows that fiancé-stealing or staying out too late are outside traces of internal struggles full of subtlety and small changes and selfishness and wishes to do good. I could say that these new things I've learned about my mother's youth unmake all that I knew of her. They are the opposite of the letter I sometimes want reminding me that I am loved. But in fact all my mother is lacking is an Eliot to write about her. Then she'll be a Maggie too. And maybe all she was saying in the gift of the book was that: we are all Maggies. I am one, you are one, she is one.

After two successful novels, Eliot was surer of herself as a writer. She found a rhythm: *Silas Marner*, then Florence; *Romola*, then Milan; *Felix Holt*, then Liège. While she was in England writing, Lewes went out in society, but Eliot stayed at home, only accepting visits from people she trusted, such as Anthony Trollope, who found one of their boys a job in the office of the Postmaster General where he worked, and Barbara, who was putting together the first women's suffrage petition and helping Emily Davies establish what would become Girton College, the first women's college of the University of Cambridge. To Barbara she wrote, in the middle of drafting *Silas Marner*, that she "preferred excommunication" to being "brought within the pale of people's personal attention." Her reticence showed too in the quiet way she supported Bodichon's activism: she met with Davies in private and gave money to Girton, but felt that if her views on women's place in society (which she might call nuanced, and I might call lukewarm) were widely known, they would be misunderstood. I am sometimes disappointed with Eliot's reluctance to speak up, because although she sets an example with her own career as a novelist, centers flawed but powerful women in her work, argues again and again that women should have access to formal education, she also wants women to know their place in society, which is complementary to that of men. Even by publishing with a male pseudonym, which she didn't have to do—her contemporaries Elizabeth Gaskell, Harriet Martineau, and Christina Rossetti didn't—she's gaming the system rather than remaking it. But I can forgive her almost anything for writing *Middlemarch*.

I suppose one of the most controversial parts of that novel for a twenty-first-century feminist like me is the fact that Dorothea Brooke, its intellectually ambitious heroine, ends up in an "unvisited tomb." Dorothea is endowed with money, status, ability, and above all idealism, but she is born into a society that can't help but misunderstand her. She is a cygnet among ducklings, a Saint Theresa without a great deed to accomplish, we are warned in the Prelude. She will be "foundress of nothing," a heroine who's no heroine at all. I remember feeling disappointed by her slide into domestic anonymity when I first read the book. I understood Dorothea's desire for more, and though I was grossed out at the thought of marrying someone like Casaubon, I understood that she might want someone to learn from if universities for women didn't exist yet. But I didn't see why she had to be punished for that desire to know, and not be allowed to achieve all she could. Florence Nightingale, reading each book of *Middlemarch* as it was released monthly in 1872, thought something like this too: why was Eliot depicting a failed reformer when there were real Octavia Hills in the world?

Although it dominates the first book of *Middlemarch*, Dorothea's story is not where Eliot began. She thought the novel was about Tertius Lydgate, an idealistic doctor arrived in a country village during the years before the Great Reform Act of 1832 to show the provincials how it's done. But she wasn't happy with the book until she saw a way of doubling and counterpointing Lydgate's fall with Dorothea's growing realization that marrying Pascal, as it were, might not fulfill her. In her own life, Eliot felt she was on the downward slope. In 1869, she glimpsed her own death when Lewes's middle son returned home from the British colony of Natal (now South Africa) with a spinal disease. She nursed him for six months, her only rest the two times a week she allowed Barbara to take her place at his bedside. "This death seems to me the beginning of our own," she wrote in her journal on the evening he died. She stopped writing the story about Lydgate, feeling that both herself and her work were "languishing," and were moreover useless in the face of the world as it was. "Am I doing anything that will add the weight of a sandgrain against the persistence of such evil?" she wrote about the Franco–Prussian War on the last day of 1870. Even when she began writing again, describing the emerging story of Dorothea hopefully as one "recorded among my possible themes ever since I began to write fiction," her sense of writing's uselessness was still on her mind: "In my private lot I am unspeakably happy, loving and beloved. But I am doing little for others."

When Eliot first began to write fiction, she wrote that "art is the nearest thing to life; it is a mode of amplifying experience and extending our contact with our fellow men beyond the bounds of our personal lot." The best thing an artist achieves is "the extension of our sympathies." And even if she doubted that at times, *Middlemarch* is proof that she didn't give up on it: if her books were only a sandgrain, they were nevertheless a sandgrain. On rereading *Middlemarch* now, no longer a young woman hoping to get into Oxford but someone who's been married and divorced, I can see more clearly that Dorothea is confusing a wish to better herself with marriage. "What a lake" Casaubon is, she thinks, "compared with my little pool!" I notice the signs of someone who doesn't know herself yet, wanting something that could never suit her. In the opening scene of the novel, Dorothea and her younger sister Celia are splitting their dead mother's jewels between them. Dorothea refuses to take anything, shuddering at what wearing a cross made of pearls "as a trinket" would do to her principles. But on opening a ring box they discover an emerald surrounded by diamonds, then notice a matching bracelet, and Dorothea conveniently remembers that "gems are used as spiritual emblems in the Revelation of St. John," and holds her hand up to the window so that the stones catch the light. "Yes! I will keep these." She is not so immune to beauty as she thought; she is not so able to renounce luxury as she imagined. (She is deeply likable in this.) Along with other glimpses of Dorothea as she is, rather than how she claims to be, Eliot extends the reader's sympathies further by giving us access to Casaubon's feelings. He had dismissed love in favor of work, but as he got older he began to see marriage differently, as a solace: "Hence he determined to abandon himself to the stream of feeling and perhaps was surprised to find what an exceedingly shallow rill it was." So much for the lake Dorothea saw in him! Before this, he could tell himself that true love would sweep him away when he found it, but now he can only suspect he's not capable of it. I can imagine his disappointment now in a way I couldn't when I was seventeen.

Like pinning out knitting to reveal the design, or holding a candle to a mirror to uncover a pattern of scratches, Eliot's narrator is always willing to try another way of seeing things. The intelligence telling the story holds no boundaries: in fact I often imagine them high up, observing from a place where boundaries don't mean much anyway. "What do I think of *Middlemarch*?" Emily Dickinson wrote to her cousin in a letter. "What do I think of glory?" There is irony in the novel, there is distance, but somehow it often results in a many-sided identification. *Middlemarch* is constructed as a moral and emotional workout: I don't think the ideal reader is supposed to skip through it unaffected. Even though I got in, I'd felt silly after my Oxford interview for treating a cornerstone of the English canon as a soap opera, and I knew that the way I identified with Dorothea wasn't something I was supposed to use when writing essays. I was reading naively, and that sort of reading was about to be trained out of me. The biggest taboo during my degree was to wonder about the sort of person a writer was from the novels they wrote, and I dread to think what would have happened if I'd turned up to a one-on-one with my tutor and said, "I don't like Casaubon." Biography, the writer's or mine, didn't matter, because books weren't about the people who wrote or read them, they were about the times the writer lived through, the history of ideas, the debates the books contributed to, and the way they changed notions of what the novel or a poem or a play could do. *Middlemarch* is more than eight hundred pages long and has lots to say about all of those subjects, and when I came to study Eliot, I read critics who traced her use of Darwin's *On the Origin of Species* and I wrote an essay about the web-like structure of the book. I was doing intellectual and literary history, and I was good at it, and I liked it. But did I also have to completely abandon the other sort of reading? I thought I did, and I had no idea that Eliot had hoped her writing would extend sympathies, as in fact it had done to me on my first reading, and every subsequent one. "If we had a keen vision and feeling of all ordinary human life," the narrator says in a ubiquitous passage of *Middlemarch*, "it would be like hearing the grass grow and the squirrel's heart beat, and we should die of that roar which lies on the other side of silence." Even in mocking her ambition, Eliot makes it sound noble to die of a compassionate cacophony. And isn't she also saying that identifying with characters, seeing their various points of view, isn't the easy path it appears to be?

On her honeymoon, Dorothea cries. She and Casaubon have gone to Rome (where Will caught sight of her in the Vatican galleries). Casaubon has worked on his book and Dorothea has been to see the ruins, the churches, the galleries, the views. After her dutiful tourism, she often prefers to end the day out of the city, under the Italian sky. She's not sure why she's crying:

she married the man she wanted to marry, and has the life of the mind she wanted. "How was it that in the weeks since her marriage, Dorothea had not distinctly observed but felt with a stifling depression, that the large vistas and wide fresh air which she had dreamed of finding in her husband's mind were replaced by ante-rooms and winding passages which seemed to lead nowhither?" In identifying with Dorothea, you are brought to strange places: it was she who imagined that her husband would enlarge and enliven her, not him and not even us. The reader can trace the connection between the woman who let sunshine find her emerald ring and the one who wants to watch a Lazio sunset, even if she can't quite yet. We are set thinking by Ladislaw noticing a "sensuous force controlled by spiritual passion" in her; we underline the phrase, we hold on to it as we read. A life of scholarly duty won't be enough for Dorothea. And as soon as we are sure of this, blame falls away, or rather descends equally on everyone. Her story challenges the very idea passed down at Oxford that books were about other books, that they were not about life. (And it doesn't surprise me that some Eliot scholars think she based the character of Casaubon on an actual Oxford don.)

I used to want desperately to be a "proper" critic, to be taken seriously, to have a full command of history and theory, but I don't want that anymore. I don't want to "admire" writing for its erudition, I want to be changed by it. I want to know what it's like to be someone else. I want to have that moment of recognition, finding something on the page I've felt but haven't put into words. I don't want just to accumulate knowledge but to be transformed by it, even if that transformation is tiny. Reading like this is at first about the possibility of changing your mind, but it can also be about changing the way you live, moving beyond what you already know, and letting that expansion affect how you live. Even at the size of a sandgrain, the shift is enough. You might speak up at the dinner table like Mary, or take up drinking wine and crying like Simone, or get up early to write like the character of Lenù in Ferrante's Neapolitan novels. You might try an open marriage or decide to have a child with a lover or determine to lie to get ahead. It is not about self-improvement but about freedom. And one of the ways you put on your freedom is by changing: becoming less of a feminist or more of one, writing more or something different or giving up altogether, gaining the courage to act according to your beliefs or condemning society from seclusion.

One of the things Eliot is saying in *Middlemarch*, I think, is that sandgrain-sized changes are worth it: "What do we live for, if it is not to make life less difficult to each other?" Dorothea's greatest achievement won't be her contribution to Casaubon's book, *The Key to All Mythologies*, but her daring in extending both sympathy and practical help to Lydgate when Middlemarch turns against him. (It is help Maggie Tulliver could have done with.) This sort of daring is within all our reach in the way being the author of a synthesizing work about Western belief isn't. Look again at the last sentence of the novel with this point of view and you see that the "unhistoric acts" that got Dorothea an "unvisited tomb" are actually the source of the "growing good of the world." You can count the number of copies a book sells, you can calculate the wealth someone leaves when they die. But the things Dorothea did are "incalculably diffusive." And I know that, because she's diffused them to me too.

I am wondering now whether Dorothea has changed me or I

have changed Dorothea. Did I really see her at seventeen when I wanted her to live up to the ideals she set herself? That was all I wanted to do too, and I doubt I would have listened to anyone who said that perfectionism of that sort wouldn't bring me happiness. This has always been a problem in my life: I won't speak unless I have planned the perfect thing to say; I won't date until I'm half a stone lighter; I won't send out my writing until I've read it so many times I'm sick of it. I've too often let perfection be the enemy of the good. No one told me at Oxford that I couldn't write an essay that took in Eliot's life, her influences, her historical context as well as my own history with her writing (an essay that might look a bit like this one); I must have told myself that. *Middlemarch*, of all novels in the canon, contains multitudes, and part of what makes it great by definition is that it can't be exhausted by a single approach. So it's not Oxford's fault, and, like Dorothea again, I surely needed to know what the scholarly path looked like in order to even tell that it wasn't for me either. So I think I must have changed Dorothea, not the other way around. There was so much I couldn't see on my first reading, as I'd guessed, because I'd barely lived. By my second, I had married believing in an intellectual partnership as much as a romantic one, I had been disappointed, I had divorced. All of this meant I could see that the younger me was no better than Dorothea, Casaubon, Lydgate, or Rosamond in *Middlemarch*, who believe that getting married will solve their problems. If I didn't think I was good enough, how would marriage solve that? OK, someone liked me enough to marry me but could that even get through if I didn't like myself? It's the wrong solution to the problem, and worse, the problem wasn't even in view if I thought I could solve it like that.

After my divorce, I went to therapy for years, first twice a week and then once a week. Instead of holidays or new shoes, I spent a pound a minute trying to work out why I'd left my marriage: I felt like bewildered Dorothea crying in Rome. But over time, what made me happy did emerge, in things I could reach reliably rather than the post-divorce thunderclaps like falling in love again or making a home on my own. On the evenings I sat in the cheap seats at the ballet because I didn't want to go home to an empty house, I would have lemon sorbet and champagne for dinner. As the only single woman at a one-year-old's birthday picnic, I could be the one to pick up a friend's daughter so that she could touch the leaves on a tree. On empty evenings, I would binge episodes of reality TV shows as if they were *Middlemarch*, forgetting my own problems in love. They were unhistoric acts, and didn't always add to the growing good of the world, but I think Dorothea would understand anyway. She had been waiting for a long time for me to catch up. It's good to have ambition—would I have even applied to Oxford from a state school without it?—but you can't be a prisoner to your ideals if you discover they don't make you happy.

And sometimes you make terrible predictions about what will make you happy. In July 1871, while Eliot was drafting *Middlemarch*, she wrote to Emanuel Deutsch, the German Jewish scholar and a friend who was just emerging from a "Slough of Despond":

Encourage Mr. Micawber's philosophy in your soul, and be sure that something will "turn up." Hopelessness has been to me, all through my life, but especially in painful years of my youth, the chief source of wasted energy with all the consequent bitterness of regret. Remember, it has happened to many to be glad that they did not commit suicide, though they once ran for the final leap, or as Mary Wollstonecraft did, wetted their garments well in the rain hoping to sink the better as they plunged. She tells how it occurred to her as she was walking in this damp shroud, that she might live to be glad that she had not put an end to herself—and so it turned out. She lived to know some real joys, and death came in time to hinder the joys from being spoiled. Which things are a parable.

Eliot wrote about Wollstonecraft in an essay just as she was thinking about beginning to write fiction, and here she is again. I wonder how many times she turned to Mary's life story in her head as encouragement, how many times she smoothed the rough edges of Mary's life into a silky pebble-parable. Mary was born again late in life as Mary Ann was, one by surviving suicide and the other by assuming a new name. They both outlived their hopelessness, and as Eliot argues here on behalf of Wollstonecraft, were rewarded for it. Maybe life isn't about anything so facile and twentieth century as working out via trial and error what makes you happy, maybe it's just about being hopeful for long enough—treating it almost as a discipline—to see something change. Book Five of *Middlemarch* is called "The Dead Hand" after the spiteful will Casaubon makes, barring his widow specifically from marrying Will, but the dead can also reach out hands to hold, as Wollstonecraft does. In Nuneaton Museum, there is a white marble sculpture of Eliot's right hand, a rose between her thumb and forefinger and a signet ring on her little finger. It is surprisingly beautiful: calm and almost balletic but with latent, coiled energy.

"No former book of mine," Eliot wrote of *Middlemarch* in her journal, a year after all its parts were published, "has been received with more enthusiasm." It literally brought flowers to her door. "I have received many assurances of its influence for good on individual minds." Eliot's fame had very nearly blotted out the fact of her living with a married man: she received visits from Tennyson, Darwin, and Henry James; she corresponded with Elizabeth Garrett Anderson and Harriet Beecher Stowe. Turgenev paid homage, as did Queen Victoria. On Sunday afternoons she sat almost in state, receiving visiting luminaries. The holiday in Bad Homburg she took once *Middlemarch* was finished gave her the first scene of her next novel, which concentrates on a society beauty, Gwendolen Harleth, and a man, Daniel Deronda, searching for his own identity, which he eventually discovers in the Jewish community. One evening in the Kursaal, she watched Byron's grand-niece at the gambling tables, and it made her "cry to see her young fresh face among the hags and brutally stupid men around her." And so *Daniel Deronda* begins: "Was she beautiful or not beautiful?" Eliot isn't normally this pithy, and I catch a sense of her confidence, a hard-won ease with herself as a writer. In that novel, written as she was touching the height of her fame, she examines what it is that makes an artist, deciding that it is a quality of soul rather than a skill set or a burning ambition or a calling or an eye for what is salable. And the artist's highest state is a sort of self-forgetting, a melting, a blurring of boundaries between herself and other people or even the landscape: a way of letting other voices take over that also comes close to a desire not to exist at all. This is a strange, appealing idea that Elena Ferrante uses too, particularly for the character of Lenù. The moments of melting in all of these books are ones I see and feel are important, though I am not always sure I understand them. I like the idea of losing myself—it's part of the pleasure of getting drunk or having sex—but it also frightens me. I think of Maggie Tulliver noticing the tidal wave coming toward her, breaking the "threads of ordinary association." That sounds scarily like losing your bearings, losing your mind. One of Eliot's biographers, Jenny Uglow, argues that this "recurs so often that one cannot help feeling it must have been a crucial experience for the author herself." Perhaps this is what neuroscientists are getting at when they refer to the flow state, which happens when you're deeply absorbed in doing something, almost anything but often making art, that allows you to forget yourself and your worries. Perhaps it is about going mad. It's interesting too that this loss of boundaries should be important to two women writers who, at the distance of centuries, needed the cover of a different name in order to write fiction. Making things up can offer them a way to smash boundaries that are rigidly enforced in reality. Eliot knows how much work can be behind the extension of sympathies, let alone the abolition of boundaries. Dorothea's defining moment, inviting Lydgate to see her and tell her the story behind the rumors about him, is hard won over more than six hundred pages.

Two years after *Daniel Deronda* was published, to reviews hostile to the Jewish part of the novels, Lewes developed cancer, and on November 30, 1878, he died. Eliot didn't leave her room for a week. She allowed letters to pile up: the first person she wrote to, in early January, was Barbara: "I am a bruised creature, and shrink even from the tenderest touch. As soon as I feel able to see anybody I will see *you*." She didn't go out for three months, and she abandoned her own writing, the half-drafted *Impressions of Theophrastus Such*, to complete Lewes's last work. In March she wrote again to Barbara. "As for the mind, I am full of occupation, but the sorrow deepens down instead of diminishing . . . for nearly 25 years I have been used to find my happiness in his. I can find it nowhere else. But we can live and be helpful without happiness, and I have had more than myriads who were and are better fitted for it."

She was joined in her grief by a friend, John Cross, who was twenty years younger than her. His mother had died a week after Lewes had. Cross, who worked as a banker, helped her to set up the George Henry Lewes Studentships that would support the study of physiology in England for the next sixty years: "That there should always, in consequence of his having lived, be a young man working in the way he liked to work, is a memorial of him that comes nearest to my feeling," she wrote to Barbara. She decided to read Dante in order to learn Italian, and Cross, also needing an occupation during his own mourning, asked to accompany her. Grieving, even with good company, even with a language to learn, is slow, mysterious, unending work. In her diary for October 3, 1879, she simply wrote: "Tears, tears."

That winter, Cross noticed his feelings had changed from friendship into love, and told Eliot. She refused him. He would ask again. And she would refuse him again. In letters, he was her "Bester Mann," her "Best loved and loving one." She asked her doctor: should I marry? He had attended Lewes in his final illness, and watched over Eliot in her grief. "Why not?" he said, and on May 6, 1880, they were married, and immediately left for a honeymoon in Italy. She was sixty-one and he was forty. Eliot's brother Isaac, who had broken with her for living in sin with Lewes, was delighted, writing after twenty-three years of silence to offer "sincere congratulations to you and Mr. Cross," hoping that marriage "will afford you much happiness and comfort." Many of her friends were baffled: why the capitulation to marrying after years of not? It was left to Barbara to be the friend we all hope we can be. She was one of the first to know, as she was one of the first Eliot let in after Lewes's death. She wrote:

> My dear I hope and I think you will be happy. Tell Johnny Cross I should have done exactly what he has done if you would have let me and I had been a man.
>
> You see I know all love is so different that I do not see it unnatural to love in new ways—not to be unfaithful to any memory. If I knew Mr. Lewes he would be as glad as I am that you have a new friend.
>
> I was glad to hear you were going to Italy but I did not guess this.
>
> My love to your friend if you will.
>
> > Your loving
> > Barbara

I can't say I don't find something glorious in Eliot, who for so long thought herself unlovable, being adored at the age of sixty-one by a younger man. It is as stupid to avoid convention for the sake of it as to court it. Eliot lost as many friends for marrying as for not marrying. "I shall be a better, more loving creature than

I could have been in solitude," Eliot wrote back to Barbara, in a sentence Dorothea might have used to explain to her sister her marriage to Ladislaw.

As for the relationship with Cross itself, it is hard to judge. On honeymoon in Venice, Johnny jumped out of the window of their hotel and into the Grand Canal. He later put it down to overexertion, but it is hard not to think of it as a self-destructive act. His recovery was slow, and they stayed on the Continent longer than they'd planned to, returning to Cross's house in Cheyne Walk in moneyed Chelsea at the beginning of December 1880. There she received friends again—Herbert Spencer and Edith Simcox, a younger feminist writer who was in love with Eliot—though Barbara had suffered two successive strokes and couldn't come. On December 19, Eliot noticed "a slight sore throat" and on December 21, she died at Cheyne Walk. She'd been married for seven months. Cross, who would go on to write an important early biography of Eliot, buried her in Highgate Cemetery, next to Lewes. Her tomb is a simple obelisk, and the flowers lying on the ground before it last time I was there indicate that it is far from unvisited.

Zora

The spring I took antidepressants for the first time, four years to the month my marriage had broken down, I couldn't rely on sleeping through the night. I prescribed myself a bath every evening. To get the water hot enough, I had to run the tap slowly, and I would roam my flat while I was waiting for the tub to fill. Some days, I would be my own turndown service, laying out a nightdress and spraying my pillow with aromatic spray; I would add things to the bath I'd read about online, like chamomile tea bags or Epsom salt or bergamot oil, or brush my skin from sole to throat with pale bristles as the wellness influencers recommended. "There must be quite a few things a hot bath can't cure," Esther Greenwood says in *The Bell Jar* (the sentence is infuriatingly cross-stitchable, instagrammable), "but I don't know many of them." I was trying the cure. But when I got into the bath, I would start crying, as if being submerged in hot water to the chin allowed me to release something the day kept in check. And I wasn't weeping with picturesquely leaking eyes but heaving with deep racking sobs that echoed off the tiles. Or I would get sweaty and red and my heart would beat fast and I would have to get out after ten minutes. Or the water had run cold and I would discover it as I stepped in, and have to take a shower instead. I kept trying. I stayed close by while the tub filled, checking I hadn't got the temperature wrong. I bought a bottle of bath foam aimed at getting babies to sleep and sunk into bubbles instead of steeping in salt. And to head off tears I would read. On one of those evenings, I picked *Their Eyes Were Watching God* by Zora Neale Hurston from my shelf.

I'd had a copy for more than a decade, carrying it from a flat shared with friends to a home bought with my husband back to a flat where I lived on my own. The edition was produced for the feminist publisher Virago's thirtieth anniversary, a hardback with a red pattern of handlike leaves and purple berries on it, with an introduction by Zadie Smith. My mother had bought it for my birthday, along with other titles in the Virago anniversary drop: Angela Carter, Muriel Spark, Barbara Pym, and Elizabeth Taylor. (I was getting better in a single respect: I'd delayed reading *The Mill on the Floss* for twenty-four years but only ten for *Their Eyes Were Watching God*.) Zadie writes about her mother giving Zora's novel to her when she was fourteen, and hating the idea that there were books she had to read because of the girl she was. When Zadie asked if she was supposed to like the novel because she's Black, her mother replied: "No—because it's really good writing." I followed Janie's life from deep within fragrant hot water, thrilled to watch her escape every wrong match until she found a resting place in herself. Why had I not known of this sort of story before? Janie tested her personality and found something out about herself through her relationships, becoming more herself by the encounter with another. Couldn't I see my own life like that? If Janie hadn't known other sorts of partnerships, she wouldn't have been able to discern the one that worked, the one for which it was worth defying gossip.

Maybe *Their Eyes Were Watching God* had found me at exactly the right time. I was fascinated by love and entirely mistrustful of it; I had a sense that all my instincts were wrong, and that the love that did and had come my way, I was unworthy of. All my relationships so far had been mistakes, I thought, and I was crying in the bath again.

Zora Neale Hurston wrote the novel—a fixture on high school syllabuses, a million-copy seller, and inspiration to a generation of Black women writers—in seven Caribbean weeks during winter 1936. She was forty-six, though most people thought she was thirty-six (I'll explain later), and was living in Haiti, to learn Creole and observe voodoo ceremonies for a book of anthropology she had won a Guggenheim fellowship for. At this midpoint in her life, she had good work, enough money, and plenty of time. "Nobody realizes more than I what a wonderful thing has happened to me," she wrote to Henry Allen Moe, the president of the Guggenheim Foundation and the future dedicatee of *Their Eyes Were Watching God*. "I have grown in every direction in these six months." And although she had left her love, Percival Punter, a graduate student more than twenty years younger than her, in New York, her feelings for him had not faded. She would direct or sublimate or relieve her emotion into *Their Eyes Were Watching God*. "The plot was far from the circumstances," Zora later recalled, "but I tried to embalm all the tenderness of my passion for him" in the novel. There is a saying in French, *reculer pour mieux sauter*, and it means that the drawing back makes the eventual leap higher. Zora retreated, and returned with a novel. In the calm recollection of what she'd felt, a transformation happened. And a bit, perhaps—the conjecture is irresistible—of the magic she'd been studying among the mambos of Haiti made it into the novel too.

Zora set *Their Eyes Were Watching God* not in the hills above Port-au-Prince, where she wrote it, but in Eatonville, Florida, where she'd grown up. Eatonville, east of Orlando, wasn't the first town in the United States to be self-governed by Black people, but it was the first one to be incorporated, "charter, mayor, council, town marshal and all." This place—"of five lakes, three croquet courts, three hundred brown skins, three hundred good swimmers, plenty guavas, two schools, and no jailhouse"—was where Zora Neale would return to again and again over the course of her seventy or so years, both in her fiction and in her life. In the first decade of the twentieth century, Southern state after Southern state passed Jim Crow laws that disenfranchised Black people from their own country. In Florida, white and Black children had been prevented from going to the same school since 1885; white and Black people hadn't been able to share a train carriage since 1865; Black men and white women who spent the night together could be fined $500. These prohibitions did not crumble until 1967, seven years after Zora's death.

Zora was born in Notasulga, Alabama, in January 1891, the fifth child and second girl to John Hurston and Lucy Potts. They were sharecroppers, until John, who was also a Baptist preacher, set out to find something better for his family. Zora was three when they moved to Eatonville, and always spoke of the place as her "native town," even though it wasn't. In other ways, though, she was pure Eatonville. As a child, she clashed with her father, who thought "it didn't do for Negroes to have too much spirit," and her grandmother, her mother's mother, who couldn't make sense of her self-assurance. "She had known slavery, and to her," Zora wrote, "my brazenness was unthinkable." But Zora hadn't known slavery and barely remembered Alabama. She would sit on the front gatepost, and ask white travelers on their way to Orlando if they wanted her to go "a piece of the way" with them. (They rarely said no.) In "Drenched in Light," one of her first stories, she wrote about a girl, "little Isis Watts, the joyful," who rode along with white travelers as her grandmother yelled at her to clean up the yard. At the end of the story, a white woman intercedes on Isis's behalf because "I want brightness and this Isis is joy itself, why she's drenched in light!" Isis is all joy and sunshine and song and dance. (These are the words Hurston uses over and again about her in the four pages or so of the story.) In an essay written a few years later, "How It Feels to Be Colored Me," Hurston remembers that white people

> liked to hear me "speak pieces" and sing and wanted to see me dance the parse-me-la, and gave me generously of their small silver for doing these things, which seemed strange to me for I wanted to do them so much that I needed bribing to stop. Only they didn't know it. The colored people gave no dimes. They deplored any joyful tendencies in me, but I was their Zora nevertheless. I belonged to them, to the nearby hotels, to the county— everybody's Zora.

She is everybody's Zora, but she belongs most to herself. She isn't doing anything she doesn't want to be doing, and she immediately sees that there is value in the life she leads and the things she knows. Zora, the first professional Black woman writer, could only have imagined a profession where there was none by noticing that what she already loved to do was worth silver coins to other people. It is the joy in a character like Isis that made her the first professional Black woman writer. Hurston is literally performing for white visitors, but she doesn't see it that way. She sees freedom and song and light. She sees herself doing what she wants to do.

If her father and grandmother counseled humility, Zora remembers her mother telling her, and all the Hurston children, to "jump at de sun." Lucy defended her daughter's right to sit under the "loving pine," her favorite tree in Eatonville, and think up stories. Zora picked up Eatonville lore from Joe Clarke's store porch, during "lying" sessions where the men of the town told folk tales. At school she read Norse tales, Roman myths, the Bible, Grimms' fairy tales. She herself fashioned dolls out of a corn cob, corn husk, and a bar of laundry soap and embroiled the characters in love triangles. She also had visions from a young age that as time went on she understood to be premonitions too.

When Zora was fourteen, Lucy became sick, becoming thinner and weaker until she was confined to her bed. Not wanting to believe she was dying, Lucy made Zora promise she wouldn't take the pillow from underneath her head, or cover the mirror, or stop the clock, which is what was done when a person had died to let the soul from the room. It was an impossible injunction, unfair even, in the face of the rest of the family who wanted the death done right. As Zora yelled for the mirror to be uncovered, "Mama was still rasping out the last morsel of her life." Zora had the sense that Lucy was "trying to speak to me. What was she trying to tell me?" Zora couldn't and wouldn't know, a torture in itself. Lucy died as the sun set. "I had failed her. It seemed as she died that the sun went down on purpose to flee away from me," she wrote thirty years later. "That hour began my wanderings. Not so much in geography, but in time. Then not so much in time as in spirit."

She'd not only lost the parent who supported her, but she now had a new memory, of not using her voice in service of her dying mother's. I can't help wondering how this affected Zora, who had believed so effortlessly that she would be listened to, in song as in reading out loud in the classroom. There were limits, it turned out, to what even a strong and clear voice could do. Lucy's children, six boys and two girls, whom she had taught at home, would be scattered across the South after her death. "Mama died at sundown and changed a world. That is, the world which had been built out of her body and her heart." And so for Zora the world of Eatonville—the Black-run town where the porches are full of stories—became entwined with the emotional world her mother had built for her. Eatonville was where she returned to do her first pieces of anthropological work. It was where she set her first novel, about a faithless preacher like her father, married to someone who died like her mother. And it was where she would set *Their Eyes Were Watching God*, that embalming of her passion for her great love.

After Lucy's funeral, Zora went upstate to school in the city of Jacksonville, and her father married again. When the money for the school fees ran out, she returned to Eatonville. One day she found her stepmother in her mother's feather bed and ended up in a fistfight that nearly killed them both. And so she left again, now working as a maid, now as a nanny, now going back to school, now leaving a job because her employer was set on enticing her to run away with him. She lived all over Florida and Tennessee, sometimes with her mother's friends, sometimes with her older brothers and sisters. In 1915, at twenty-four, she took a job as a dresser for an opera singer touring with a Gilbert and Sullivan production. As an important part of a company of actors, her confidence grew exponentially again (and the money didn't hurt). When her opera singer left the stage in order to marry, Zora began going to high school at night, knocking a decade off her age at enrollment. (Her biographers are often angry at her for lying about her age, but she didn't get the chance to finish school because of her mother's death, which is hardly fair either.) She was aiming at Howard University in Washington, DC: "It is to the Negro what Harvard is to the whites," she explained in her memoir. When she got in at the age of twenty-eight, she felt "the ladder under her feet" for the first time. She majored in English and worked to support herself as a manicurist in a barber shop near the US Capitol. Her clients were bankers, senators, journalists, and congressmen: "I learned things from holding the hands of men like that."

At Howard, she met Herbert Sheen, whom she would eventually marry, and began writing stories and articles, first for the university newspapers, and then for *Opportunity* magazine in New York, which had been founded to document race barriers but quickly became the journal of the Harlem Renaissance. *Opportunity* launched the writing careers of Zora, Langston Hughes, Claude McKay, and Countee Cullen, among others, via its annual literary contest. Zora sent them "Drenched in Light," and on receiving a letter from the editor asking for more, she turned up in New York City "with $1.50, no job, no friends and a lot of hope." She won a prize in the contest, and attracted attention: she was given a job as a secretary to Fannie Hurst, who had written the novel *Imitation of Life* and would become a lifelong friend, and a scholarship to Barnard to study anthropology under Alain Locke, the first African American Rhodes scholar and an elder statesman of the Harlem scene. (In attending a white college, she was one of only three hundred Black women doing so in the US in the early 1920s.) Arriving at the *Opportunity* competition after-party, she reportedly flung a colorful scarf around her neck and bellowed the name of her play—"*Coloooooor Struuuckkkkk!*"—out loud. The Isis Watts spirit was back.

I began the search for a home of my own. I looked at tens of flats, every Saturday morning and often on my lunchtimes too. And then I found one. There was a tiny room for writing that looked over a garden, in which I would plant roses and lavender. The living room was painted in a pink that felt fresh and warm at once, and windows on both sides let in cubic meters of light. I had a gas range to cook on, a bath to fill with hot water, and a bedroom tucked cozily at the back of the house. I dreamed of sharing the place with lovers, family, friends, the children I knew, filling it with new memories. I wanted parties there, dinners, Christmases. I fantasized about the things I would write in my study: could I write that novel I longed to? But it wasn't easy to live there alone: there were cupboard doors I didn't know how to rehang; there was no one there if I cried; the pretty sash windows let heat escape, so I often ended my days curled up on the sofa in a blanket instead. I was a gentrifier in a neighborhood that a generation ago had been affordable; I lived solo in a flat meant for a family. I had made space in my life for new things to come in, but when were they coming? When

I read Zora, cheerfully moving through the world toward the right life for her, I felt envious, stuck. I wanted to know how to move through life with ease.

It would later be historicized as the Harlem Renaissance, but Zora simply lived it: she would go to "rent parties"—because wages were too low for rents, there were parties in apartments with music and cocktails, with a 50-cent entry fee—all around the intersection of Seventh Avenue and 135th Street. "When Zora was there," the poet Sterling Brown remembered, "she *was* the party." With friends, she started a magazine, *Fire!!*, which disappeared after one issue. She worked on a play with Langston Hughes, becoming close to him. People slept with each other in a free and unstigmatized way, and sex parties were held too. Zora was still writing to Herbert, but he remembered she didn't require fidelity of him, and perhaps she also didn't expect that of herself. There were plays and poetry readings, dinners and lectures. She was photographed. But it is almost as if the living overtook the writing: her antics generated "Zora Stories," anecdotes Harlemites passed around, making her a figure in society rather than a serious writer. In 1927 she perhaps sensed the shift, and left New York for Eatonville, to collect the sort of folklore she grew up hearing. This would become the pattern of her writing life: back and forth between literary New York and porches in Florida; collecting Black stories for her anthropological work on the one hand and writing her own on the other. She was also reunited with Herbert after five years apart, and married him in Florida that May, feeling "assailed by doubts" on the wedding day itself. Did she love him, or was he just a habit?

Her story-collecting was funded by money from Barnard as well as from Charlotte Osgood Mason, her patron and that of many writers and artists in Harlem, including Hughes. (Zora's letters include many to her patrons, and disappointingly few to her lovers and close friends.) Zora became interested in hoodoo, learning enough from surviving practitioners in New Orleans to become a priestess herself, and was given the name Zora the Rain-Bringer. But the New York money dried up during the Depression, she divorced Herbert after all, and decided to return to Florida, to give herself the time and space to write fiction again. She drafted *Jonah's Gourd Vine* on a wobbly card table in a two-room house in Sanford, making a cameo appearance in her parents' story as Isis from "Drenched in Light." She owed $18 in back rent when she received a telegram from Lippincott in New York accepting the novel and offering her $200 for publication.

"It was unheard of for a young Black girl to aspire to be a writer," the poet Margaret Walker later said. "Only one person had even tried." And that was Zora. She was forty-three (though not everyone knew it) when *Jonah's Gourd Vine* was published in 1934, and it was followed a year later by *Mules and Men*, her first book of anthropology. *Mules and Men* opens with an account of a "toe party" in Wood Bridge, near Eatonville, where the men choose a woman to spend the evening with from a parade of their toes. Charlie Jones picks Zora and treats her to hot peanuts and home-brewed coon dick in a jar ("the minute it touched my lips, the top of my head blew off") but the dance floor was already empty by the time they got on it. At the end of the night, she collects a song: "Ruther be in Tampa with the Whip-poor-will/ Than to be 'round here—/ Honey with a hundred-dollar bill." In Florida, her life and her writing fed each other in a way that wasn't so easy in New York. She'd applied for a Guggenheim fellowship to continue her story-collecting during her graduate studies at Columbia, but she found out she had been turned down. She didn't know that her friends in New York had told the Guggenheim judges that Zora was a genius—but unreliable.

It was at this impasse that Zora fell in love. Percy Punter was also studying at Columbia, and twenty-three years old. She was forty-four, seemingly thirty-four. They had first met three years before, when Zora was married. Then she was directing *The Great Day*, a revue of songs and stories she'd collected during her travels. Punter sang in the revue, and she remembered him for being "tall, dark brown, magnificently built." And as she got to know him for the second time, she was drawn in by his independence of mind: "When a man keeps beating me to the draw mentally, he begins to get glamorous." She fell in love as if she'd made "a parachute jump." Punter was insecure, perhaps jealous of how in demand Zora was, and needed proof of her devotion: he asked her to marry him, leave New York, and give up her work. "I really wanted to do anything he wanted me to do, but that one thing I could not do." And yet they couldn't leave one another alone, even as they could not compromise. They came to blows. When Zora heard she had won a Guggenheim, having reapplied after her rejection, she left for Jamaica and Haiti "to work hard on my research to smother my feelings. But the thing would not down."

Their Eyes Were Watching God opens with Janie Crawford walking back into Eatonville after a funeral. Everyone is wondering where she's been and what has happened to her. The men notice her "pugnacious breasts," the women her "muddy overalls," though only her best friend Phoeby approaches her to hear the story, with a plate of mulatto rice. Janie eats; Phoeby protests the rice would have been better with more bacon grease. Janie's returned from working in the Everglades with her partner Tea Cake, though now he's "gone. And dat's the only reason you see me back here." Janie wants to tell her story, not just because rumors have already started to fly, but so that her friend understands her: "Phoeby, we been kissin'-friends for twenty years, so Ah depend on you for a good thought. And Ah'm talking to you from dat standpoint." And she is talking: Hurston alternates between dialect, as an anthropologist might, and an elegant, wise, third-person voice, almost out of a folktale. She's using her Eatonville and her Columbia sides, creating a style suited to someone who believes that "Negro reality is a hundred times more imaginative and entertaining than anything that has ever been hatched up over a typewriter." She is rooted, and yet entirely herself.

"Ah know exactly what Ah got to tell yuh," Janie begins, "but it's hard to know where to start at." The narrative has already started in fact, with the image. "Janie saw her life like a great tree in leaf with things suffered, things enjoyed, things done and undone. Dawn and doom was in the branches." I thought of the Loving Pine of her Florida childhood, and the Tree of Hope in Harlem at the corner of 7th and 131st, which performers would rub for luck. I thought too of *The Bell Jar*'s imaginary fig tree: the branches with their ripening figs offering everything and nothing. Janie is being brought up in West Florida by her grandmother, who is waiting watchfully to see who is interested in taking on and marrying her granddaughter. (Her own daughter, Janie's mother, disappeared years before, having fallen in love without getting married, or as her grandmother puts it, having "hugged and kissed and felt around with first one man and then another.") Janie's grandmother wants her to marry the older, "decent," "good man" Logan Killicks, knowing that her death will leave Janie with no protection—"de nigger woman is de mule uh de world so fur as Ah can see," is her own worldview—and that someone who can give Janie a home is good enough. For Janie, sitting underneath a blossoming pear tree dreaming of kissing a classmate rather than "ole skull-head" Killicks, she'll do what she must, and hope for love to arrive.

It does, but not in the shape of Killicks, or even of the man for whom she leaves Killicks. "There are years that ask questions and years that answer," the narrator says. "Did marriage compel love like the sun the day?" This is the question to which Janie will find the answer in her first marriage. When Joe Starks rolls into town, leaving her loveless contract with Killicks makes emotional, if not yet practical, sense. Her pear-blossom dream had died long before and she hadn't expected to be able to make an escape. Janie has dough in the skillet for Killicks when she sees that by staying with him, she's losing time: "A feeling of sudden newness and change came over her. Janie hurried out of the front gate and turned south. Even if Joe was not there waiting for her, the change was bound to do her good." And immediately, it does: "The morning road air was like a new dress . . . Her old thoughts were going to come in handy now, but new words would have to be made and said to fit them." (I haven't said yet how consistently well dressed Zora was: not just that flung colored scarf on her first weeks in New York City but flapper dresses, navel-skimming beads, a dark fedora with a curving brim.) The air can't have changed, and Janie isn't perhaps in love with Joe Starks, but sometimes moving away from something you know isn't working matters more than what you're moving toward—the boldness itself is what makes the air feel like a new dress. I felt that too, and I did buy new dresses, almost as soon as I knew I needed a new life. I wore black velvet and red silk instead of shapeless jumper dresses. I let my clothes be tighter and my shoulders naked. I bought a perfume with amber notes. I was hopeful. Janie's boldness makes the idea that there is some better love out there possible; it keeps faith with the vision she had under the pear tree.

Joe and Janie are heading toward Eatonville before it was Eatonville, as Zora's parents once did. Joe builds a general store and then proposes himself as "mayor–postmaster–landlord–storekeeper," and that means Janie becomes "Mrs. Mayor Starks" and has a reputation to burnish. The pressure that comes with being First Lady of Eatonville—to be seen and not heard, not to join in the lying sessions on the store porch, to add up the prices for a pound and a half of bacon and a half-pound of lard in her head, to wear her long hair tied up in public—begins to tell on Janie, who stages silent rebellions against the work she has to do but isn't suited for. But she's also finding out what she is good at. When she speaks in favor of her husband's freeing of a mule which is being baited by the men of Eatonville—"Abraham Lincoln," she tells the townspeople, "he had de whole United States tuh rule so he freed de Negroes. You got uh town so you freed uh mule. You have tuh have power tuh free things and dat makes you lak uh king uh something"—it's obvious to all that she's a "born orator." Keeping up appearances is a "strain," and speaking her mind is a relief. She loved listening to the boast-flirting and the debates about everything and nothing going on among those gathered on the porch, when she was still allowed to.

She's cooking one evening for Joe, as she once did for Logan. Dinner has gone wrong—the fish is raw at the bone and the rice is burnt—and he explodes, slapping her face. Cheeks hot, she sees that she's no longer "petal-open" with her husband: "She had no more blossomy openings dusting pollen over her man, neither any glistening young fruit where the petals used to be." This love has not borne fruit. (Conventionally, this metaphor would mean children, but here it seems to mean a full, ripened love. Zora would have no children, and she seems not to have written about it, and perhaps it didn't bother her very much.) Feelings have a natural flowering, and a natural failure to thrive. Janie has a dim sense that there must be something beyond her marriage to Joe Starks, even if there are other women, perhaps most, who would jostle and cajole to be the wife of the mayor of the first incorporated Black town in America. "She was saving up feelings for some man she had never seen," is how the narrator puts it, with that wise, age-old, all-encompassing voice that either knows that better love is around the corner, because they're the narrator after all, or simply the truth universally acknowledged that being single and open to whatever good, petal-open love that comes her way makes more sense than staying in a relationship she knows can't and won't suit her.

Janie's way out of her marriage isn't clear. At thirty-five, she thinks she's too old for another divorce, and there's at least a roof over her head. "She didn't read books," the narrator says, "so she didn't know that she was the world and the heavens boiled down to a drop." (I underlined this sentence in my copy as I read in the bath, my mood lifting so very slowly but definitely lifting: I read books, and maybe one day I could think of myself as the heavens in a drop instead of a depressive dripping wet from her bath cure.) And then plot intervenes and Joe conveniently sickens. I say conveniently, but he did all he could to speed things along: he refuses Janie's help, and won't let the doctor come from Orlando to see him and prescribe something for his failing kidneys. In his last moments, he allows Janie to come to his side. "You wasn't satisfied wid me de way Ah was. Naw!" she says to him. "Mah own mind had tuh be squeezed and crowded out tuh make room for yours in me."

After the funeral, she lets her hair down, and the suitors start calling:

> Janie laughed at all these well-wishers because she knew that they knew plenty of women alone; that she was not the first one they had ever seen. But most of the others were poor. Besides she liked being lonesome for a change. This freedom feeling was fine. These men didn't represent a thing she wanted to know about. She had already experienced them through Logan and Joe. She felt like slapping some of them for sitting around grinning at her like a pack of chessy cats, trying to make out they looked like love.

Her relationships have shown Janie what she doesn't want, but have given her enough status and money and time to work out what she does. Maybe all she wants to do right then is laugh. Tea Cake comes into the store at 5:30 p.m. one day, looking to buy cigarettes. Janie sells him some Camels; he asks for a "lil piece uh fire" too. She hands him two matches and asks him why he isn't at the ball game like everybody else. "Well, Ah see somebody else besides me ain't dere. Ah just sold some cigarettes." They laugh, and they won't stop. They play checkers, they drink Coca-Cola, they eat pound cake, they go trout fishing—in short, they play. In the evenings, Tea Cake sings the blues, lulling her to sleep, and when she wakes, he is combing her let-down hair. "He looked like the love thoughts of women," the narrator says. "He could be a bee to a blossom—a pear-tree blossom in the spring. He seemed to be crushing scent out of the world with his footsteps." Janie finally has her blossomy love.

When I told my old boss I was getting divorced, she said: "Well, you did get married in a very desultory way." I puzzled over the comment for a long time, but she had hit on something. I was missing joy, excitement, fun. It's good to be sensible when you are investing your pension, but if desultory becomes your permanent mood? It seems obvious now, and I don't blame my husband for it. In the years since my divorce, I have lighted on that blossomy, foamy feeling more often. I have found it more easily outside the sort of relationship where you share a bank account, thrash out Christmas plans, and discuss what's for dinner. (That daily discussion about dinner was one of the things I hated most about being married, as I hadn't yet found my own way of enjoying cooking and planning meals, let alone doing it jointly. It had been a question my mother asked me, and I was often stumped for an answer as a child: I knew we couldn't have pizza every night.) With men who aren't my husband, or who don't want to be, I can stay up all night talking and drinking and listening to music and having sex. I can kiss on manicured lawns, drink prosecco in bed, read poetry at dawn, dance naked in heels, paint my lips red. And the question soon comes: can you make a life from this? Early intoxicating love is one thing, but what about dinner on a Tuesday in March? I was worried about replicating the things I found confining about being married. I had a beautiful home now, but did I know how to live in it with someone else? I was scared of getting trapped again, and I couldn't see what possibilities there might be in a joint life.

But I was learning. I held a party for my summer birthday: I warmed pizza and chilled rosé and turned the patio into a jungly dance floor, going so late that the neighbors behind started yelling. We had Easter Sunday lunch around my dining table, my little brother cooking lamb, my father sneaking around the corner for potted daffodils, my mother quite ill but accepting the dinner spoon by spoon. I held brunch for Melanie and our university girlfriends, warming croissants and brewing coffee while their babies sprawled over the carpet, clutching my wooden spoons in their little fat hands. I made overnighting friends "divorce pasta": a lemon and Parmesan spaghetti I'd made for myself so many times that I could give my full attention to what they were saying as I cooked. I rolled out my yoga mat in the mornings—it was Melanie, I think, with the wisdom earned from her own single years, who reminded me of what I could do with a yoga mat of my own—and I read on the sofa while dal bubbled on the stove. I cried in the bath, on the sofa, in the garden. I watched formulaic rom-coms. I danced in front of the bathroom mirror when I got back drunk. It wasn't that I didn't know how to make a life, I discovered, it just wasn't easy. I had to be patient, and I had to try new things, and have them fail sometimes. I had to work out what was right for me.

From the stability I made for myself, I could glance up and let other people into my life. After a few years of living alone, not always happily, Željka moving in was a delight. She joined me for yoga in the mornings, and she showed me how to deal with the last vegetables in the weekly delivery. (This involves vegan mayo and hot sauce.) I learned that there are a million solutions to what to have for dinner, and I'm finding the ones that suit me. I'm growing up, or into myself, or something. And I could apply what I learned with Željka to whatever new arrangement I found, couldn't I? Should I be fortunate to find that blossomy feeling again, I could let it guide me. One gets so tired and disillusioned at the end of a relationship that it's easy to forget that the weird, mysterious energy of falling in love gives you all you need to rearrange your life. And that all these problems of living are never-ending, which is to say that neither being married nor being single is the solution to them.

It's almost because Janie seems to be having so much fun that her friends start counseling against her relationship with Tea Cake. Surely he's trying to get her money? And what about her husband, so recently dead? But Janie is tired of living by society's rules—she's done that and it hasn't made her happy. "Dis ain't no business proposition, and no race after property and titles," she tells Phoeby. "Dis is uh love game. Ah done lived Grandma's way, now Ah means tuh live mine." She has a sense of rightness in her own feelings. Her relationship with Tea Cake is figured as an expression of her independence, rather than the loss of it. And although this love will provoke Janie to jealousy, and bring her into the cane fields in the Everglades as well as the eye of a hurricane, she'll also come to understand that these feelings, for this man, allowed her soul to crawl "out from its hiding place." Huddled in the dark during the storm, Janie wants to outlive the tempest, and have her life with Tea Cake. "They seemed to be staring at the dark, but their eyes were watching God."

Tea Cake, described earlier in the novel as a "glance from

God," is bitten by a rabid dog in the floodwaters, and can't get an antidote in time. His death puts Janie in the courthouse before it lands her back home in Eatonville. Over that plate of mulatto rice with not enough bacon grease, she tells Phoeby how she survived, and what to tell the gossips. She and Tea Cake were in love, and "love ain't somethin' lak uh grindstone dat's de same thing everywhere and do de same thing tuh everything it touch. Love is lak de sea. It's uh movin' thing, but still and all, it takes its shape from de shore it meets, and it's different with every shore." She knows something about love three relationships later: it isn't pear blossom, or even a grindstone, but the changing, moving sea. It's also something that adapts according to the capacity of the lovers, and the way they can love. When I despair of finding love again, friends keep faith for me, and remind me that all I've learned can only make the next thing better. That night, in her own bed again, she sees that she'll never be without Tea Cake: "He could never be dead until she herself had finished feeling and thinking. The kiss of his memory made pictures of love and light against the wall. Here was peace. She pulled in her horizon like a great fish net. Pulled it from around the waist of the world and draped it over her shoulder. So much of life in its meshes! She called in her soul to come and see."

It isn't recorded what Percy Punter thought when he read *Their Eyes Were Watching God*, but we know he left his number with Zora's publisher. (This is one of the more delicious gaps in Zora's biography: was it like the Richard Linklater movie *Before Sunset*, when Jesse brings Céline back into his life by writing a novel about the twenty-four hours they spent together in Vienna and

Before Sunrise a decade before?) It took her months "to get up my courage" to call. And when she did, she "found out that he was a sucker for me, and he found out that I was in his bag." Their love had withstood violence, separation, and novelization, and though Zora, writing in 1945 with a Janie-like thought, said she couldn't know what was next for them both, she at least had had the "satisfaction of knowing that I have loved and been loved by the perfect man."

It's when Janie meets Tea Cake that *Their Eyes Were Watching God* soars, and we can see what Janie's struggles (and they are far from over at that point in the novel) have been heading toward. It is where we can see the imprint of Zora's tenderness toward Percy. In 1974, when Hurston's work was being rediscovered after a long period of obscurity, June Jordan called *Their Eyes Were Watching God* the "most successful, convincing, and exemplary novel of Blacklove that we have. Period"—a judgment that would surely have thrilled Zora. She herself described her novel to a friend in a way that suggests, at least to me, a myth or a parable of a woman who just wants to live:

My next book is to be a novel about a woman who was from childhood hungry for life and the earth, but because she had beautiful hair, was always being skotched upon a flag-pole by the men who loved her and forced to sit there. At forty she got her chance at mud. Mud, lush and fecund with a buck Negro called Teacake [*sic*]. He took her down into the Everglades where people worked and sweated and loved and died violently, where no such thing as flag-poles for women existed.

The novel could be an exemplar of Blacklove, but it might also be an early attempt to tell stories about women who leave marriages but don't die for it, as the heroines of *Anna Karenina* and *Madame Bovary* die. Anna and Emma, and their novels, dominate the canon for good reason, but they and their creators are unable to imagine happy endings in the nineteenth-century white bourgeois worlds they inhabit. I love that Zora uses the word "mud" to describe the place Janie goes with Tea Cake: she doesn't need to be clean and raised up above other women, she needs to laugh and to work. I didn't know how much I needed Janie Crawford until I read about her. I needed to see divorces that felt like expansion. I often felt I'd failed the test of marriage, even as I knew that leaving this particular relationship was right for me. At friends' weddings I was an ill omen, even though everyone knows that 40 to 50 percent of marriages end in divorce. Society understands partnership: grandmothers sigh with relief, the government owes you a tax break, other couples invite you to dinner. I moved through the world with less friction when I was married.

Their Eyes Were Watching God got good reviews in the *New York Times* and the *Herald Tribune*, a telegram from Edna St. Vincent Millay, and brought its author interviews and commissions for the *Saturday Review of Literature*, but the acclaim didn't extend to her male peers. Alain Locke called it "folklore fiction" and asked when Hurston was going to "come to grips with motive fiction and social document fiction?" Richard Wright, about to bring out his book of stories, *Uncle Tom's Children*, but still years from publishing the pathbreaking *Native Son*, argued that Hurston's novel wasn't serious, as it portrayed Black people in a "safe and narrow orbit in which America likes to see the Negro live: between laughter and tears." It's true, I think, that Hurston wasn't writing a protest novel, but it's not true that the only way to be political in fiction is by foregrounding current social conditions and problems. "The sensory sweep of her novel," Wright wrote, "carries no theme, no message, no thought." Perhaps, by contrast, they weren't messages Wright was able to hear.

It's often been said that focusing on women's lives ought to wait until society-wide inequalities are addressed, as if there could be a perfect order to reform, as if race, sex, and class could be separated out. (Another way of putting this argument is that if we address class inequalities, ones of sex and race will be swept along too.) And I can understand why Wright felt a more direct approach to be so urgent: then, as now, Black men and women were dying in disproportionate numbers. Bigger Thomas, the protagonist of *Native Son*, kills the daughter of his white employer and is in turn killed for his crime by the state, but the reader gets to see the whole story, from the rats in his single room on the South Side of Chicago to the conversations he has with his lawyer before he is executed. But in dismissing Hurston's novel, severing it from her own life as a woman and from her work collecting Black stories in the US and the Caribbean, a whole strand of Black literature disappears from view. June Jordan wondered why these strands have to be set against each other: "I do not accept that Wright and Hurston should be perceived, properly, as antipathetic in the well-springs of their work," she wrote in *Black World/Negro Digest*, "Bigger Thomas, the whole living and dying and creation of him, teaches as much about the necessity of love, of being able to love without being, therefore, destroyed, as Hurston's Janie Starks." What might be the effect on Black literature, and the movement for Black rights, if we set these writers against each other? There is a loss of complexity, a one-eyedness, a simplification. We can allow Wright his convictions, and understand also his need to clear a little space for himself, without leaving Hurston's mulatto rice, her dialogue-dialect, her pear blossom behind completely.

This is not to say that Hurston was particularly progressive in her politics: she would go on to work on a campaign for a Black Republican governor, Grant Reynolds, and she was almost pro-segregation, using Eatonville as an example of the benefits of living in an all-Black environment. "I am not tragically colored," she wrote in 1928. "From what I had read and heard, Negroes were supposed to write about the Race Problem," she commented in 1945. "I was and am thoroughly sick of the subject. My interest lies in what makes a man or a woman do suchand-so, regardless of his color." (I think of Zadie turning away from *Their Eyes Were Watching God* because she was *supposed* to like it.) There is a part of me disappointed in Zora, which wishes she had written about race. Because she knew both the store porch in Eatonville and the ivory towers of Columbia, her view would be valuable. Why wouldn't she want to fight for her own, and others', freedom? But Zora's idiosyncrasy, whatever it was in her that spurred her to try to make a living out of collecting and writing Black stories when no woman had done so before, is also the thing that stops her from falling in with the correct political views of the time. And without that quality, even if it was counterproductive, there is no Zora at all.

After the success of *Their Eyes Were Watching God*, in quick succession Lippincott brought out both *Tell My Horse*, the book that resulted from her research trips in Jamaica and Haiti, focusing particularly on voodoo, and *Moses, Man of the Mountain*, the novel she'd been working on for years, a retelling of Moses's story in her own Black vernacular. In writing a book about opposing tyrannical powers in the period leading up to the Second World War, when pressure was beginning to be put on writers to stop talking about the things they didn't like about America and unite against a common enemy, Hurston was being more daring than she appeared. Hurston's taking up of myth at this point in history is a little like Sartre, Beauvoir, and Camus using it to cloak their own ideas during the Nazi occupation of Paris—luckily it seems that Western censors on both sides of the Atlantic weren't very good at spotting allegory.

Zora was living in Florida again, working for the Federal Writers' Project on their guide to the Sunshine State. As a "Back to Work" initiative for writers, part of FDR's New Deal, a volume was being written for each state in the US—Richard Wright, Saul Bellow, and Ralph Ellison all contributed—and Hurston knew more than anyone about her corner of Florida. Her colleagues in the Jacksonville FWP office remember her charisma ("she just had it") and that she smoked in the office when she wasn't supposed to. In June 1939, she married Albert Price, a twenty-three-year-old working for the FWP, though the marriage lasted six weeks.

It's hard to write about the last twenty years of Zora's life. She didn't find happiness like Mary Wollstonecraft or get a last chance at love like George Eliot. Sad, meaningless things started happening to her. She married again, briefly, in 1944. Punter is back in her life in 1945, while she's writing the memoir her publishers demanded, *Dust Tracks on a Road*, but disappears sooner than I'd like. She moved publishers, from Lippincott to Scribner's, to work with the star editor of his generation,

Maxwell Perkins, but Perkins died before they could begin collaborating. Her last published novel, *Seraph on the Suwanee*, her only novel about white characters, told the story of a woman who is too insecure to be happy in love. Just as that novel came out, she was brought to court in New York by the mother of a young boy who claimed Zora molested him while she was organizing a "Block Mothers" communal childcare initiative. This tangle, a harrowing one for Hurston, wouldn't be unraveled for years. (His testimony turned out to be false.) She lived on a boat, worked occasionally as a maid, and reported on the trial of Ruby McCollum, a Black woman who murdered her white lover in Florida. She took a university job and had to leave when she had an affair with one of her students. She kept writing to different publishers in New York, offering novels, and kept getting knocked back. She wrote horoscopes; she grew vegetables to save money on groceries; she got behind on the rent.

Her last home was in Fort Pierce, Florida, and is now preserved. It must be one of the smallest US National Historic Landmarks, a painfully modest white concrete oblong (which was painted pea green when Zora lived there). She wrote on her typewriter, surrounded by bookshelves made of fruit crates, and grew gardenias out back. Her landlord, a doctor who was from Eatonville too, often waived the rent or stumped up for groceries. He would drop by just to talk: "She was a well-read, well-traveled woman who always had ideas about what was going on." Zora was working on a book about Herod, but barely wrote letters: she'd lost contact with her friends in New York. Her health began to suffer. She applied for welfare for medication for hypertension, and then she applied for help to buy food. After a stroke in 1959, she moved into a nursing home, and after a second in January 1960, she died. There wasn't enough money for a funeral until a call was put out: Lippincott and Scribner's sent $100 each and the undertaker donated the plot. Foamy white flowers covered the steel casket, and the choir from the local school sang, but there would be no headstone, not for a decade at least.

I lost count of how many American friends told me they'd read *Their Eyes Were Watching God* in high school, but I still meet people who haven't heard of her, or who tell me about her as a new discovery, someone I would be interested in. When I try and think about why I didn't read the novel in my late teens, whether it was on the syllabus or not, I can't say it wasn't racism of a sort, whether institutional or my own. It makes me sad that it took me so long to get to Zora, that the idea of Janie and of Zora herself wasn't something I carried through my life as I tried to live it, often so badly. Why was Zora forgotten by so many? Sometimes party Zora overshadowed writer Zora. Her political conservatism can't have been appealing in the civil rights era, which took flight a few years after her death. As the first Black woman writing professionally for a living, perhaps what she was doing wasn't legible: this pioneer could also look chaotic. But it wasn't just me that took too long to find her.

In 1975, Alice Walker wrote an article for Gloria Steinem at *Ms.* magazine about a trip to Eatonville and Fort Pierce "in Search of Zora Neale Hurston." Walker knew Zora's novels backward and forward and had wanted to talk to people who knew her. While in Florida she went to find Zora's grave to pay her respects. She waded into the overgrown yard, her skirt tucked into her knickers. Insects bit her bare legs; snakes lurked.

"Zo-ra!" she shouted. "I hope you don't think I'm going to stand out here all day, with these snakes watching me and these ants having a field day. In fact, I'm going to call you just one or two more times." And then she found what she was looking for. She wasn't sure at first, because all it appeared to be was a sunken rectangle six feet long. Hmm. She decided Zora needed an actual headstone, and asked the engraver to add "A Genius of the South," a line from Jean Toomer, to her name, date, and three professions. Walker said she didn't cry on finding Zora; she reminded us that Zora wasn't the crying type.

I know the instinct that brought Walker to the overgrown cemetery, because I keep finding similar feelings bringing me graveside. There is homage to pay, a connection to make, a heroine to laurel. Freud thought memorials helped people forget— leave the memory in stone, and get on with life—but I wonder if that really was what Walker was doing, and what I am doing. I often go to the dead (Zo-ra! Geor-ge! Ma-ry!) to tell them things, and ask for things, even impossible things like persuading someone I love to come back. Not heroines, but household goddesses. I find myself using their lives in different ways: they ask questions of me, they push me, they comfort me when they're silly or funny or getting too much bad luck. They are most alive in their writing, but at their graves I'm reminded that they were just mortal, and I remember again that they're only women. So maybe Freud isn't exactly right that monuments are about forgetting. Zora began to be remembered when Walker put up a gravestone. Her grave now stands on a mown lawn, with an information placard by it, item number four on the Zora Neale Hurston Dust Tracks Heritage Trail.

I felt relieved when I found out that Toni Morrison, too,

hadn't read Zora until the 1970s. When asked in an interview in 1994 why she read Zora so late, Morrison replied: "I was just ill-read, that's all, because I had gone to schools where . . . [I was] ill-taught. And they didn't have any books in my libraries so it was a long time before I had the thrill of being introduced to them, after I had written, you see." I love that word "thrill" because I've spent so much of my life feeling guilty about not having read certain books yet (always yet), not thinking that if I'd read everything, there would be no more thrill. Later in Morrison's life, Zora comes up casually and habitually, as if she were always there. There are paths unimaginable without her. But it was the discovery of Janie that set me right, and I can't say, for me, that the discovery truly came at the wrong time. Within a year of that first reading, I was reducing my dose of antidepressants with a tiny plastic guillotine and being able to look at the love I lost, as love from which I also gained.

Virginia

I noticed someone wearing a fur coat on the subway and I thought of Virginia Woolf. I had arrived in New York City a month before and was on my way to meet my friend Sam for pizza and a movie, and I think the fur was supposed to be monkey, black and long rather than short and rufflable, and it was matted, likely fake. On the day Woolf died, Friday, March 28, 1941, she had gone out of the house for a walk before lunch, then doubled back on herself to get a walking stick and put on her fur coat. She'd rescued the coat earlier that year from the ruins of her London home, which had been bombed during the Blitz; that morning she would put stones in its pockets, and go into the Ouse. Her body was spotted by children playing on the banks of the river twenty days later. The drenched fur coat looked like the floating trunk of a tree.

She had thought she was going mad again, she wrote in a last letter to her husband, Leonard, and that this time she wouldn't recover. She couldn't concentrate, she heard voices, she couldn't write: nothing could dissuade her. The last few years had brought the death of many of her friends—Lytton Strachey, Roger Fry, Dora Carrington, as well as her nephew Julian in the Spanish Civil War—and Hitler's intensifying assault on England's south coast (planes even came down in the fields around her Sussex home; her study in London was now open to the air). When she was ill before, she had been advised to rest, drink milk, avoid anything that might upset her. If it was lucky that she was ill in the time before electroshock therapy, society hadn't yet (and still hasn't) met mental illness with the compassion and patience and inching encouragement it ought. Woolf doubted that she could fight her own thoughts every day for what could be up to two years. In the harsh light of the New York City subway car, stainless steel and blue plastic gleaming, I could see that the woman in the fur coat had chosen to wear fur because she did have some sort of faith in the future and in the evening that would unfold for her once she got to Manhattan. That was what Woolf no longer had in the spring of 1941. She didn't know that the allies would win the war. She couldn't believe that even if she had no hope herself, her circumstances, her mood, would change—this is true only because nothing stays the same, even if you want it to.

Reading Woolf again during my first weeks in New York I had a sense of newness every day. Perhaps it spilled over from real life: I was delighted by America as a one-day, one-week, then one-month-old New Yorker, by the flavors of seltzer in the grocery store, by the view of the Brooklyn Bridge and the Statue of Liberty on my commute, by the bright dry sunshine of my first American fall. I noticed the way the woman vaccinating me presented the vial before she filled the syringe in front of my eyes (in England, this preparation had happened in advance, out of sight, for efficiency, and I suppose because a country with universal healthcare expected you to trust it more); I noticed the way the concrete sidewalks were smoother and wider than the tiled pavements in England; I noticed the rats scuttling underneath the trash bags left out on the street in the evenings. I felt spoiled with novelty, and even the hardest parts of navigating the systems of a new country, like going to the Social Security office in freezing mist at 7:15 a.m., retained charm somehow because of it.

But the new was also in what I was reading. I had read Woolf before but I'd never really got on with her. Her books felt austere and sort of blurry, written from a position secure within the British bohemian elite. In the past, I had felt I was striving to be included, thought worthy and intellectual, by reading them. I sometimes found the whole Bloomsbury thing not just distant but also kind of embarrassing, all decorative scarves and elegant dissension. I knew I was missing something, even as I was at a loss how to come near it.

I had first read Woolf when I was sixteen. My family had moved to Dover from the suburbs and when I started at the girls' grammar school, my English teacher gave me a short handwritten list of important English novels. I darted around in it, never quite finding time to read *The Pilgrim's Progress* but deciding to tackle the so-called difficult prose of Virginia Woolf. My teacher had told me not to worry too much about understanding *To the Lighthouse*, just to let it wash over me. I read it dutifully to the end, feeling that I'd experienced something beautiful but nothing I could be very sure of. They didn't get to the lighthouse, or did they? My teacher's advice was annoying because it's not in fact a difficult book, but it was good advice in that it helped me not be scared of something so unfamiliar. I suspected Woolf would look down on someone like me, a provincial schoolgirl who persevered rather than questioned.

When I took a job in Bloomsbury after university, I began again with her. It felt like a dereliction not to have read her properly and I decided to tackle the novels in chronological order, something I told myself was important for my education. There were still blood relatives of Woolf's around, and I even met some of them; the history, the aesthetics, even the gossip all seemed to come extremely close. On this attempt, I only got to *Mrs. Dalloway*; I didn't abandon the project consciously, I just didn't go on. Sometimes my little brother would tease me: weren't you supposed to be reading all of Woolf in order? Where did you get to again? He was right. It was a willful undertaking, meant as an accomplishment, understood as homework. The least intellectually exciting way to read anything.

So I waited. And then I tried again on the subway from Brooklyn to Manhattan. In the mornings, I would take out one of her novels and find the dialogue and action hard and sharp and precise, the details almost otherworldly, both appropriate and yet unexpected. In the evenings, it was harder to resist the temptation to pick up my phone instead, but if I opened Woolf, I found the books fuzzier, warmer, funnier, but less piercing than in the morning. At night in bed, they changed again, and I would notice melancholy notes. It was like a perfume changing over the day, ripening and fading. I always found something to surprise me as I moved from book to book over her career, dipping into an essay, a story, or an autobiographical sketch as I went. When she had a new idea, she searched for a new form for it. She wrote novels about a single day, and a hundred years. She depicted the matriarch of an English village and someone suffering from shell shock. She broke her novels in two and roamed freely through her characters' thoughts. She was constantly looking for possibilities in her writing, revising her sense of what she could and wanted to say in it, testing herself, questioning ideas that were passed down from her father's generation, competing with the women writers around her in a not necessarily generous way. The questing could be restless, apart from it didn't feel like that to me in New York. It felt alive.

In noticing the fur coat on the subway uptown, I noticed I was noticing—and it felt suddenly unfair that I had the pleasure of being charmed by the new. I had so much novelty, a lot of it from reading Woolf's novels, and she had lost her own faith in the future. How was it that this sense could ebb away or straightforwardly vanish with very little warning? I had it now, but when I was crying in the bath in England I didn't have it. Was I maybe experiencing modernism? We tie that make-it-new impulse to the early twentieth century, but it could be that modernism also comes in waves over our little lives.

During my first weeks in New York, many people asked me why I'd decided to come to their city. I found the question hard to answer, and still haven't developed a satisfying response. I knew that I'd needed a fresh start. My life had been so sad: watching my mother fade away had been grueling; my divorce exhilarating then confusing; depression had exhausted me. I'd changed because of the events in my life and it felt like I was better fitted to American openness: I was embarrassing the English with my need to earnestly remake my life, but Americans understood wanting a life of one's own. I had friends in the US: Lidija, whom I met working in London, had come out to New York City years ago and now had an American passport, an

American boyfriend, an American apartment. My move could be read as alarmingly ambitious, but in truth I didn't want to go upward but outward. When I was younger, I had wanted to write a book, any book—but all the losses I'd experienced made me want simpler things. My ambition wasn't like Plath's, who shined up her CV with a Fulbright Scholarship to Cambridge, it was more like Beauvoir's, who was fascinated by the ways of ordinary Americans in a New Mexico diner. What I most wanted was to be happier, along with the room to work out what that looked like for myself. More prosaic conditions came into it too: my mother had moved to a care home and my father shifted from asking for my help to encouraging me to live my life; my brothers had less need of me as they established their own families. What did I need? I'd lived in Paris when I was twenty-one and knew that a foreign country could be utterly charming for the small things that presented themselves in the course of a normal day. People kept asking and my answer got more unwieldy: because of Care Bears, "Like a Virgin," Tab Clear, *My So-Called Life*, denim dungarees, *The Catcher in the Rye*, Sylvia Plath. I realized my reply could whittle itself down to "because I was born! I wanted change and newness because I was born!"

I hadn't thought of newness as sustaining before, or as important to happiness. But I kept discovering that I was happy in New York, in tiny and large ways, and so it was in the subway car that I understood why Woolf felt she couldn't live without the feeling, once she'd stopped believing that it would come again. I'd cried earlier that day on reading Hermione Lee's account of Woolf's suicide, and I understood then why I had: not just because I would have to let Woolf go as I came to the end of the biography, but for Woolf as a woman, and for me myself, who had been so lost. I too had felt that nothing would change—but I had been wrong. And I was so relieved to be wrong.

It wasn't her fault—it is never anyone's fault—that Woolf was born into the family she was. Her father, Leslie Stephen, was editor of the *Dictionary of National Biography*, and was friends with George Meredith and Thomas Hardy; her mother was his second wife, Julia Prinsep, whose aunt was Julia Margaret Cameron. England is small, but it is not so small that Virginia Woolfs are born every day: she was connected to some of the most accomplished people then living. She was born on January 25, 1882, a younger sister to Vanessa and Thoby, though she wouldn't be the baby of the family—Adrian would arrive in October of the following year. Her childhood was split in two from the beginning, between long bright summers at St. Ives and dark, rigid winters in Hyde Park Gate, by a sexual assault she endured from one of her older stepbrothers, and then definitively broken by the death of her mother when Virginia was thirteen. The unbereaved Leslie Stephen was demanding, but the grieving man was bullying. He mourned in a grandiose way that left no space for his children's feelings, and he demanded their company at a moment when they needed to make their own way in the world. And although he encouraged Virginia in her reading and pushed her to write, he didn't arrange for any formal education, a decision that would echo down her life.

I'd always thought of Woolf as deeply entrenched in Oxbridge, and believed wrongly that the lectures that became *A*

Room of One's Own were given to women students at Newnham College, Cambridge, because she'd been invited back as an alumna. It turns out that she took some classes in history and in Greek at King's College London, but she never read for an undergraduate degree. She made herself intellectually formidable because she was angry, and she became even more aware of what she'd missed out on when her older brother Thoby went to Cambridge. She read four books at a time as a teenager, and still held herself to those standards years later, particularly when she became a working reviewer. It was a quest fueled by insecurity, which meant she could never definitively say it was over (none of us can). Once you know this about her, you see it surging up in her books—from the worries about women's writing in *To the Lighthouse* to the barely concealed rage in *A Room of One's Own*—and it changes her tone. It seems incredible to me that I have more formal education than her, just as it seems astonishing that she couldn't always see what she had gained from finding out for herself what good writing was. Woolf had the run of her father's library, access to his friends, and, through Thoby, would come to know and tussle with other Oxbridge-trained minds. She was also never poor, and had the support and inspiration of her older sister, Vanessa. But she would have to make so much of her life herself.

In 1904, when she was twenty-two, her father died, and she stopped writing. She thought she heard birds outside speaking in Greek and feared she was going mad as she had after her mother's death. She attempted suicide. Her siblings gathered her up and together they set about changing things: they moved to Bloomsbury, at the other end of London from Kensington, and they lived in light with Thoby's friends coming in and out, discussing, painting, gossiping, writing. They encouraged her to keep writing. She first appeared in print that year, when the *Guardian* published her review of *The Son of Royal Langbrith* by William Dean Howells. Woolf would later say that the end of her father's life was in some measure the beginning of her own. "His life would have entirely ended mine . . . No writing. No books. Inconceivable." She took a room at the top of the house as her study, framing a letter of George Eliot's she'd taken from Hyde Park Gate as encouragement (as she began writing her first novel, *The Voyage Out*, she reassured herself that Eliot didn't publish her first until "near 40 I think," as people would say to me of Toni Morrison too). She came off initially as a sad girl—at a party she once sat in the corner reading Alfred Lord Tennyson's *In Memoriam* while Vanessa danced all night—but as her confidence grew, she became garrulous and charming. When Thoby died unexpectedly, and Vanessa married Clive Bell and began having babies, Virginia attempted to make a new life once more, sharing a house in Brunswick Square with Duncan Grant, John Maynard Keynes, her younger brother, Adrian, and Leonard Woolf, who had started to become more important to her.

Woolf proposed in January 1912, but thirty-year-old Virginia was unsure of her answer until late April, when they first kissed on the cliffs above Eastbourne. She wrote to him on May Day, dithering still, worried that she was unstable, that he wanted her too much, that marriage was too conventional, that she felt no physical attraction to him, that she ran hot and cold, that he felt too foreign. "We both of us want a marriage that is a tremendous living thing, always alive, always hot, not dead and easy in parts as most marriages are. We ask a great deal of life, don't we? Perhaps we shall get it; then, how splendid!" On the threshold of convention, she hesitated, hoping that in this interzone between marriage and not-marriage, they could make something new out of the institution: a modernist marriage. They wed that August in St. Pancras Town Hall, during a thunderstorm, and maybe they did get the sort of partnership Virginia wanted. It was a marriage that gave her room to fall in love with women, that could care for her when she was sick, that produced the Hogarth Press, that allowed her to write eight novels and many other books before she fell ill for the last time. It has never felt like a romantic match to me—Lee proposes that it was brokered by Strachey, and notes that it was never passionate—but what Virginia wrote in her last letter to him, that no one could have done more than he had done, seems right. He reminds me of Lewes, Eliot's partner, in that he took his responsibility to Virginia's writing seriously. Lewes protected Eliot from other people's opinions, and Leonard was Virginia's crucial first reader. *To the Lighthouse*, he said, was a "masterpiece." *The Waves* was also a "masterpiece," and the "best of your books." It barely matters that he repeated himself in his praise because he kept her writing. I wouldn't want to say that these men were male muses, as I suppose I'm cynical about the role of the female muse—who wants to be a Véra, even to a Nabokov, anymore?—but I am interested in marriages that are set up in a way that supports the writing and the happiness of both people in it. I collect anecdotes, which I then idealize: Mary and Percy Shelley wrote a book together on their honeymoon; Kazuo Ishiguro reads his work in progress to his wife, Lorna, at the end of the day; Elsa and Norman Rush treat Norman's novels like a family business. My own experience of being married to another writer was full of disguised envy; I know such alliances are delicate and difficult. Yet I keep hoping I can find something that might work for me; I keep looking for examples that work for others. It's an old habit, wanting to learn something from books that I need to try out in life, to go over a thing in my head many times that I know must be made in the world.

The Woolfs began a life together. "In the morning we write 750 words each," Leonard wrote to Strachey in 1913, "in the afternoons we dig; between tea and dinner we write 500 words each." But they were tested almost immediately when Virginia became ill, triggered by finishing *The Voyage Out*. He took care of her, following the doctors' advice, which meant rest in all senses: physical, mental, and emotional. The cure for madness then was agonizing, as it was for Plath. (Wollstonecraft seems to have escaped the doctors.) I think it makes most sense to take Lee's line about her illness, and recognize Woolf's courage in facing these recurrent episodes in her life, and the good effects of the decisions that were taken in response to it. They moved to Richmond and bought a printing press so that Virginia might have a hobby; loading type into trays ready for printing books was meant to be soothing, and it was. Having her own press also encouraged her to write, and in the way she wanted to. Her initial move away from the conventional style of her first two novels, the story "The Mark on the Wall," came out of those conditions: she described to her friend Ethel Smyth how the conventional and the experimental coexisted in her until one outpaced the other. *Night and Day* she wrote in permitted half-hour bursts while she was still ill—"bad as the book is, it composed my mind"—but, confined to bed for the rest of the day, she thought up poems, phrases, stories.

These little pieces in *Monday or Tuesday* were written by way of diversion; they were the treats I allowed myself when I had done my exercise in the conventional style. I shall never forget the day I wrote "The Mark on the Wall"—all in a flash, as if flying, after being kept stone breaking for months . . . How I trembled with excitement; and then Leonard came in, and I drank my milk, and concealed my excitement, and wrote I suppose another page of that interminable *Night and Day* (which some say is my best book).

She's writing this letter in 1930, having changed her prose into something less codified, a form that embodied "all my deposit of experience in a shape that fitted it." It is a moment a little like Eliot's breakthrough—though that was crowned with a kiss, not subdued by a glass of milk—but for Virginia, there is a trace of danger, as if she's been caught indulging in intellectual stimulation. (Plath would know too how important it was to look calm and capable for your family.) But it's exciting even to read in a letter: imagine what it must have felt like, to have written "The Mark on the Wall" in a flash.

If the end of her life was winter—death, war, loss, aging—the period in the 1920s following her recovery was summer. She unfurled in her forties, romantically and in her writing, much as Eliot, Hurston, Beauvoir, and Morrison did. She met and fell in love with Vita Sackville-West, and she wrote many of the enduring books: *Mrs. Dalloway*, which was followed by *To the Lighthouse*, which was followed by *Orlando*, which was followed by *A Room of One's Own*. These experiences wrapped around each other: the brightening spark of falling in love, the relief of writing through some of her preoccupation with her parents, the experience of lecturing at Cambridge and elucidating some of the obstacles women face when they sit down to write. Vita was married and the more famous writer when they met, genuinely aristocratic rather than part of the intellectual aristocracy as Virginia was. Their relationship proceeded slowly, by letter and visit, holiday and love note, until Virginia fell ill and Vita started planning a trip to Persia. Virginia had started thinking of Vita as her lighthouse, but "fitful, sudden, remote." What would it feel like not to be able to see each other at all? They began sleeping together not long after, during a weekend spent alone together at Long Barn, Vita's home in Kent before Knole. On the first night, Vita wrote to her husband: "She said she depends on me. She is so vulnerable under all her brilliance." On the second, after staying up until 3 a.m. making love, she wrote: "I love her, but couldn't fall in love with her, so don't be nervous!" But they had fallen in love: they both said that their relationship had broken down more walls, more ramparts within both than anyone had ever done before.

When Vita did leave for Persia (with another lover), Virginia immersed herself in the writing of *To the Lighthouse*. "Like a child," Virginia wrote to Vita, "I think if you were here, I should be happy." The center of gravity of Virginia's life was with Leonard and Vanessa, but it seems to me somehow that Vita re-enchanted life for her. They never lost contact—Vita was sending her butter to supplement war rations a few months before she died, and she was the first person Leonard wrote to when it sunk in that his wife would not be back from her morning walk—but their relationship mellowed into friendship. For these few years though, as *To the Lighthouse*, *Orlando*, and *A*

Room of One's Own were taking shape, Vita was necessary to Virginia, and there was a flourishing within Woolf. It wasn't that her happiness tipped over into her prose, it was rather that she lived more intensely, and that was the quality that made it into her books. It was the way that she saw things that changed.

I can feel the change most in *To the Lighthouse*. Form and content, intellect and feeling are in balance, and time is perhaps the most important protagonist in the story. It is a much less mysterious book to me now, at thirty-nine, than it was at sixteen. It is about grief. I didn't get it when I was younger, but I hadn't experienced grief then. In "Modern Fiction," an essay from 1925, Woolf argued that writing can come nearer to life by sweeping away some of the conventions that help orient a reader. "Let us record the atoms as they fall upon the mind in the order in which they fall," she proposed. "Let us trace the pattern, however disconnected and incoherent in appearance, which each sight or incident scores upon the consciousness." It is a tiny, nano-sized manifesto—is she thinking of the little bit of ivory Austen said was all the space one needed to write a novel?—in which fidelity to life is placed before convention, like the ideas about marriage she floats in her consideration of Leonard's proposal. The mystery, the difficulty even, of the prose is purposeful, because it reflects the enduring mystery of other minds.

From the first page of *To the Lighthouse*, which was written in 1926, a year after "Modern Fiction" was reworked, we are dealing with pulses of thought and feeling among family and friends while they summer in Scotland. The first words of the novel are spoken by its matriarch, Mrs. Ramsay, to her son,

James, who has asked to visit the lighthouse. The weather, as so often on British summer holidays, won't guarantee them the excursion, something Mr. Ramsay won't hide from his son. But his mother is more obliging. "Yes, of course, if it's fine to-morrow," his mother says. "But you'll have to be up with the lark." This utterance, the novel's first, is a force, or whatever it is that causes an atom to fall on all the minds in the novel in turn. It falls on James's, who is cutting pictures out of a store catalogue, and the effect is to "fringe" the refrigerator under his scissors with "joy." Then James's reaction affects his mother's mind, as his concentrated frown allows her to dream of the day he'll be "all red and ermine on the Bench." The prelapsarian holiday mood attaches to, even originates out of, the mother.

Mrs. Ramsay is the suffusing presence of the first part of the novel. Virginia admitted the portrait was drawn from her own mother, but she also used parts of her sister Vanessa's character, who by 1925 was a mother of two boys and a girl. What I notice most in the portrait, psychologically speaking, is that Woolf imagines her mother as a peer rather than an elder. I've often wished to know people at other times of their lives—to have known a lover when he was younger, for example—but it is possible only in fiction. Doing this for a parent is an act that can help a child grow up or let go, if they can see the things their parents did as simply part of the hurt they inherited. Woolf wrote that she was obsessed by her mother until she was forty-four, when *To the Lighthouse* offered her an outlet:

Then one day walking around Tavistock Square I made up, as I sometimes make up my books, *To the Lighthouse*;

in a great, apparently involuntary, rush. One thing burst into another. Blowing bubbles out of a pipe gives the feeling of the rapid crowd of ideas and scenes which blew out of my mind, so that my lips seemed syllabling of their own accord as I walked. What blew the bubbles? Why then? I have no notion. But I wrote the book very quickly; and when it was written, I ceased to be obsessed by my mother. I no longer hear her voice; I do not see her.

I suppose that I did for myself what psychoanalysts do for their patients. I expressed some very long felt and deeply felt emotion. And in expressing it I explained it and then laid it to rest.

Reading Woolf's account of the beginnings of *To the Lighthouse*, it is strange to me that anyone ever talks of books apart from a writer's life and her obsessions, as we did at university. Even if a book is about everything else, it is never not about the life the writer lived.

One of the things I liked most about it this time around was its emotional atmosphere. Mrs. Ramsay observes the happiness of a young woman at her table who has just received a marriage proposal, and she thinks not of herself, but of her daughter. "You will be as happy as she is one of these days," Mrs. Ramsay says to her daughter, Prue, in her mind. "You will be much happier, she added, because you are my daughter, she meant; her own daughter must be happier than other people's daughters." Ten pages later, Prue thinks a tessellating thought: "That is the thing itself, she felt, as if there were only one person like that in the world; her mother." Her thoughts lie behind her suggestion for an outing, an after-dinner walk across the sand:

"Thinking what a chance it was for Minta and Paul and Lily to see her, and feeling what an extraordinary stroke of fortune it was for her to have her, and how she would never grow up and never leave home, she said, like a child, 'We thought of going down to the beach to watch the waves.'" This emotional call and response, echoed in the final scene of the section where Mrs. Ramsay and Mr. Ramsay don't say they love each other and also say they love each other, is something the reader sees rather than the characters. Woolf the writer has orchestrated an unsayable yet always said love between Prue and her mother, perhaps so that Woolf the mourning daughter has the portrait to hand (that is, on the page), whenever she needs it, the reassurance that an absent mother is not an unloving mother. Mrs. Ramsay experiences happiness like light, "in waves of pure lemon." Her "simplicity fathomed what clever people falsified." This warmth feels to me like a trace of grief, the mark of the emotional stakes of the book for its writer. I don't much disagree with Vanessa, who wrote, referring to their mother: "You have made one feel the extraordinary beauty of her character, which must be the most difficult thing in the world to do. It was like meeting her again with oneself grown up and on equal terms and it seems to me the most astonishing feat of creation to have been able to see her in such a way." But part of the reason Mrs. Ramsay is so indelible is the shape of the novel, another of Woolf's feats of creation.

As my mother became ill, it was the atmosphere around her I missed most. I was particularly scared of the moment I knew would come, when she would look at me, her own daughter, and not recognize me. The Christmas five years after her diagnosis, as I was helping her put her coat on to go on a walk, narrating what I was doing as mothers do to children—"your son George bought you that dress"—she said: "Oh, that's why he likes me so much! That's why he gives clothes!" and I realized she was there already; she might not know who I was. I don't know why, in fact it now seems to me cruel, but on the walk I turned it into a game. Who am I, Mum? Am I your mum, Trixie? Or am I your son Richard's girlfriend, Phu? "You're kind and you're pretty," she answered, and I laughed. In the five years since she said that, I've often thought it good enough for me. Even when she didn't know who I was I told myself: she liked me. And I remind myself still, with Woolf, that a mother is always a mystery; she has lived so much of her life before you were even born.

No one my age had a parent with Alzheimer's, but I had an older friend whose partner had died of it. She told me something I didn't believe at the time: that I could have another relationship with my mother, and that it would be something I would be grateful for in the future. She urged me to visit her more; I went every weekend during the furloughs of depression that followed my divorce. I often couldn't see the point in getting up, but there I had to, because Dad was out and Mum couldn't get washed and dressed without me. I helped her in the shower, singing bad renditions of Madonna, Michael Jackson, and Wham! songs when she got flustered with drying herself and putting on face cream and brushing her teeth and pulling up her tights. (Approximate versions of 1980s pop aren't prescribed for Alzheimer's, but music very much is.) I found new ways of being with her. In the summer, I read the Ischia scenes from Ferrante to her as she dozed on a lounger in our sunny back garden. And I read Beauvoir in French out loud to her too. (One of my first memories of my mother's glory is her arguing with a hotel manager in French one summer holiday.) We swung side by side in the children's playground, her worrying that we would get caught. I put a bib around her neck, cut up her food, and gave her a spoon instead of a fork. In the evening, Dad showed me how to put her in pajamas, brush her teeth, give her her tablets, and sit with her while she fell asleep. She liked childish humor, and all of my dad's bad jokes—"You're a princess," he'd say as he helped her on with her boots, "you get everything done for you"—and banging the table to Nina Simone's "My Baby Just Cares for Me."

Woolf described the structure of *To the Lighthouse* as two blocks joined by a tunnel—she drew a sketch, like a puzzle piece, to show what she meant—and it is in that tunnel, that narrow dark four years' space, that the First World War happens and Mrs. Ramsay dies. There is a symmetrical beauty to the pattern: the summer of the failed trip to the lighthouse, time passes, then the summer of the successful trip to the lighthouse. The days are long but the years are short. And even though there is change and loss over the novel's short span, there is nevertheless a unity of mood, as Mrs. Ramsay's absence is as strong as her presence. The abandoned holiday house grows mold, sheds plaster, lets the rain in. The plot happens, but in square brackets. Objects rot and warp and grow haunted and shunnable in front of us. There is distance. We notice the impersonality of nature: go to the beach and "ask the sea and sky what message they reported or what vision they affirmed" and discover not that nature tries to complete what man began but that "with equal complacence she saw his misery, condoned his meanness, and acquiesced in his torture." It is natural that a mother should die suddenly, a daughter not survive childbirth, and a son be hit by a shell—and yet it also isn't. The outrage is personal, and yet such things happen to people every day. So against the psychological engine of the novel, what Woolf sometimes feared was its sentimentality, there is this other determining and abstract force, one that wants to find a shape for feeling. There is something touching about these two impulses competing, and sometimes, I thought as I read, they are not in opposition at all.

The difficulty I was told I didn't need to struggle with when I was younger doesn't now seem one. Perhaps it is simply that I've read more, and perhaps because I see the difficulty has meaning in itself. The prose isn't transparent because minds are also not like that, and nothing worth knowing is like that either. I can now connect Woolf's style with what she was trying to say: that something was knotted up and hard to reach because that's how our minds often treat things that are unassimilable. Her experiments in fiction aren't about intimidating the reader, but bringing her close, showing the workings of disordered and vulnerable minds, or the operation of memory over time, or how centuries of accreted oppression act on a woman when she sits down to write something.

One thing I do remember from my first reading of *To the Lighthouse* is Lily Briscoe, the youngish woman artist who spends much of the novel painting. She's not part of the family, and not getting proposed to, but she is attempting to capture the things she sees and thinks and feels on canvas. Mrs. Ramsay has an organizing effect on her family and friends; Lily, like Woolf, is attempting to organize life into art. At first they don't see that they're allies: Mrs. Ramsay is patronizing, and Lily is adoring; Mrs. Ramsay holds that "an unmarried woman has missed the best of life," and Lily simply feels that "she liked to be alone; she liked to be herself." Lily might be small, inconspicuous, and dressed in gray right now, but at forty she could outshine them all: "There was in Lily a thread of something; a flare of something; something of her own that Mrs. Ramsay liked very much indeed, but no man would, she feared."

The contrast between Lily and Mrs. Ramsay feels initially like a generational difference, another split the book is interested in. They are not mother and daughter, apart from in the sense that Mrs. Ramsay is mother to everyone in the novel, and they don't believe the same things, yet they understand each other. When I told my mother I was getting divorced, I also apologized to her: she was longing to be a grandmother, and I couldn't stay married to my husband, who wanted children. At that moment, I was about to publish my first book, and I didn't think I wanted children at all. With switchblade logic I thought of as motherly (though I know that not all mothers do this), she brought my new values into harmony with her own. It was after her Alzheimer's diagnosis, but she still managed to listen and to say: "Your book is your baby." When I remember this, I'm often in awe that she was able to find a way to love me, even as I was telling her I wasn't going to give her what she wanted, an experience she had wanted for us both. And there would be no time to change my mind, because she would soon be gone. Yet she accepted it, and me, as I was.

Woolf had hoped to have children, but doctors advised against it following her breakdowns. (She was a terrific aunt:

happy to be teased, generous with money, lavish with time, and instinctively wise.) She often tells herself in her diaries and letters not to pretend that books are a replacement for the loss of her own offspring, something that feels instinctively true to me, even when I heard babies being compared to books by my own mother. No matter what I write—not least these essay-attempts to capture some tones and thoughts from half a life of unsystematic reading—there's no bettering or doing over or outpacing life. It is only that time has passed in writing and reading instead of doing other things. It doesn't feel like I've chosen this over that because I think it's more important: I have done what's possible for me to do, and I accept my limits. I get older and paths disappear. Mrs. Ramsay fears that no man would love Lily, then she immediately thinks that Lily would be a good romantic match for someone at the table; that life was "terrible, hostile, and quick to pounce on you if you gave it a chance," and that "no happiness lasted—she knew that." And perhaps because she holds opposing positions, she can find room to admire, and even love, Lily. We don't always love the things that are most like us, and in loving what we don't expect to, we often change our minds. Perhaps Woolf's portrait of Mrs. Ramsay is cubist, willing to show us the depressive, the ur-mother, the submissive, the matchmaker-meddler, the knitter, the ghost. A mother in all her shades and moods: a person, finally, rather than a mother.

While I was losing my mother, I felt an urge to capture her. My father bought a camcorder and made videos of our family holidays. I wrote down things she said in my phone, on scraps of paper, in emails to myself: the time I put on an old floral wrap dress of hers and she said: "It's beautiful. Proper dress. I love you, Jo"; the time I turned on the water for her shower and she recoiled: "This is very very very fire." After weekends caring for her, I would often find myself in tears back in London when what I'd seen a few days before sunk in. I took long, dark, wet walks and listened to music while I cried. Friends suggested that it might help to write about it, and I did, haltingly. But when I tried to capture her, I found I wrote about myself, and what it felt like to lose her. My account of her disease from diagnosis to the moment before she went into a care home didn't seem to capture what she was like as a woman in the way Woolf captures Mrs. Ramsay. When my essay about her was published, friends read it and wrote to me, often through their own tears, and I didn't feel comforted. I was losing my mother, whom I still needed, for no reason. I didn't make her live again on the page, I didn't lay to rest some very long and deeply felt emotion as Woolf did. I'd kicked up dust and scared myself. I took myself to the doctor, and she listened while I sobbed and then prescribed sertraline to help lift me out of depression.

I'd lost a great deal, but mum was still there. We relinquished her reluctantly to a care home and my relationship with her adapted again. I visited her there solo one Sunday afternoon, about eighteen months after she moved in, and I found her lying on her sofa. I opened the window to let air into the over-heated room, then I curled myself against her and cried for all I had lost, heaving and gasping and letting myself go completely. My hot tears fell onto her chest, where I'd laid my head, and her dress absorbed them. I'd cared for her for years, had been her daughter for even more, all my life, and I knew we didn't have much time left. I wanted to be mothered again. As she clutched my shoulder, her hand was as steady and sure about what I needed as it ever was.

One irony in the plot of *To the Lighthouse* is that Lily, the not-daughter, arranges the return to the lighthouse, and inherits Mrs. Ramsay's position in the third part of the novel. While the children, "coerced, their spirits subdued," bear witness to their father's outsized grief, Lily slips the blood tie and is able to paint. On arriving at the house, she'd not felt much, but in the process of considering color and shape, she has room at last to be visited by the ghosts she longs to see. At first, Lily feels again the "old horror . . . to want and want and not to have" rising to her lips as she cries "Mrs. Ramsay! Mrs. Ramsay!" to the one person who can't come. She feels that the way her emotion is being stirred works against the painting, ruining the balance: "There was something perhaps wrong with the design? Was it, she wondered, that the line of the wall wanted breaking, was it that the mass of the trees was too heavy? She smiled ironically; for had she not thought, when she began, that she had solved her problem?" But then, suddenly, almost unwilled, her art-making allows a vision to spring up. "Mrs. Ramsay—it was part of her perfect goodness to Lily—sat there quite simply, in the chair, flicked her needles to and fro, knitted her reddish-brown stocking, cast her shadow on the step. There she sat." The ghost is not showy like that of Hamlet's father, but an encouraging presence, finishing the socks she wanted to give to the light-house keeper's son no doubt, and is somehow proof that Lily is on the right track. The ghost accepts what Lily is doing; the ghost decides not to ask for anything more. Lily is the only one of the group who has created the conditions for Mrs. Ramsay to visit her, and that quiet fact is also an argument for Woolf's own art, even as she and Lily worry about shape and form. The novel ends not at the lighthouse, even though the family does at last make it there, but with Lily's finished picture. The last line of the novel belongs to both Lily and Mrs. Ramsay: "I have had my vision." And it is almost as if Woolf is speaking too, laying down a burden.

Virginia's last note to Leonard is about as famous as anything she wrote—if you don't know it yet, stop reading here, google, and you can see it in her handwriting; go to see a new ballet based on her life and hear it read by a famous actress—but perhaps only because we never got to read the other note she left, to her sister Vanessa. That may have been better still. Woolf lost her mother, unfairly, at thirteen, but she had a sister who shared her commitment to making art, and she wasn't the only person Woolf had—in fact her world was full of sisters, half-sisters, mother figures, ancestresses (and later lovers and admirers). There was a letter written by George Eliot hanging over her first writing desk, remember. When she was reading Eliot in preparation for the essay in which she declares *Middlemarch* a novel for grown-ups, she has a sense that "no one else has ever known her as I know her." There is a bond there, almost an accidental alliance like the one between Lily and Mrs. Ramsay in *To the Lighthouse*. She goes further still in *A Room of One's Own*: "We think back through our mothers if we are women." Woolf's argument is often reduced to its most practical suggestion, that women writers need a room of their own and enough independent wealth to live on, when her point is more that these things are the minimum makeweight against centuries of patriarchy, the engine for all the accumulated instincts that stop even women with a room of their own from writing freely once inside it. I hope that Woolf wouldn't be horrified that I have borrowed and changed her title for my own book, and one of the reasons I can hope that she would see me as an errant daughter rather than a traitor is that she was also saying that there are different ways of living from the ones women have been offered. Like Elena Ferrante would do later, Woolf is lamenting the short, halting nature of women's traditions, and usefully sets out the contours of the literary one for those who might want to be part of it. The mothers are all dead, and so off we go to the cemetery again. "Masterpieces are not single and solitary births," she writes,

> they are the outcome of many years of thinking in common, of thinking by the body of the people, so that the experience of the mass is behind the single voice. Jane Austen should have laid a wreath upon the grave of Fanny Burney, and George Eliot done homage to the robust shade of Eliza Carter—the valiant old woman who tied a bell to her bedstead in order that she might wake early and learn Greek. All women together ought to let flowers fall upon the tomb of Aphra Behn which is, most scandalously but rather appropriately, in Westminster Abbey, for it was she who earned them the right to speak their minds.

It is not that there is some sort of magical sisterhood, but that voices must accumulate before a single one can speak. It is not that solidarity produces change, not quite that, but that there is safety in numbers. Underneath the homages and the flowers, the gentle ribbing and the overidentification, is an idea that instead of reading books in order to learn about history or science or cultural trends, women might draw benefit from thinking of themselves as being involved in a long conversation, in which they both listen and talk, and even manage in this way, over time, to establish a tradition.

There is a sense when you read Woolf's essays that she thinks literary criticism would at its best be something like that, a conversation between like-minded and not-so-like-minded people over time. Almost by evolution, the conversation would refine what books are really for. Like Simone de Beauvoir, like Mary Wollstonecraft, like Zora Neale Hurston, like Sylvia Plath, she wrote in different genres, crossing the arbitrary lines drawn by who knows what person and when. (A man, surely.) But Woolf did also offer thoughts about what books did for her, and what they should do generally, and they are thoughts I find much more useful now than the academic models I was taught at university.

"Like most uneducated Englishwomen," she quipped in *A Room of One's Own*, "I like reading," and she was referring to herself when she called her collections of essays *The Common Reader*. She veered between pride and shame at never having sat for a degree, though surely she also sensed that a qualification could only lead, many years after graduation, to the unpicking of what you had learned at the university. In "How Should One Read a Book?" she thought that the best way was for the reader to imagine that she herself was writing the book she was reading, sympathizing with the author about the choices that have to be made. She let an "after-reading" take place once she'd turned the last page, allowing a book to shift shape in her memory, and made judgments only in comparison to other things she had read, not according to the fashionable opinion. In "An Unwritten Novel," a short story, she would go further still. The narrator frenziedly imagines herself into the life of a woman sitting across a train carriage from her, ending up by the sea at Eastbourne embracing the "adorable world!" As Woolf wrote it, she wondered if she did not deal "in autobiography & call it fiction?" I think it's more that she was trying on other ways of being: you discover who you are by knowing who you are not. You get lost in another life for long enough to see what's missing from your own—and what you are going to do about it.

I don't think that Woolf wrote, as Eliot did, with a nineteenth-century purpose to enlarge the heart. But toward the end of her life, she mounted arguments more frequently—*Three Guineas* an angry one against war and the society that keeps engaging in it; *A Room of One's Own* a sparkling one about all the things that hold women back—and we've seen that the writing of her books changed her. She knew what value forging a path had for those who came after her; she knew things could change. (Women had the franchise now, and millions of Germans voted for Hitler.) That she did know this makes her loss of faith in newness before her death less bearable. I know she was ill, which makes perspective impossible to come by. When you are wondering how to get through the night, it is no comfort to be told that things will change in time. But Woolf's writing embodies newness no matter if she lost faith with it, and it's still available to me a century later as a month-old New Yorker.

Woolf knew that life stories were altered by time passing: "These facts are not like the facts of science—once they are discovered, always the same. They are subject to changes of opinion; opinions change as the times change." I could approach Woolf now because she didn't seem so impeccable anymore. Between my first reading and my subway sessions, during the years of not reading her, I visited Monk's House in the village of Rodmell in Sussex, her country home, which is now a museum run by the National Trust. You entered through the gift shop, where every item's colors had been elegantly faded. I couldn't buy anything: it all felt so queasy. The house itself was crammed with things, but not her things really, as her husband had lived in the house for twenty-eight years after her death. In the back garden her writing hut had been left, every side looking out onto green fields or green garden or green trees, but the room itself, with its desk and scattered papers, was enclosed in glass by the National Trust custodians. I could walk around the hut and peer in, but not go into the room and be there to kneel down or lean over and try to see what she saw. I was in the place where she wrote and I felt as far away from her as ever.

From the garden, you could walk into her bedroom (at some point husband and wife stopped sharing a room and Virginia slept in a room of her own that gave directly onto the garden), and arched around the door were pink roses in full bloom. That was the first glimpse I ever had of Virginia Woolf: someone who wanted to fall out of bed into a tangle of scented flowers, someone who had loved women but stayed faithful to her husband, someone who had worried about her sadness returning, about her writing drying up, and who cared enough about clothes to give her niece, Angelica, a clothing allowance of £100 a year. She had taught me that to live was to keep responding to events as they arose, to let relationships—like the one with my mother as she got ill—change even if that scared me. And I had to let myself grow and change too: ambition to fade, depression to lift. In that moment under the roses, Woolf suddenly seemed to live. I took a picture and texted it to my crush, not really telling him what I had discovered (my texts to him hovered between mysterious and confusing) but wanting to mark the dawn of a thought anyway. Woolf's life and death had been so hardened by time that it had been difficult to believe, until I saw them, that roses had bloomed in the spring for her too.

Five minutes' walk from my new apartment in Brooklyn, I discovered, as a five-month-old New Yorker, Woolf was there. Devika, one of my closest friends, was visiting from London, and I took her to the Brooklyn Museum. I'd met Devika on the first day of university, when we discovered a mutual love of Marlboro Lights and the band Ash. Throughout university we smoked, got drunk, discussed books, talked about boys. We went to each other's weddings; I held her son when he was a few days old; she talked me through my divorce; and when I started taking antidepressants, she was the one who offered me oven pizza, Netflix, and her spare room every Monday evening. She has sensed what I needed as I lost my mother. When I left London I made her promise to visit me at least once a year; we talk on the phone most weeks. Here she was at last in Brooklyn, and our relationship was changing again. We stepped into the museum and discovered that Judy Chicago's *Dinner Party* (1974–79) has a permanent home there, and Woolf her everlasting place at that table. Chicago's place settings are for giantesses, the plates are metamorphosing into a vulva, the china goblets are waiting stoutly for their wine. The forks are improbably enormous. "Virginia Woolf" is embroidered on a yellow-green cloth, the V fading into blue waves. Was I so far from a life of my own? Perhaps I was coming closer. I could travel halfway across the world, I could explore, I could be renewed, and yet not abandon myself, and yet find new things that felt right.

Simone

Almost from the moment she published *The Second Sex* in November 1949, Simone de Beauvoir was asked why she'd never written a female character who lived a free life, the sort she envisioned in her final chapter, "The Independent Woman." If the mother of twentieth-century feminism couldn't imagine a free woman, who could? At first she would answer brusquely. "I've shown women as they are," she told the *Paris Review*, "as divided human beings, and not as they ought to be." (She'd said as much in an epigraph borrowed from Sartre: "À moitié victimes, à moitié complices, comme tout le monde.") But in a later interview she answered the same question angrily:

> The history of my life itself is a kind of problematic, and I don't have to give solutions to people and people don't have a right to wait for solutions from me. It is in this measure, occasionally, that what you call my celebrity—in short, people's attention—has bothered me. There is a certain demandingness that I find a little stupid, because it imprisons me, completely fixing me in a kind of feminist concrete block.

I know what that feminist concrete block looks like—it has a turban, it wears a black polo neck, it works at the Café de Flore, it has contingent lovers around one essential love, it drinks, it dances, it travels, it talks, it marches, it writes—and I have loved that concrete block as long as I've known it existed. It was partly the glamour of that myth that led me to read Beauvoir in the first place, working through both volumes of *Le Deuxième Sexe* at twenty-one, leaving hopeful questions about the future in the margins: would it always be true that "men don't like tomboys, or bluestockings, or clever women; too much daring, education, intelligence or character scares them?" Like so many other women, I wanted a feminist heroine, and Beauvoir seemed to fit: she had written a work of lasting value and she'd lived a life disdainful of convention—what more could one ask for? Surely that was why she'd written four volumes of memoir: to show us all, in an act of unprecedented generosity, how she'd freed herself. When she was buried in the Cimetière du Montparnasse, the waiters lined up outside La Coupole to see her coffin pass. A man carrying his toddler on his shoulders in the funeral throng told Beauvoir's first biographer, Deirdre Bair, that he wanted to be able to tell his daughter when she was older that they'd paid homage to a great woman. (Engraved over the columns of the Panthéon, a short walk from La Coupole, is the line "Aux Grands Hommes, la Patrie reconnaissante.")

But since April 1986, when Beauvoir died, the idea of her as a feminist heroine has faded. Her letters to Sartre, published four years later, showed her seducing her pupils and then passing them on to Sartre, in a bad modernist version of *Les Liaisons dangereuses*. She carried on a ten-year affair with the husband of one of her female lovers without the woman knowing. The publication of her letters to Nelson Algren in 1997 made the relationship she had with Sartre look passionless, as did the photo that emerged in 2008 of Beauvoir at forty-two, pinning her hair up in Algren's bathroom wearing just a pair of heels. And her insistence that Sartre was the philosopher, not her—because she hadn't invented a new system as he had done—looks too modest: he often took ideas from her novels, it now seems, not the other way around.

I wanted my heroine back. I needed her. Reading *Le Deuxième Sexe* had been one of the great discoveries of my final year at university, one of my first experiences of intellectual confidence. I read a lot of that enormous, two-volume book in the flat of my husband when he was still my boyfriend, but I kept the experience for myself rather than sharing it with him. Beauvoir always felt like mine. I hadn't read her four-volume autobiography—*Memoirs of a Dutiful Daughter*, *The Prime of Life*, *Force of Circumstance*, and *All Said and Done*—so I ordered secondhand copies online hoping, among other things, to have her restored to me. I read her in twenty-page increments as my stamina, lowered by depression, built again. She spoke this time as a woman who had attempted to live freely, and she felt like an aunt, a mother, an elder. I found that she hadn't claimed any superhuman status for herself: "I wanted to make myself exist for others by conveying, as directly as I could, the taste of my own life," she wrote at the very end of *Memoirs of a Dutiful Daughter*. Simone "communicates emotionally at once," Sartre wrote. "People are always involved with her by virtue of what she says." She herself said that she wrote about her life to ask: "What have I done with my freedom?" She wasn't seeking exoneration or canonization, but to live—with all the messiness that implied—on the page. She didn't even come to memoir until late in her life. Could she have been unsure what value there was in telling her own stories when philosophy and fiction could offer people rather more than her own example? And if I hadn't grown out of wanting to learn a lesson from her life, might the real lesson be the harder one—to value her for the mistakes she made as much as for what she achieved, and to accept that they might even be intertwined?

Memoirs of a Dutiful Daughter came out in France in 1958, when Beauvoir was fifty. It began at the beginning, with her birth in the early hours of January 9, 1908, above the Café de la Rotonde in Montparnasse. There were red silk hangings over the stained-glass doors in the apartment where she grew up, chandeliers, and a mother who, Proustianly, kissed her goodnight in perfumed black velvet before going to dinner. In the summer, the family visited her paternal grandfather's estate, Meyrignac, near Tulle, where there were magnolia trees, a stream with waterlilies and goldfish, peacocks, and wisteria. She was the favorite, even though her parents had wished for a boy—a wish that was even more evident when her sister Hélène, or Poupette, was born. Two days a week she went to a private Catholic school, Le Cours Désir (her mother's influence), and she liked reading more than anything else (her father's). "I was a madly gay little girl," she writes, though what I noticed most in her description of her childhood wasn't her happiness but her confidence. She had appalling handwriting (Sartre used to complain about it) and always "made a mess of hems," but "as soon as I was able to think for myself, I found myself possessed of infinite power . . . when I was asleep, the earth disappeared; it had need of me in order to be seen, discovered and understood." Her confidence, which never left her ("I have almost always felt happy and well adjusted," she said at sixty-four, "and I have trusted in my star"), is astonishing. I have never known a woman, in person or in print, who talks about herself the way Simone de Beauvoir does. That preternatural conviction makes sense of the teenage Simone rejecting God and the social code of the bourgeoisie she was born into; the woman in her twenties believing that she was her lover's essential love despite evidence to the contrary; the thirty-something deciding to write a book about the female condition; the fifty-year-old producing a 2,000-page autobiography. One day, while drying the dishes her mother was washing, she caught sight of the wives in the windows opposite doing the same thing, and had a vision of domestic life as a horrifying *mise en abyme*. "There had been people who had done things," she said to herself. "I, too, would do things." Jo in *Little Women* helped her work out what things to do, as did Maggie in *The Mill on the Floss* (she didn't discover Sand or Colette until later). And so did a new girl at school, Elisabeth Mabille, whom she called Zaza.

Zaza arrived at Le Cours Désir when Simone was ten: she'd been educated at home until burns caused by an accident when roasting potatoes led to a year's convalescence, and her falling behind with her studies. This appealed to Simone: "She at once seemed to me a very finished person." Zaza was skinny and dark, better than Simone at schoolwork, could make caramel and do cartwheels, and used to stick her tongue out during school piano recitals. With Zaza, Simone had "real conversations" for the first time, the kind she thought her mother and father had with each other. They became "the two inseparables." (Elena

Ferrante mentions the protagonist of *The Days of Abandonment* reading Beauvoir's late novella "The Woman Destroyed"; but, to me, Zaza and Simone could be foresisters of Lila and Lenù of the Neapolitan quartet.) After a day at Meyrignac eating apples and reading Balzac, both supposedly sinful activities, Simone discerned that she had lost the faith she once thought would send her to a convent—how could she believe in God and sin against him without feeling any guilt? She replaced love of God with another sort, for her cousin Jacques, whom she thought of as something like le grand Meaulnes. Jacques, older, better read, and willing to take her to bars, would disappear for weeks on end, and Simone, now studying philosophy at the Sorbonne (the École Normale was still barred to women), would work at the Bibliothèque Sainte-Geneviève, and take herself to the Louvre, to Chaplin movies, to see Madame Pitoëff in *Saint Joan*. "I would wander all over Paris, my eyes no longer brimming with tears, but looking at everything." She began writing novels, abandoning one, "Éliane," after nine pages, and sneaking out for a gin fizz at the Jockey with Poupette: after one drink her "loneliness evaporated." She came across Simone Weil (they didn't get on); she made friends, most of them male students at the Normale. Zaza fell in love with one of them, the once and future Maurice Merleau-Ponty, despite her parents' opposition, and although Simone thought later that she had fallen in love with the "image" of Jacques rather than the man himself, she still wished he were in Paris and not in Algeria doing military service. One group of normaliens, known for "brutality" (they threw water bombs on students "returning home at night in evening dress"), was the "little band" of Paul Nizan, René Maheu, and Jean-Paul Sartre. Sartre was rumored to be "the worst of the lot."

Beauvoir was preparing for her exams, full of love for Zaza, constantly addressing herself in her diary to the absent Jacques, and giddy for the married Maheu. She began to talk philosophy with the "petite bande" in the bars and gardens of the Latin Quarter, while ostensibly revising for the agrégation that would guarantee her a teaching post somewhere in France. She called Maheu her Lama (he gave Simone her lifelong nickname, Castor, French for "beaver," because she was "always fussing and working"), and admired everything about him, from the way he popped his collar to the way he teased her. "You're interested in everything," she records him saying in her diary for summer 1929. "That's why I reproach you." (Maheu seems to have been the first person she slept with, though she protested to Bair that she was still a well-brought-up Catholic girl at this point.)

Sartre's early attempts to capture Beauvoir's attention fell flat. "Sartre gave me as a gift some absurd pieces of porcelain won for me last night and a vile twopenny novel for my sister," she wrote in her diary. Seven days later, over cocktails at the Falstaff, she was beginning to reassess the situation: "Lama makes a woman feel attached to him just by softly caressing her neck, Sartre by showing her heart to her—which one more surely enslaves her?" Five days after that, she wrote of Sartre: "Intellectual need for his presence, and emotional turmoil in facing his affection. Doubts, upset, exaltation. I would like him to force me to be a real somebody, and I am afraid." Sartre brought her the results of the agrégation (he came first, she second), and announced that from "now on"—it was June 1929—"I'm going to take you under my wing." Beauvoir was twenty-one. He urged her to try to "preserve what was best in me: my love of personal freedom, my passion for life, my curiosity, my determination to be a writer"; she thought she had found the "dream companion I had longed for since I was 15." Jacques had returned from Algeria and got engaged, as he told Simone sheepishly, after a three-week courtship. His marriage, she later noted, turned out to be one of "moderate rapture"; their families stopped talking, but for years afterward she would catch sight of him in the bars of Montparnasse, "lonely, puffy-faced, with watering eyes, obviously the worse for drink."

Zaza was preparing with "frenzied" optimism to go to Berlin (her parents had thought separation the best way to discourage the match with Merleau-Ponty), where she foresaw a year of love letters and reading Stendhal. But the day after Simone and Zaza had said goodbye, Zaza fell ill. Delirious, with a temperature of 104 degrees, she turned up at Merleau-Ponty's door and demanded his mother explain why she didn't want them to marry. When Merleau-Ponty himself arrived, she turned on him too: "Why have you never kissed me?" He kissed her. Under pressure, both sets of parents backed down: the marriage could go ahead, but first Zaza had to get well. She was transferred to a clinic in Saint-Cloud—"my violin, Ponty, Simone, champagne," she would cry out over and over. Four days later, she died. The next time Simone saw Zaza she was laid out on a funeral bier, surrounded by flowers and candles, her face thin and yellow. The doctors blamed meningitis or encephalitis; no one knew for sure. "We have fought together," Beauvoir wrote, "against the revolting fate that had lain ahead of us, and for a long time I believed I had paid for my own freedom with her death."

This astonishing sentence—"whoah Simone," I wrote in the margin—is where Beauvoir ends *Memoirs of a Dutiful Daughter*. It's one of the most novel-like endings of all her books: best friend dead, first love engaged to someone else, the faith and social class into which she was born abandoned.

Beauvoir had in fact already tried out Zaza's story as a novel—in 120 pages she wrote in 1954 at the age of forty-six—but she left the completed book in a drawer. *The Inseparables*, finally published in 2020, makes the fictional Zaza, called Andrée, worldly but obedient to her Catholic family's bourgeois traditions; Sylvie, the fictional Simone, watches the tragedy unfold from a class below. The teenage girls are alone one night when Andrée admits that falling in love has utterly changed how she thought about herself. She had thought she was "so ugly, so clumsy, so uninteresting." Sylvie reacts strongly to this. "You never knew it, but from the day I met you, you were everything to me. I had decided that if you died, I would immediately die as well." Andrée is confused: "I thought your books and your studies were all that was really important to you." The intensity recalls that of Mary Wollstonecraft and Fanny Blood, of Lila and Lenù—and in all three cases it also approaches a love affair.

This insight of Beauvoir's seems psychologically right to me: that one of our first experiences of love as young women is close friendship. I suppose it's now a cliché to say that the greatest love stories in our lives might be with our friends. Beauvoir was lucky in this: Zaza loved her, and died loving her. The feelings were clear even if the circumstances were unfair. Until relatively recently, my experience of female friendship was much more painful. I left my first best friend—she was blond to my brunette, and we played in a tent glowing red inside—behind at five years old when my family moved away. Next I was part of a trio of girls, giving me the illusion of being well resourced, and the frequent experience of being left out. As a teenager, I was absorbed into a group of indie kids: we discovered drinking and dancing and snogging together; we dyed our hair, strategized about crushes, made mixtapes, stayed at each other's houses all weekend. My family moved again and I left them behind as a way to commit to the new place, where I found a new best friend instantly—and was just as quickly dumped by her. I saw myself as someone who was useful to others rather than a person who could be loved for who she was.

Both Lidija and Devika remember me before my divorce as poised, others say I was stuck up. I longed for a best friend I could be wholly myself with, and was susceptible to people who worked hard to be friends for longer than was good for me. At university, I made friends much more slowly. I needed to, say, have an argument and find a way back (or not). I needed time to unfold; I still do. (One of my sixth-form friends had called me "Crème Brûlée," caramel-hard at first glance but cream-soft underneath.) All of my closest friends now have seen me cry; they have heard me say I love them; they have seen me angry, withdrawn, vicious, and petty; they have had to remind me to behave better. They have stood with me while I was messy, and I have tried my best to stand with them when they have needed me.

Andrée's assumption in *The Inseparables*, that books were enough for Sylvie, has the force of a lover's complaint. Andrée is the most important person in Sylvie's life at that point and her opinion matters. Being poised must attract as many people as it puts off, but when I'm taken with someone, the idea that they'd prefer someone to laugh at their jokes rather than analyze everything haunts me, as it haunts Lenù, Sylvie, and Mary. Books do serve in an emotional crisis, and in curious ways: Lenù in particular can draw people to her with what she writes, can bury herself in books when her crush falls for someone else, can muddle a suitor's intellectual status with love, can use her writing to make her passion last. Beauvoir would struggle wherever she loved, and writing could be a refuge for her, a routine, an escape but never quite enough on its own. In *The Inseparables*, Sylvie's attention is occupied by Andrée's romantic entanglements, while in life, Simone had Sartre waiting in the Jardin du Luxembourg to talk about Plato—and a career as a writer and thinker within reach.

In the epilogue to *Force of Circumstance*, Beauvoir said that there had been "one undoubted success in my life: my relationship with Sartre." She explained that they had only once, and only for one night, been at odds. They reasoned together, shared the same body of reference: "We might almost be said to think in common." She added that this might seem to contradict what she says about how important independence should be to women in *The Second Sex*, but she made a distinction: "I insist that women be independent, yet I have never been alone." That delicate, perhaps utopian balance—togetherness not encroaching on independence—was present in the way she and Sartre conceived of their relationship from the beginning: theirs being the essential love, they wouldn't lie to each other about contingent lovers. They would try this "lease" for two years while they were both in Paris, and then renegotiate, in the belief that they would be separated for two or three more years. Beauvoir remembered feeling "a flicker of fear" over this arrangement, a feeling she immediately subdued. Scholars including Toril Moi have seen her acceptance of the pact as a strategy for dealing with her fear of losing Sartre, but she seems to have suffered all the same. Bair says that nearly all Beauvoir's friends remember her sometimes leaving the café table during evenings with the "family"—Beauvoir and Sartre's name for the group of ex and current lovers they socialized with—to "go and sit alone at another table to consume vast quantities of wine and sob uncontrollably." Beauvoir herself talks of the jealousy she suffered the first time Sartre took another lover, and of the moment "my heart's old armour of optimism fell away" when he told her of the weeks he'd spent in New York falling in love with Dolores Vanetti, to whom he would propose marriage. If writing a novel (*She Came to Stay*) about sharing a lover that ends in the established woman killing the newcomer isn't a sign of distress, what is? Generations of feminists have asked the question never expressed better than by Angela Carter: "Why is a nice girl like Simone wasting her time sucking up to a boring old fart like J-P?"

At the end of the first year of the Sartre–Beauvoir pact—marked by that first experience of jealousy, which she dispelled by walking up and down the Butte Montmartre—Beauvoir was sent to Marseille to teach. Sartre proposed to her so that they wouldn't have to be separated. "I may say that not for one moment was I tempted to fall in with his suggestions," Beauvoir writes in *The Prime of Life*, adding that "the task of preserving my independence was not particularly onerous; I would have regarded it as highly artificial to equate Sartre's absence with my own freedom—a thing I could only find, honestly, within my own head and heart." Twelve years later, she wrote about this "important decision" in different terms: "I very strongly wished not to leave Sartre. I chose what was the hardest course for me at that moment in order to safeguard the future." There is a complex idea of independence here: it can't be defined by leaving Sartre, and yet it can't be achieved by staying with him when she wanted to. "If any man had proved sufficiently self-centerd and commonplace to attempt my subjugation," she writes about the fear of abandoning herself to love, a fear that comes up again and again, "I would have judged him, found him wanting, and left him." Perhaps Beauvoir's independence was achieved in the way she describes it in *The Prime of Life*, by working determinedly at her teaching at the lycée during the week and hiking in the calanques and the Côte d'Azur at the weekends, "daily and unaided fashioning my own happiness."

The next year she was in Rouen and Sartre not too far away in Le Havre, where he was beginning to set down the thoughts that would result in *Nausea*. When they went back to Paris they would meet friends over apricot cocktails to elaborate Husserl's phenomenology into a philosophy of everyday life. Beauvoir began seven novels in this period, abandoning them all. She feared that the writing life she longed for would never materialize; when she was drunk, she would cry and then argue with Sartre, insisting that drunkenness let her see the truth: "the joy of being, the horror of being no more" (Sartre didn't agree). She began a relationship with one of her pupils in Rouen, Olga Kosakiewicz (Beauvoir was twenty-seven, Olga seventeen); Olga, the first lover she and Sartre shared, remained a part of the "family" until she died. Around this time, Sartre took an injection of mescaline to pull him out of a depression and found himself trailed by imaginary lobsters. Beauvoir, deeply unsettled, said she "preferred the idea of Sartre angling for Olga's emotional favors to his slow collapse from some hallucinatory psychosis," though the idea of living in a trio for years "frankly terrified" her. Almost in reply to Sartre's desire for Olga, Beauvoir took up with one of Sartre's students, Jacques-Laurent Bost ("I slept with little Bost three days ago," she wrote to Sartre. "It was I who propositioned him, of course"), and continued to sleep with him for a decade. Olga, who would hate the way she was written about in *She Came to Stay*, barely spoke publicly of her relationship with the pair, saying almost nothing to Bair. She soon extricated herself, transferring her affections to Bost, whom she would eventually marry. Bost's affair with Beauvoir was kept secret from Olga—and omitted from her memoirs, but not from *She Came to Stay*, a frequent Beauvoirian move.

In 1938, *Nausea* was published to acclaim (it was Beauvoir who had suggested that Sartre present his ideas in a novel rather than an essay) while Beauvoir's collection of short stories, *When Things of the Spirit Come First*, was turned down twice. She began relationships with some of her other pupils, among them Nathalie Sorokine (who called her "a clock in a refrigerator" for the way she divided her time between her lovers and her work, brooking no deviation), and Bianca Bienenfeld, whom Sartre seduced (once Beauvoir had told him how to go about it). He also began a relationship with Olga's sister, Wanda. Beauvoir told Sartre that the situation had become "grimy": Bianca was dependent and desperate, convinced Beauvoir loved Sartre more than her. Beauvoir admitted that she had behaved disgracefully and encouraged Bianca to put herself at the center of her own life, perhaps as she had tried to do when suffering from jealousy herself. It takes discipline to remind yourself that comparison demeans all parties: we can forget that one person is never just the same as another. (There is a particularly nasty letter to Sartre in which Beauvoir describes Bianca's "pungent faecal odour" during their "embraces"—perhaps another tactic Beauvoir used to separate herself psychically from those she felt were coming too close to her.)

When the war began in September 1939, both Bost and Sartre went into service. Beauvoir fell into a depression, left Paris, came back again. She got used to food shortages, didn't wash much, and waited for letters that inevitably got misdelivered. Sartre broke up with Bianca by letter, exacerbating her distress: "I never blamed you for making the break, since after all that's what I'd advised you to do," Beauvoir wrote to him, "but I blamed us—myself as much as you, actually—in the past, in the future, in the absolute: the way we treat people." In 1993, after the letters to Sartre were published, Bianca wrote a memoir, *Mémoires d'une jeune fille dérangée*—a riff on Beauvoir's title. She'd felt abandoned by the couple during the war (she was Jewish) and began to recover only when she married one of Sartre's pupils, was analyzed by Lacan, and achieved some distance from the "family." In December 1945, after an evening spent talking to Bianca, Beauvoir was full of remorse: "She's suffering from an intense and dreadful attack of neurasthenia, and it's our fault I think. It's the very indirect but profound aftershock of the business between her and us. She's the only person to whom we've really done harm, but we have harmed her."

Beauvoir was the co-architect of Bianca's suffering: the women and men who got involved as contingents weren't fully responsible for what happened to them. The harm to Bianca was lasting and intense, and Beauvoir's cruelty is difficult to forgive in the woman who would write the ethics of existentialism (Sartre never got that far) and say in her plays, essays, novels, and memoirs that reciprocal relationships were what mattered most in life. I struggle with knowing about Beauvoir's repeated relationships with people younger than and overawed by her, the betrayal, the abandonment. (Sorokine's mother pressed charges for debauchery, and Beauvoir was dismissed from teaching in 1943 by the Vichy authorities, which was seen as a feather in the *résistante*'s cap rather than a sin against sexual mores.) But Beauvoir never entered into this sort of trio after Bianca; she recognized she had hurt someone she loved; it seems that she was the one to call a halt to the griminess. In *The Prime of Life*, reflecting on the pact thirty-one years later, she says: "There is no timeless formula which guarantees all couples achieving a perfect state of understanding; it is up to the interested parties themselves to decide just what sort of agreement they want to reach. They have no a priori rights or duties." Now we have the letters, the diaries, and the testimony of the "thirds," we can see the pact being renegotiated in real time, as they decide what suffering each can bear (Sartre was also jealous, particularly when Olga wouldn't sleep with him) and allow the experiment in love to play out. In certain moods I can agree with Beauvoir that her relationship with Sartre was the greatest success in her life—it was certainly hard-won, which is perhaps what gave it its value.

Since 1941, when Sartre was released from a Nazi POW camp and returned to Paris, the old band had been meeting in a group they called Socialism and Liberty. They talked, wrote, printed and distributed leaflets, but mostly they lay in wait: "If the democracies won, it would be essential for the left to have a new programme; it was our job, by pooling our ideas, discussions and research, to bring such a programme into being." But other underground groups were more successful than theirs, and by 1943, Sartre and Beauvoir found themselves reduced, politically, to a state of "total impotence." She held that it was an intellectual's duty not to write for collaborationist papers, and so she didn't, but she did accept a job at Radio Vichy producing a program about medieval music, and she had signed the Vichy oath—declaring she wasn't Jewish—when still working as a teacher. After the failure of Socialism and Liberty, Sartre and Beauvoir expressed their opposition in their writing: Sartre produced *Being and Nothingness*, *The Flies*, and *No Exit*; the "grimy" period earlier in the war had brought Beauvoir the subject of her first novel, *She Came to Stay*, and during her mornings at Café des Trois Mousquetaires on the rue de la Gaîté she began a second, *The Blood of Others*, set among Resistance fighters.

When *She Came to Stay* was published in 1943, followed a year later by her philosophical essay *Pyrrhus and Cinéas*, Beauvoir's life as a public intellectual began. After the liberation of Paris in August 1944, the city boomed: "So many obstacles had been overcome that none now seemed insuperable." Beauvoir might find herself listening to Romain Gary at the Rhumerie, or at a cocktail party with Elsa Triolet and Louis Aragon, or drinking whisky with Hemingway until dawn in his room at the Ritz, or talking to Nathalie Sarraute, or waiting in a cinema queue with Violette Leduc, or sitting on a snowy curb at two in the morning while Camus "meditated pathetically" on love. Beauvoir and Sartre set up a journal, *Les Temps modernes* (named for the Chaplin movie), with Michel Leiris, Merleau-Ponty, and

Raymond Aron on the editorial committee, and she went to the Ministry of Information to beg for a quota of paper. *The Blood of Others* came out, the first issues of *Les Temps modernes* were published, her play, *Les Bouches inutiles*, was put on, and her stock rose again. She became the literary equivalent of Dior's New Look, and a tabloid figure: being called "la grande Sartreuse" or "Notre-Dame de Sartre" made her laugh, but she found it "repugnant" to be looked up and down like a "dissolute woman."

She wrote in the mornings in her room in La Louisiane, a private hotel on the rue de Seine, with a cigarette in one hand and a fountain pen in the other, stopped for lunch with Sartre and the family, then returned at 4:30 p.m. "into this room that's still thick with smoke from the morning, the paper already covered in green ink lying on the desk," to write again before dinner. And she'd found a new question, born out of her admiration for *L'Âge d'homme*, in which Leiris tried to trace his initiation into manhood, and from seeing the mysterious *Lady and the Unicorn* tapestries, just brought out from wartime storage: "What has it meant to me to be a woman?" At first, she protested to Sartre that her sex "just hasn't counted." Look again, he said. "You weren't brought up in the same way as a boy would have been." She looked again, and "it was a revelation: this world was a masculine world, my childhood had been nourished by myths forged by men, and I hadn't reacted to them in at all the same way I should have done if I had been a boy." In fact, her interest had begun earlier: in 1943, when Paris was still occupied, she had spent time with some of the surrealist women, now in their forties. "They told me a great deal; I began to take stock of the difficulties, deceptive advantages, traps and manifold obstacles that most women encounter on their path."

The war years were the only time she entertained the idea of herself as a housewife: she records that she scraped the maggots off a joint of pork and made turnip sauerkraut. Now, desperate to travel again, she arranged a four-month lecture trip to America. (Such journeys would be a fixture of Beauvoir's postwar life: she would visit China, Brazil, Russia, Egypt, Israel, Palestine, and Japan as well as making many shorter trips to European countries, spending every summer in Rome.) Sartre had already been to the US, and now Dolores was getting a divorce and coming to Paris. Beauvoir was scared of the depth of their connection; it seemed better for the two women to swap countries. She landed in New York City in January 1947 and went straight out into the "supernatural light" of Broadway, freed from "the past and the future, a pure presence." *Vogue* threw her a party, the *New Yorker* described her as the "prettiest existentialist you ever saw," and she lunched her way around Manhattan, becoming close to Richard Wright and his wife, Ellen (left-wing Americans who criticized their country in a way that made you love it more), before taking off for Vassar, then Chicago, California, Texas, New Orleans, and New Mexico.

She'd been told to look up Nelson Algren, the writer of a well-received collection of short stories, *The Neon Wilderness*, when she got to Chicago, but when she rang a "surly voice" told her she had the wrong number. She rang again, and again the voice said that she had the wrong number. She rang a third time; he hung up. After "a melancholy supper at a drugstore counter" she rang a fourth time, this time leaving a message with the operator, and when Algren heard the names of their mutual friends, he at last softened and said he'd meet her in the lobby in half an hour. (In *The Mandarins*, the character based on Algren picks the phone up on the first try.) They spent the evening in West Madison among the "bums, drunks and old ruined beauties"—"it is beautiful," Simone told Nelson—and then talked about Malraux's novels until one in the morning with a "peroxided blond" who ran a shelter for down-and-outs. Beauvoir returned to Chicago at the end of the lecture tour.

The first day of her reunion with Algren at his home on Wabansia Avenue was, she explained in *Force of Circumstance*, "very much like the one Anne and Lewis spent together in *The Mandarins*," the novel dedicated to Algren: "embarrassment, impatience, misunderstanding, fatigue, and finally the intoxication of deep understanding." In the novel, Beauvoir describes the psychoanalyst Anne Dubreuilh entirely renewed by her encounter with the writer Lewis Brogan:

> His desire transformed me. I who for so long a time had been without taste, without form, again possessed breasts, a belly, a sex, flesh; I was as nourishing as bread, as fragrant as earth. It was so miraculous that I didn't think of measuring my time or my pleasure; I know only that before we fell asleep I could hear the gentle chirpings of dawn.

The next day he gave her a "clunky silver band," as Bair calls it, a Mexican ring that Beauvoir told her was "supposed to be my wedding ring and I am going to be buried with it." The day he gave her that ring became their anniversary. Her friends in New York warned her that he was "unstable, moody, even neurotic," but she "liked being the only one who understood him." She wept on the plane back to Paris when she found the poem her "beloved husband" had written inside the copy of his book he'd given her, and during her stopover she wrote to him in her idiosyncratic English: "I love you. There is no more to say. You take me in your arms and I cling to you and I kiss you as I kissed you." Back in France, she moved away from Paris to avoid Dolores, gave up work on her "essay on Woman," and used orphenadrine, a muscle relaxant, to blunt her self-questioning over Algren. "Wouldn't it be better to give up the whole thing?" she asked herself. But she kept writing to him, telling him that "I feel I am tied to you by hundreds and hundreds of ties, and they will never be broken," and trying to make him understand that while he would always have the love of his "Wabansia wife," he could never have her life, which was in Paris. By September, she was back in Chicago.

Bair spent seven years talking to Beauvoir about her life and remembers the story of the affair with Algren as the only time she became "girlish, flirtatious, gloriously happy, and deeply sad—all in the single telling." Sometimes it's hard to remember that this thirty-nine-year-old woman writing as "your loving frog-wife" to "my own beloved Nelson" was also drafting *The Second Sex*: "The mornings are so hard, my love, when I open my eyes and you are not there," she wrote to him on her return to Paris at the end of September 1947. "Last year my life here was full and rich, now everything is empty." Although Beauvoir maintained to the last that she couldn't have left France, I often think she should have: while in love with Nelson she wrote *The Second Sex*, about falling in love with Nelson she wrote *The Mandarins*. Why else would you need to be free, if not to do what you want to do? Over the next five years Algren asked her again and again to marry him, and then remarried his ex-wife, rejecting Beauvoir's offer of friendship: "I can never offer you less than love." When the remarriage failed eight years later, he visited Paris and they found a sort of harmony again: visiting the Crazy Horse and the Lapin Agile, going to the Musée Grévin and listening to Bessie Smith, seeing Seville and Athens and Istanbul and Marseille. "I wasn't tearing myself to pieces, as I used to, at the thought that our intimacy had no future," she wrote in *Force of Circumstance*; their relationship was "completed, saved from destruction, as though we were already dead." It wasn't quite dead for him: he was furious about what she said about their affair in her memoirs, writing in *Harper's Magazine* in 1964 that "anybody who can experience love contingently has a mind that has recently snapped. How can love be contingent? Contingent upon what?" They stopped writing to each other that year, but when Beauvoir was buried, more than twenty years later, she was wearing Algren's ring, as she said she would.

I once went to a fancy dress party as Beauvoir: I wound a black-and-white scarf around my head as a turban, but nevertheless I kept having to explain. I now think this might have pleased Beauvoir, who didn't want to be remembered for a hairstyle she'd adopted to hide dirty hair during the Occupation, but had hoped, from the age of twenty and far beyond, "to make myself loved through my books." Twelve years after she published *The Second Sex* in 1949 she was still receiving letters from women who told her that it had "saved me"; psychiatrists, she heard, gave it to their patients. It was the book that brought her the most satisfaction; she was gratified that younger women now wrote as "the eye-that-looks, as subject, consciousness, freedom." (Less pleased were Norman Mailer, whose first wife divorced him after reading it; the pope, who banned it; and François Mauriac, who told a contributor to *Les Temps modernes* that "your employer's vagina has no secrets from me.")

The Second Sex germinated in conversations with Sartre, was changed by Beauvoir's experience of love with Algren, owed a lot to the understanding of the US civil rights movement she gained from Richard Wright, and was given its title by Bost. It's a long book with a simple proposition, one of those elegant thoughts it's both easy to remember, impossible to exhaust, and much contested: "One is not born but rather becomes a woman." The idea is still alive for me: if one becomes a woman, I reason, then it is right for trans women to be considered women. And it is a hopeful one: women are trapped, mutilated (one of Beauvoir's favorite words), complicit, steeped in bad faith not because that's their nature but because that is how the world has schooled them—or, rather, not schooled them. The world has, can, and must change.

It's also a curious book, with a strange history. I was struck by the fact that although its structure can be laid out logically on a contents page—the first volume covers what has been said about women by biology, psychoanalysis, historical materialism, history, and literature; the second goes through the ages and archetypes of woman before finally considering what it might take for them to become independent—it reads as if it was assembled from personal experience: Beauvoir's travels, her discussions, her reading, and her understanding of existentialism. It seems homemade, like a patchwork quilt. She calls the woman in love a jailer, a paranoiac, a slave, a person involved in a desperate psychological attempt to "survive by accepting the dependence to which she is condemned"; yet she also imagines an "authentic love," "a human interrelation" founded on accepting the other "with all his idio-syncrasies, his limitations and his basic gratuitousness." (I think of Beauvoir saying she wasn't offended at Algren's "bluntness" when he was asked about the US publication of *The Mandarins*: "I knew all about his moods.") For a book that invigorated a liberation movement, it spends a great deal of time elaborating on the ways woman is everywhere in chains; independence is only glimpsed. The intellectually free woman fears losing love, so makes "a show of elegance and frivolity" instead of "naturalness and simplicity"; she cultivates competence when "discussions, extracurricular read-ing, a walk with the mind freely wandering" would do more to encourage originality; she is new to the country, and so is "afraid to disarrange, to investigate, to explode." *The Second Sex* has sold a million copies in English, but anglophones have only been able to see it cloudily: the first silently edited English translation was made in 1953 by a zoologist who didn't know philosophy; the new one, first published in the US in 2009, was made not by Beauvoir scholars but by translators whose previous work included cookery books. But it is, for better or worse, where modern feminism begins, and though I long for a world where it is no longer useful, I use Beauvoir's application of Hegel's master-slave dialectic—woman is doubly oppressed, first because she's a slave and second because she works to identify with her master's view of her as a slave—most weeks, and on bad weeks most days.

Giving up Algren, Beauvoir gave up on love. "I'll never sleep again warmed by another's body," she said to herself, and tried to accept it. "I suddenly found myself on the other side of a line," she wrote in *Force of Circumstance*. "I stood there, bewil-dered by astonishment and regret." She learned to drive; on a spring road trip to Provence, behind the wheel on her own for the first time, she felt as exhilarated as she had when walking in Marseille as a young woman. She finished the enormous novel that was becoming *The Mandarins*, giving herself the "pleasure" of transposing into "a fictional world an occurrence," her time with Algren, "that meant so much to me." She makes Anne and Lewis's time together sexy—with both bad sex, which is to say perfunctory and given into, and good sex, which renews their faith in love—and yet also captures the difficulties of their relationship. The second time the lovers meet, Lewis is both 20 minutes late (as he'd got the time of her arrival wrong) and 40 minutes early (as that was how long he'd planned to wait in the airport before her touchdown in Chicago). Time warps, drags, stretches out: they're too old when they meet to really be together; they can't work out why there is both not enough and too much time; they don't know how to weave their relationship into an ordinary day. It is almost because their affair is so future-less that Anne can bring so much of herself into it, without fear. At one point, when she declares she can't make a life with him in America, he concedes that he loves her for this too, and she bursts into tears in his arms. He says:

"It's funny but sometimes you seem like a very wise woman, and sometimes you're just like a little child."

"I suppose I'm really a stupid woman," I said. "But if you love me, I don't care."

"I love you, my stupid little Gauloise," Lewis said.

This tiny exchange, written in the clichés lovers speak in (I can't work out whether "frog-wife" is worse or better than "stupid little

Gauloise"; they both make me wince), also captures the attraction and impossibility of the encounter. In love, Anne can be a little girl and a grown woman with a life of her own, and she can also slip both roles and be free—but this freedom is dependent on his admiration. I don't think anyone is incomplete without a partner, but there are certain ideas a person can have about themselves that cannot shift until they are accepted and appreciated by another. Anne says she's stupid here, not Lewis. He transforms her doubt about herself into something he can love.

One of the curious things about Beauvoir's work is the way she mixes genres: her novels have the tang of memoir, her memoirs have the finish of a novel, her essays have the tone of conversation, her conversation has the severity of a lecture (as you can see on YouTube, she never smiles or uses a plain French word when a recondite one would do), her letters have the feel of pillow talk. This has often meant that her novels look more like *romans-à-clef* than they are, and that her memoirs are taken as gospel. (It has led to funnier misunderstandings too: when Beauvoir published "The Woman Destroyed" in *Elle* magazine, hundreds of readers wrote in to say how sorry they felt for its protagonist, whose husband had left her. Beauvoir had to explain that she had intended merely to alert them to the danger in not having resources of your own.) It's as if she pursues the idea first, then bends the rules of the genre to fit what she has to say. She'll tell the reader she can skip the account of her travels to Brazil if she likes, or let her semi-fictional characters talk for pages before they do anything. Over time, her sentences became plainer and her turn of phrase more vivid. As a body of work, hers feels accidental, prolix, and messy: not the work of a concrete block, but of a woman.

If there was pleasure in putting some of her time with Algren down on the page, perhaps it also helped to write about the last summer they spent together in America. Lewis had fallen out of love with Anne, but Anne still loved him, arriving for a lakeside holiday with Parisian silks and perfume. They have sex but it's "without a word, without a kiss," and Anne spends the rest of the night crying on the sofa. She lives in hope that summer, not able to hate him, trying to let swimming in the lake, reading books, the glossy sky, and a combination of Benzedrine and whisky blunt the obvious truth that the relationship was over. She sympathizes with him, even thinking at times that he made the only decision he could: "How he must have wanted a woman completely his! For a moment, he had thought he had escaped solitude; he had dared to wish for something other than security. And he had been duped, he had suffered, he had recovered." But the intellectual acceptance doesn't and couldn't make her happy. As the book ends, she is tormented still. "Who knows? Perhaps one day I'll be happy again. Who knows?" Beauvoir doesn't give Anne a happy ending, but she doesn't condemn her either.

In 1954, when she was forty-six, *The Mandarins* won the Prix Goncourt, and Beauvoir became only the second woman the jury could agree on in fifty years (Elsa Triolet was the first). She refused to "exhibit herself" to the press, skipping the traditional scrum at Drouant for lunch with members of the family, including Claude Lanzmann—her new lover, the first, contingent or essential, she'd moved in with. She credited Lanzmann with having "freed me from my age," and he encouraged her to keep going on *The Mandarins*; Beauvoir would lend him money to begin filming *Shoah*. Sartre's role in her life had changed: they still worked together in the afternoons, and still summered together in Rome, but since her time with Algren she had a new freedom from him. After winning the Goncourt (and buying her first apartment with the resulting royalties) she began writing her memoirs, in which Sartre makes many comic appearances: he dresses up in drag and is pursued by an American lesbian, steals a skull from an ancient ossuary, rolls down the slope he's supposed to be sleeping on, encourages Simone to overtake dawdling Italian drivers ("Pass him, go on, pass him!"), tries sashimi for the first time, then Japanese whisky for the first time, then can't eat anything for two days. Some complained that she was demeaning a great man, but Beauvoir, true to form, thought that the telling of these things only made him more lovable.

The end of her life was marked by intolerable losses and a resurgence of political activism. The Algerian War soured her view of France, and brought her out onto the streets again and again. She saw herself differently as she aged: "I loathe my appearance now," she wrote at fifty-five, and wrote a book, *Old Age*, in the manner of *The Second Sex*. As she approached sixty, Lanzmann moved out, though he remained part of the family; five years later, Beauvoir's mother died. Beauvoir hadn't been close to her mother since her late teens, when she broke with Catholicism, but the experience of caring for her during her six-week illness, while concealing from her the diagnosis of untreatable intestinal cancer, brought about an intense period of grieving—and the short, brutal, and beautiful memoir *A Very Easy Death*. Françoise de Beauvoir had "lived against herself," continually rebelling "against the restraints and privations that she inflicted upon herself." Her life could have been used as an example of a woman oppressed by society, living proof of the arguments put forward in *The Second Sex*. But at the end things became tender and simple, and Beauvoir could make her happy by feeding her tea with a spoon, crumbling biscuit into each mouthful. After her mother's death, Beauvoir looked again at a photo of the eighteen-year-old Simone with the forty-year-old Françoise around the time they broke with each other: "I am so sorry for them—for me because I am so young and I understand nothing; for her because her future is closed and she has never understood anything."

It was at this point that she became close to Sylvie Le Bon, a philosophy student thirty-three years her junior, who had written to her in admiration a few years earlier and was studying at the Normale (now open to women). When Beauvoir broke down after seeing her mother in a hospital bed for the first time, Sartre had helped her analyze her feelings, but he hadn't dried her tears. Sylvie was different: she accompanied Beauvoir on trips to Rome and New York, did her shopping, watered down her whisky, and eventually became her literary executor. There were other rumors too. When Bair asked Beauvoir about the nature of their relationship, she exploded: "We are not lesbian! . . . Oh sure, we kiss on the lips, we hug, we touch each other's breasts, but we don't do anything . . . down there! So you can't call us lesbians!" You can take the girl out of the Catholic bourgeoisie, but you can't take the Catholic bourgeoisie out of the girl.

Her fiction in the late 1960s became more radical: she wanted to show the bourgeois the flimsy basis on which they'd built their lives. In *Les Belles Images* (1966), Laurence, who works in advertising, comes to recognize that her life is empty, but doesn't know how to reshape it into something better. "I've always run along a set of rails. I've never decided anything; not even my marriage, nor my profession, nor my affair with Lucien—that came and went in spite of me. Things happen to me, that's all. What to do?" In "The Woman Destroyed," the story published in *Elle* in 1967, we read the diary of Monique, whose husband leaves her for "pretty, dashing, bitchy, available" Noëllie. Having no experience of life other than taking care of her family, Monique crumbles, clinging to handwriting analysis, horoscopes, and a Miss Lonelyhearts column to bring him back. But five months later, like Anne in *The Mandarins*, she teeters on the edge of a new, truer, life. Beauvoir's attempts at exploring these problems using fiction were spectacularly unsuccessful, partly because she was understood as a portraitist when she was trying to be an activist. Her points were made better when she used herself as an example; in her memoirs, she is more than anything else the reader's friend. (And she herself was good at friendship, keeping female friends for decades and holding on to her lovers once desire faded.) As a self-portraitist, she knows how hard living can be and how impossible the puzzles love presents us with are.

Both Beauvoir and Sartre supported the occupation of the Sorbonne in 1968, wandering the corridors, joining in the discussions about the Palestinian question. Beauvoir was hopeful: "For the first time in thirty-five years the question of a revolution and of a transition to socialism had been raised in an advanced capitalist country." It was what she had been waiting for since Algeria. As the *événements* faded, she became involved with feminist organizing. The Mouvement de libération des femmes (MLF) was born in August 1970, when nine women including Christiane Rochefort and Monique Wittig attempted to lay a floral sheaf for the unknown soldier's wife at the Arc de Triomphe. Their bedsheet and bamboo banners read: "*Il y a plus inconnu que le soldat inconnu, sa femme*" ("more unknown than the Unknown Soldier is his wife"). In 1971, in support of the MLF's campaign for free abortion, Beauvoir signed the "Manifeste des 343," declaring in that week's *Nouvel Observateur* that, along with Catherine Deneuve, Delphine Seyrig, and Marguerite Duras—as well as Olga, her own sister, and dozens of secretaries, office workers, and housewives—she had had an abortion. She marched on the Assemblée Nationale with the MLF, let them hold meetings at her flat, read the *SCUM Manifesto*, *The Feminine Mystique*, *The Dialectic of Sex*, *Sexual Politics*, and *The Female Eunuch*, and changed her position. In *The Second Sex* in 1949, she had written that "by and large, we have won the game." Now, after 1968, she declared "myself a feminist. No, we have not won the game: in fact we have won almost nothing since 1950." She saw that women were primarily devoted to "the act of wiping—of wiping babies, the sick, the old"; she saw that a socialist revolution that didn't bring women along with it wasn't worthy of the name (in this she admired Juliet Mitchell's analysis in *Woman's Estate*); she wished "for the abolition of the family," calling herself an "activist for voluntary motherhood," but didn't want to be shut up in a "feminine ghetto" and barred from having relationships with men. By 1975, Simone Veil had introduced a modern abortion law in France, and Beauvoir moved on to try to change the laws governing divorce. She also edited a column in *Les Temps modernes* called "Everyday Sexism."

Sartre died in April 1980. Beauvoir had to be stopped from embracing his corpse—his bedsores were gangrenous—but when the nurse found a sheet to drape over him she climbed up anyway, fell asleep on his dead body, and stayed there until morning. The thousands of followers behind his flower-piled Citroën hearse brought Montparnasse to a standstill; Beauvoir washed Valium down with whisky to get through his funeral and had to be given a chair when she got to the graveside. She contracted pneumonia a few days later, and while she was in hospital they found cirrhosis and motor neuron damage; it was months before she regained balance mentally and physically. Her last volume of memoirs, *All Said and Done*, isn't arranged chronologically, but according to the things she lived for: relationships and friendships first, then writing, reading, movies, music and painting, then travel and finally politics. (My favorite part of it is her list of dreams: it's comforting to know that she had a recurring nightmare in which she couldn't find a loo.) Those things brought her back to life: to her Sylvie was like Zaza reborn, or herself reincarnated; she made a last trip to New York, where she visited Kate Millett's feminist Christmas-tree-growing artists' commune; she wrote about Sartre's death and collaborated with Bair on her biography; she campaigned for a law against sexism and gave a series of interviews to Alice Schwarzer about her feminism. She took to receiving people at home in a red bathrobe, like the one her mother had worn during her last illness. When she was taken into intensive care with another bout of pneumonia in spring 1986, she tried to persuade her nurse not to vote for Jean-Marie Le Pen. She died on April 14. At her funeral, of all the passages of all the books she'd written, Lanzmann chose to read the last paragraph of *Force of Circumstance*:

> I loathe the thought of annihilating myself quite as much now as I ever did. I think with sadness of all the books

I've read, all the places I've seen, all the knowledge I've amassed and that will be no more. All the music, all the paintings, all the culture, so many places: and suddenly nothing. They made no honey, those things, they can provide no one with any nourishment. At the most, if my books are still read, the reader will think: There wasn't much she didn't see! But that unique sum of things, the experience that I lived, with all its order and all its randomness—the Opera of Peking, the arena of Huelva, the candomblé in Bahia, the dunes of El-Oued, Wabansia Avenue, the dawns in Provence, Tiryns, Castro talking to five thousand Cubans, a sulphur sky over a sea of clouds, the purple holly, the white nights of Leningrad, the bells of the Liberation, an orange moon over Piraeus, a red sun rising over the desert, Torcello, Rome, all the things I've talked about, others I have left unspoken—there is no place where it will all live again.

From the grave, Beauvoir clinches the argument. Life isn't supposed to be lived as some kind of example to others; all it is, all it can be, is a crashing together of moments. Simone went deep into those moments; her curiosity barely wavered. Her idea of a career is what I hope mine can still be: seeing the world, changing it if you can, writing novels and essays and memoirs, taking other younger women with you, loving deeply when you find love. For me, all that outlives the particularity of her life. Beauvoir couldn't come again—and thank God. But I have my heroine back, freed from her concrete block.

Sylvia

Four Augusts after I was divorced, I went on holiday to New-comb Hollow Beach on Cape Cod, where Sylvia Plath had spent her "Platinum Summer" of 1954. Not just gold, but platinum: she had survived a suicide attempt the previous August, and what better summer than the one you thought you'd never see? Lidija had come with me to the Cape. We had no vehicle and so, on our last day, we walked to the beach on the weed-grown verge under cover of pine trees, often in single file to avoid fast cars. Eventually we emerged onto the edge of this tendril of Massachusetts where Plath spent some of her happiest and freest times. The sun was sinking, and the sky was pink where it met the sea, rising up through tangerine, lemon, and pistachio to an ever-darker blue. We let loose our hair, we took off our shoes, we allowed the edge of the waves to foam over our toes. We'd heard there were sharks, so even this contact with the waters of Cape Cod Bay felt daring. The late summer day had been hot; I was fresh at last. I could not see where the beach ended.

We have developed many myths about Sylvia Plath since her death by suicide in 1963, but she had myths about herself too. She invented Lady Lazarus, who executed her comeback "in broad day" to shouts of "a miracle!" She gave life to Esther Greenwood, whose stay at an asylum lifts her depression enough to hear the "old brag of my heart": "I am I am I am." On her thirtieth birthday, Plath imagined herself riding through the Devon landscape on a horse, shedding "dead hands, dead stringencies" and announcing "I am the arrow." Both her novel, *The Bell Jar*, and *Ariel*, the collection of poems she completed before her death, are as much about rising again as they are about oblivion. She'd intended *Ariel* to start on the word "love" and end on the word "spring," and when her husband, Ted Hughes, as her accidental executor, reordered the collection for publication after her death, removing some poems he didn't like and promoting those he did, a parade of mythic women, ones who survive, ones who protest, ones who defy, vanished.

When I returned to Sylvia Plath's writing while I was trying to work out why my marriage ended, I discovered another Sylvia. I got married in pink partly under the influence of her, partly because my mother had also married, though not knowing or caring about Plath, in a pink knitted dress in 1977. (Both Sylvia and my mother borrowed the outfits from their mothers.) I had felt cowed, dazzled, overawed, scared, amazed by the woman writer I'd first read at seventeen, before I'd even had my first serious boyfriend. I liked my life to touch hers, then. I would (I do still) stop by her last flat in Fitzroy Road when in Primrose Hill, and look up at what was once her window. I wanted so much to claim her that I found myself mounting the argument that she was English, because she wrote her best work in London and Devon. But I also read her again because I suspected that something in me, some wrong idea I'd nursed, had started with her. I began with her first known letter and followed the thread chronologically through the journal, poems, fiction as she wrote them. This time around, her efforts to rise again seemed clearer to me. Her interest in the arts of living well—cooking, dressing, sewing, painting—were part of this, as were the poems she sent right back out again when they were rejected. I discovered Sylvia the divorcée, someone I hadn't known existed, right there between Sylvia the wife and Sylvia the depressive.

I discovered something else too: that her myth had less hold over me than it once did. There was something so sad about her life: it felt juvenile now, stupid even, to be taking a mid-century American woman's concerns as my own. Her intensity had not always served her well, and she'd exhausted herself trying so much harder than she needed to. She was bad at female friendship because everyone was a rival. I wanted my life to feel easier, less like I was trying to live up to an impossible ideal. And Plath couldn't help with that.

Plath's first surviving letter is to her father, Otto. She was seven. "I am coming home soon," she told him on a visit to her maternal grandparents in February 1940. "Are you as glad as I am?" It is also her only letter to him. He died nine months later, following complications after the amputation of a gangrenous leg: the result of undiagnosed diabetes. If discovered in time, diabetes was controllable in the late 1930s, but Otto had feared cancer and refused to go to the doctor. On the night her husband died, Aurelia Plath remembered thinking: "All this needn't have happened." Otto had been born in Germany, but arrived in Manhattan at fifteen. He studied entomology, writing a thesis at Harvard, published as *Bumblebees and Their Ways*, and taught at Boston University. There he met Aurelia, who was one of his students. During the First World War, Otto had lost his job and been questioned by the FBI about his loyalties to his adopted country, and his sense that he couldn't trust the people and institutions around him stayed with him, coloring Sylvia's childhood.

After his death, Aurelia moved Sylvia and her younger brother, Warren, to Wellesley, Massachusetts, so that her parents could help while she worked to keep her fatherless family afloat. At thirteen, Plath wrote to her mother from summer camp nearly every day. She reassured Aurelia by listing everything she ate ("Two bowls of noodle soup, one slice of bread, two help-ings of potatoes and cabbage"), updating her on her activities ("How I love metal work!"), sending poems she'd written for the camp newspaper ("The lake is a creature/Quiet, yet wild"), sharing her accounting (blueberry sales and pocket money from Grampy and Grammy on one side, a sketchbook and stamps on the other), and telling her she was happy over and over again, to the point that you wonder if she was. Aurelia worked hard, and she expected her children to excel academically. More-over, they had to fit in. Sylvia was already sending poems and stories out.

Through her writing, she acquired a fan, Eddie Cohen, after he read a story she published in *Seventeen* the summer before she went to Smith College on a scholarship. "I consider my story not far from the usual *Seventeen* drivel," she wrote. "Why is it that my particular brand of drivel rates such subtle flattery?" Replying to his reply, she started to flirt: "I like to think of myself as original and unconventional . . . my biggest trouble is that fellows look at me and think that no serious thought has ever troubled my little head." And then to worry—"Oh, Ed, don't laugh at me . . . I'm so pathetically intense. I just can't be any other way"—about the politics behind mutually assured destruction: "Even if you're for Pacifism, you're a communist. They are so small-minded that they can't give anyone credit for wanting life and peace even more than world-domination. I get stared at in horror when I suggest that we are as guilty in this as Russia is; that we are warmongers too."

The letters to her mother multiplied when she arrived at Smith. On September 26, 1950, two days after she got there, she wrote to her mother four times. (Is there such a thing as a helicopter child?) "I still can't believe I'm a Smith Girl!" she signed off. She took English, art, French, and botany and worried constantly about her workload, complaining that she has "to keep on like the White Queen to stay in the same place." When she got a B– in her first English paper, it made her feel "slightly sick." Sylvia Plath had to be good at everything. "God, let me think clearly and brightly," she wrote in her journal, "let me live, love and say it well in good sentences, let me someday see who I am." A farm boy gave her a kiss in the summer but she longed for more than going "from date to date in soggy desire." She went to see *A Streetcar Named Desire*, bought "'Vivid' lipstick—goes beautifully with my orange top"—drew a hot bath, took a sleeping pill and got eight hours. When she learned her scholarship had been endowed by Olive Higgins Prouty, a Smith graduate and the author of the novel *Now, Voyager*, she hoped she was good enough to deserve it. She was studying *The Mayor of Casterbridge*, and trying to "twist out a chunk of my life and put it on paper," as she told Prouty, under the influence of, in turn, Edna St. Vincent Millay, Sinclair Lewis, Theodore Roethke, Virginia Woolf, and Stephen Vincent Bénet.

When her friend Ann Davidow left Smith after one term, Plath's first letter to her, written through tears, told her that although she'd come third in the nationwide *Seventeen* short story contest, "what the hell do I care about artificial black & white 'success' if I haven't got a soul but my own perplexed self to talk to? God, Davy, I can't say how much I miss you." In her next letters to Ann, she had bucked up, and described visiting the son of family friends, Dick Norton, who was now a medical student at Yale. (Dick would become the model for Buddy Willard in *The Bell Jar*.) "Yale junior prom! Honestly, that Dick practically floored me!" she wrote to Ann. "Well, I got dressed up to kill in my old white formal, and evidently things took a quick turn from the platonic to the . . . well, you know." In her journals she fills in the dots: she let the "stiff white net slip to the floor," lifted a warm cat purring to her bare breast and then to "bed, and again the luxury of dark. Still the blood and flesh of me were electric and singing quietly. But it ebbed and ebbed and dark and sleep and oblivion came and came, surging, surging, surging inward, lapping and drowning with no-name, no-identity, none at all." Later that summer, she also dated Dick's brother Perry, though Dick had told her he'd like to marry her once he was at Harvard Medical School, a "let's wait and keep our fingers crossed deal," as she put it to Ann. She kept dating. "Always the dream," she wrote in her journal the next year, "loving two boys in one day differently for different times. Kissing both and loving both."

There is a greediness to all this, a relentlessness, a desire to have it all. But only men can have it all, she wrote in her journal:

> My consuming desire to mingle with road crews, sailors and soldiers, bar room regulars—to be part of a scene, anonymous, listening, recording—all is spoiled by the fact that I am a girl, a female always in danger of assault and battery . . . I want to talk to everybody I can as deeply as I can. I want to be able to sleep in an open field, to travel west, to walk freely at night.

At seventeen, she had told her journal: "I think I would like to call myself 'The girl who wanted to be God.'" And she would retain this intensity across her whole career. I'm sure this is one of the things I found liberating about her when I was seventeen, that she wanted so much and so baldly, so unashamedly. I looked at my own depressed English coastal town, and I wanted more, and didn't want to feel so guilty about it. Plath's ambition, though it was stranger and wilder and more antique than mine, legitimized the things I wanted. I uselessly longed and hoped and wrote instead of dating, writing fiction and applying for summer schools. I didn't think I was allowed to live the life of a writer, although that was what I wanted. Who did I think I was? I should aim for something I could get. But in reach were things I didn't want. My longing was punctuated with bursts of desire that lasted long enough to complete the form for Oxford. In those moments, I had some Plath in me. I wasn't waiting for permission that would never come.

Though I found some of the poetry hard to understand the first times I read Plath, I do remember feeling more than knowing that this was the real thing. "Daddy" shouldn't work: who could write a poem about fathers and husbands and Nazis and pretty red hearts, about Freud and Viennese beer and the Cape Cod beaches? Who would? Yet she pulls it off, and we are slack-jawed and mildly horrified. Marianne Moore would say that she is "too unrelenting" in *The Colossus*, her first book of poems; Robert Lowell would put the same thought another way by saying that in *Ariel* she was playing "Russian Roulette with six cartridges in the cylinder." Helen Vendler called "Daddy," wonderfully, "a tantrum of style." I also remember feeling at seventeen that I was liking something it was a cliché for me to like. I thought she was for girls like me who were told that they thought too much, who scribbled their feelings in a spiral-bound notebook they hid in the drawer of their bedside table. As well as a reminder that being like that was dangerous.

Dick was "out" soon enough, and other boys in, like Myron Lotz, for whom she writes the villanelle "Mad Girl's Love Song": "I shut my eyes and the world drops dead/I lift my lids and all is born again/(I think I made you up inside my head)." This poem, one of Plath's early favorites, is not in the *Collected*—Hughes left much of the early work out of the Pulitzer-winning volume. Her resistance to her mother was growing. Aurelia, she told her brother, "is an abnormally altruistic person, and I have realized lately that we have to fight against her selflessness as we would fight against a deadly disease." The "great god Gordon" Lameyer, a tall, handsome, American-jawed—I might as well say it—hunk, arrived in spring 1953, along with acceptances of three poems by *Harper's Magazine* (though they didn't take "Mad Girl's Love Song"), and the news that she had won a stint as guest editor at *Mademoiselle* in New York that June. In NYC she saw Tanaquil Le Clercq dance Balanchine, got ptomaine poisoning (which had her wanting "to die very badly for a day"), and interviewed Marianne Moore. By July, she was back home, writing Joycean love letters to Gordon, who had joined the navy. Her letter prose, usually loose and chatty, was changing, becoming fancier, swirling with in-jokes. But in her journal, she documented her disappointment at not being accepted for Frank O'Connor's writing seminar at Harvard as it leaked into every area of her life. It infuses her sentences too, which flicker between the first and second person:

> You looked around and saw everybody either married or busy and happy and thinking and being creative, and you felt scared, sick, lethargic, worst of all, not wanting to cope. You saw visions of yourself in a strait jacket, and a drain on the family, murdering your mother in actuality, killing the edifice of love and respect—built up over the years in the hearts of other people . . . Fear, big & ugly & sniveling. Fear of not succeeding intellectually and academically: the worst blow to security. Fear of failing to live up to the fast & furious prize-winning pace of these last years—and any kind of creative life. Perverse desire to retreat into not caring. I am incapable of loving or feeling now: self-induced.

She would turn this state into the image of the fig tree in *The Bell Jar*. Esther Greenwood returns home from what was supposed to be "the time of her life" in New York, one of twelve women from across America who had won a contest to work at a fashion magazine for a month. But magazine life seems shallow—the girls there think the Rosenbergs *should* be electrocuted—and her boyfriend Buddy is a hypocrite who slept with a waitress last summer. "I couldn't stand the idea of a woman having to have a single pure life and a man being able to have a double life, one pure and one not." *This* was what she'd been aiming at for nineteen years? Better to drop "clean out of the race." Esther imagines sitting in the crotch of the fig tree watching all the branches of her life—romantic, intellectual, academic, editorial, maternal—grow, bear fruit, ripen, and then, "just because I wouldn't make up my mind which figs I would choose," wither, until finally the dried-up figs fall at her feet.

Plath portrays 1950s America bitterly, and is cynical of even the best—a Yale-educated husband, a job in the big city, fancy clothes, parties with important people—that world could offer. Postwar America wasn't yet ready to let its daughters live as they wanted to. Back at home Esther learns she hasn't won a place on the writing course she hoped would erase the memory of New York, and a bell jar descends. Everywhere she goes, she is "stewing in her own sour air." The attempt to lift the bell jar will take her to one mental hospital after another, one psychiatrist after another, and finally to the electroshock chamber, where they grease her temples and let blue volts fly.

In 1953, Plath noted to herself: "You are afraid of being alone with your own mind." She didn't tell her friends about the way she was feeling in her letters until she herself was hospitalized. She wrote to Gordon on the first day of outpatient electroshock treatment, though she said nothing about it. She attempted suicide on August 24, and was found, barely alive, two days later. She received clumsy, floundering care—analysis, ECT, insulin shots, medication—in public Massachusetts hospitals, before landing, courtesy of Prouty, at the genteel-shabby private institution McLean, where Lowell went in some of his manic phases. She was analyzed there by the thirty-year-old Ruth Beuscher, who believed Sylvia had foundered while trying to reconcile her literary ambition with the call toward marriage. (Beuscher would share Plath's medical records with biographers after her death, and even at McLean she wasn't truthful when she promised there would be no more shock treatment.)

On Christmas Day, she wrote to Gordon to thank him for a copy of *Axel's Castle*, Edmund Wilson's study of the Symbolist poets: "Your letters, which I am just now growing able to fully appreciate, have made me want, more than any other single thing, to find my way back to the world which I am again sure I can love with a deep intensity once more."

After Christmas, she wrote a long letter to Eddie Cohen, frankly and clearly and quietly describing what had happened to her:

> I was sterile, empty, unlived, and unwise, and UNREAD . . .
> I became unable to sleep; I became immune to increased doses of sleeping pills. I underwent a rather brief and traumatic experience of badly given shock treatments on an outpatient basis. Pretty soon, the only doubt in my mind was the precise time and method of committing suicide. The only alternative I could see was an eternity of hell for the rest of my life in a mental hospital, and I was going to make use of my last ounce of free choice and choose a quick clean ending.

She tried to drown herself, "but that didn't work," and then she swallowed fifty sleeping pills on "the dark sheltered ledge in our basement," having left a note for her mother saying she had gone for a long walk. "I swallowed quantities and quantities and blissfully succumbed to the whirling blackness that I honestly believed was eternal oblivion." But she vomited the pills up, and was found when her brother was angered by a beagle howling outside of the house, and went to investigate. "I need more than anything right now what is, of course, most impossible; someone to love me, to be with me at night when I wake up in shuddering horror and fear of the cement tunnels leading down to the shock room, to comfort me with an assurance that no psychiatrist can quite manage to convey." She thought, she hoped, that the worst was over.

Gordon was going back over their discussions the previous summer, and he wrote to apologize for saying that "'men create art; women create people.' When I think back on it it seems to me such a crass and mean statement . . . I realized that women had not been given any near approximations of the opportunity for learning as man had until practically this century." Women writers need to know about their foremothers so they can answer back in conversations like these: yes, George Eliot and Virginia Woolf and Mary Wollstonecraft and Zora Neale Hurston and Simone de Beauvoir existed, and everything they wrote was in spite of the societies that were skeptical of their desire to write, and to live the way they did. How can you know what you could be without some knowledge of those who have done what you fear you can't? In *The Bell Jar*, Esther is warned that having babies will remove the desire to write poetry entirely.

In the new year, Plath was back at Smith, and in June she summered on the Cape with Gordon. It is through Gordon's faithful eyes that we see Plath in those immortal photos of the Platinum Summer: blond hair, red lipstick, and white bikini on creamy Massachusetts sand, alive when she could have been dead. Some have recently complained of objectification but I don't see it—when I was younger I simply saw the glamour, and now I feel her joy like a triumph. That summer, she got to be "a giddy gilded creature who careened around corners at the wheel of a yellow convertible and stayed up till six in the morning because the conversation and bourbonandwater were too good to terminate," as she said, reminiscing to Gordon afterward. In summer 2021, Plath's daughter Frieda put a tranche of her mother's possessions up for auction, including the tarot deck Ted gave Sylvia, their love letters, and their wedding rings. I was tempted by nothing—those are charged objects—apart from one thing: a snap from July 1954, right in the middle of the Platinum Summer. It is mostly of the sea and sky, but Sylvia is in the bottom left corner, smiling out of her blond bob. She is walking toward Gordon in a halter-neck, high-waisted white bikini, and her left hand swings out loose. She really does look happy. I planned to frame it in white wood under conservation glass and hang it above my desk. Rise again, rise again, rise again, it would say. And I bid on it, and I even seemed to be winning on my own birthday in July. I don't know that I'm sad, really, to have lost it (it went for multiples of what I could afford) but I know that if I was ever to be guardian of a part of Plath's life, it would be something from that summer, that Platinum Phoenix Summer.

She won a Fulbright to read for an English degree in two

years instead of three at Newnham College, Cambridge. In September 1955, she sent her first letter to Aurelia from England: "The 'bobbies' are all young, handsome, and exquisitely bred; I think they've all gone to Oxford." She went to the British Museum and to see *Waiting for Godot* and loved Foyles. In Cambridge, she bought Lucie Rie pots for her rooms and threw herself into studying, dating, acting. But women to admire, and to be friends with, were scarce. At Newnham, the dons were "all very brilliant or learned (quite a different thing) in their specialized ways, but I feel that all their experience is secondary, and this to me is tantamount to a kind of living death."

At the end of the year she went to Nice to meet Richard Sassoon, a Yale student she'd got to know in America the year before. He wasn't a blond navy hunk, but French, dark and ordinary-looking in the one picture we have of him from the 1950s: he has never spoken publicly about Sylvia, and the only letters we have are the ones she kept a copy of. She had written to him with her usual seductions: "do you realize that the name sassoon is the most beautiful name in the world. It has lots of seas of grass en masse and persian moon alone in rococo lagoon of woodwind tune where passes the ebony monsoon . . . I only want the moon that sounds in a name and the son of man that bears that name." The upbeat voice of the letters has been compared with that in her journals to make an argument about Plath's instability (as if that weren't an advantage for an artist), but she often sounds like her journal self in her letters to her boyfriends, and the playful way she writes to Sassoon is a relief after pages of advertising prose carefully targeted for an anxious mother. They walked the Promenade des Anglais together, but broke up by the end of the trip. "Will Richard ever need me again?" she wondered in her journal. "Part of my bargain is that I will be silent until he does." On February 20 she wrote "Winter Landscape, with Rooks," one of her first mature poems.

On February 25, 1956, she went to a party in Cambridge for a new magazine, the *St. Botolph's Review*, and "the worst thing happened, that big dark, hunky boy, the only one there huge enough for me . . . came over and was looking hard in my eyes and it was Ted Hughes." She recited his poems to him: "you like?" he replied. He snatched her red headband and kissed her, despite having a girlfriend who was in the other room; she bit him on the cheek "long and hard" enough to draw blood. "Until someone can create worlds with me the way Richard can," she told her mother a fortnight later, "I am essentially unavailable"; "Pursuit," her first poem about Ted, was enclosed: "There is a panther stalks me down/One day I'll have my death of him." A week after that, she told Aurelia: "Gordon has the body but Richard has the soul. And I live in both worlds." But by April she had chosen Hughes: "I have never known anything like it: for the first time in my life I can use all my knowing and laughing and force and writing to the hilt all the time, everything." On Bloomsday, they were married in Bloomsbury. Sylvia was twenty-three, and the plan was set:

> He is going to be a brilliant poet . . . I shall be one of the few women poets in the world who is fully a rejoicing woman, not a bitter or frustrated or warped man-imitator, which ruins most of them in the end. I am a woman, and glad of it, and my songs shall be of fertility of the earth and the people in it through waste, sorrow and death.

There is a moment in *Tess of the D'Urbervilles* when Hardy has Tess notice that among all the days of the year that mean something to her, there is one "which lay sly and unseen," the one on which she'll die: "Why did she not feel the chill of each yearly encounter with such a cold relation?" Reading Plath's letters, you feel the chill. Her birthday is October 27, her wedding day June 16, the day of the *St. Botolph's Review* party February 25, Ted's birthday August 17, Frieda's April 1, her son Nick's January 17, and the day she would die February 11, 1963. When she meets Ted—which is not the same as saying it is his fault—her death comes into view. He first drew her horoscope four and a half months into the marriage. Sylvia had "Saturn in 29 of Capricorn, on the cusp of the 12th, which is suicidal—especially opposite Mars in the 6th. All Correct." The Hugheses also liked to commune with spirits using a Ouija board (they mostly asked which poems of theirs would be accepted, though the spirits did once tell Plath to write about Lorelei, whose song in German legend lures men to their death). They believed in fate, even if we don't.

The Plath–Hughes marriage doesn't at first seem damned. They honeymooned in pre–package holiday Benidorm, going to the market in the morning, making love in the afternoon, reading and writing at night. Plath returned to Cambridge to finish her degree, and fearful her marriage would mean the withdrawal of her Fulbright grant, got Ted to stay away. *Poetry* magazine took her love poems: a good omen. "We shall be living proof that great writing comes from a pure, faithful, joyous creative bed. I love you; I will live like an intellectual nun without you; I need no one but you," she wrote to him in a letter that also detailed her errands and the conversation over the dinner table at Newnham. On the same day he wrote with two plots for short stories, an account of reading Wallace Stevens aloud, and an admission: "I neglected you. That's one of my most tormenting thoughts that I didn't suck and lick and nibble you all night long and it's a thought I shall never let myself in for again once I've had the chance to mend it." She commented on one of the plots: "Obviously she doesn't love her husband. She should delight to be raped on the floor."

Theirs was a fusional marriage: emotionally, physically, editorially. Plath was ambitious for both of them as professional writers in a way that seemed gauche, and perhaps even distasteful, in disguise-the-effort England, and she also, it seems to me, had a Lawrentian belief in love as one of her mediums as an artist. They were mutually nurturing in their shoptalk, on which we can eavesdrop in the letters. Ted queried the word "clearcut" in a new poem of Sylvia's, but added: "There's a terrific interplay of images and movement,—it 'comes off'—vile phrase—perfectly." She sent him details of poetry contests he should enter. They complained about editors; about one who says an animal story of Ted's is "abstract in conception," Sylvia said: "Well, what, for god's sake isn't?" and she fantasized about the *New Yorker* begging them for poems. But they were also just terribly, terrifyingly in love, dependent on each other to survive emotionally. "I feel so mere and fractional without you," she wrote when she couldn't stand it any longer, and proposed confessing to the Fulbright commission what they'd done. "I am married to you & I would work & write best in living with you. I waste so much strength in simply fighting my tears for you." Ted agreed: "To spend our first year—which is longer than most marriages last anyway—apart seems mad . . . I can hardly remember you without feeling almost sick and getting aching erections. I shall pour all this into you on Saturday and fill you and fill myself with you and kill myself on you." He moved back to Cambridge.

As she worked toward her finals, they lived in rooms in Eltisley Avenue, painting the first walls of their married life pale blue and raging about the "old smug commercial colonialism" of the Tories when the British bombed Egypt during the Suez Crisis. The winter seemed long. *The Hawk in the Rain* won the *Harper's* poetry prize; Ted believed that "Sylvia is my luck completely." She baked her own disappointment at rejections into orange chiffon pies and started writing a novel about Cambridge. "My life," she wrote in her journal, "will not be lived until there are novels and stories which relive it perpetually in time." They moved to America so that Plath could take up a job teaching English at Smith, but she was soon exhausted by working, and miserable that she didn't have enough time to write. She read instead: James, Woolf ("I shall go better than she. No children until I have done it"), and Lawrence. "Why do I feel I would have known & loved Lawrence—how many women must think this and be wrong!" They had a lot of morning sex.

In June 1958, she had her first poem accepted by the *New Yorker*. "Mussel Hunter at Rock Harbor" moves from the perspective of the hunter to that of the hunted, "dull blue and/ Conspicuous." She argued with the editor to have "river's/ Backtracking tail" instead of "backtrack tail" but agreed to the commas he added. The poem's acceptance was an encouraging way to embark on her first year of living by her writing, a year in which she was also being analyzed by Beuscher again as well as trying to get pregnant. She and Ted brought home a baby bird from a walk in a Boston park one day, but when the diet of milk and raw ground steak failed to build the bird up, Ted gassed it in a shoebox; one of their two goldfish died and the other was set free in a Boston pond; you fear for Sappho, the kitten they adopted.

When Sylvia became pregnant, they decided to come back to England, moving into a flat in Chalcot Square in North London in January 1960. Frieda was born at home and had her first bath in Sylvia's biggest Pyrex dish. "I don't know when I've been so happy," she wrote home. Ted had held a mirror so she could see Frieda being born. The poems Sylvia wrote that year were, she insisted, "bagatelles, light verse, not poems," though the *New Yorker* liked them. They accepted "Two Campers in Cloud Country," based on a moment from an American road trip they made the summer before. Away from the "labeled elms, the tame tea-roses," in a landscape of "man-shaming" clouds, "it is comfortable, for a change, to mean so little." Plath never worried about the changing climate in the way we do, but she read Rachel Carson's early work about the sea, and emblems of the natural world—elms and laburnums, blackberry bushes, poppies, the moon—appear again and again in the late poems. She was amassing a collection, and *The Colossus* was published in London a week after her twenty-eighth birthday. Ted looked after Frieda, their "living mutually created poem," in the mornings so that she could work, mostly on *The Bell Jar*, and in the afternoons she took the baby so that he could write. (At the beginning of their marriage, they had shared a writing table; her Rombauer—the American classic *The Joy of Cooking*—at his elbow as he wrote.) Ted later told their son,

Nick, that this period of their marriage was like "living inside a Damart sock."

Early in 1961 there was a miniature burst of creativity, presaging the one that would last for the final six months of her life. In a "low mid-winter slump," Plath's second pregnancy miscarried on February 6. (In a letter written late in 1962, Plath would tell Beuscher that Ted "beat me up physically" a couple of days before the miscarriage.) She took solace in Frieda's lalala, in typing Ted's play and in the Bergman movies they were showing at the Everyman in Hampstead. "We've had a sprinkling of clear invigorating blue days this week & I've had Frieda out in the park while I sat on a bench and read this week's *New Yorker*," she wrote to her mother on February 9 and 10. On the eleventh, she composed "Parliament Hill Fields": "Your absence is inconspicuous;/Nobody can tell what I lack," the first stanza ends. The speaker's winter walk home takes in a crocodile of small girls, a pink plastic barrette, a cloudbank, "I suppose it's pointless to think of you at all," writhen trees, the moon's whitening crook, blueing hills, and finally the lit house. In "Two Campers" the landscape pressed in on the poet, turning her into a fossil; here the poet's mood makes every forgotten hair clip significant. A nature poem has become a Romantic meditation. "The old dregs, the old difficulties take me to wife."

In March, she had her appendix out. She was brought orange juice, milk, and steak sandwiches by Ted every day: "To see him come in at visiting times, about twice as tall as all the little stumpy people with his handsome kind smiling face is the most beautiful sight in the world to me," she wrote to her mother. On her first night in hospital he also brought a letter from the *New*

Yorker proposing she have a "First Reading" contract with the magazine. "I had to laugh," Plath wrote, "as I send all my poems first there anyway." She read Agatha Christie and looked at the flowers sent by Ted's parents, Ted, and his editor at Faber. And she listens: "The British have an amazing 'stiff upper-lipness'— they don't fuss or complain or whine—except in a joking way & even women in toe to shoulder casts discuss family, newspaper topics & so on with amazing resoluteness. I've been filling my notebook with impressions and character studies." In her journal, which begins with a line good enough for poetry ("Still whole, I interest nobody"), she detailed her flowers, "daffodils, pink & red tulips, the hot purple & red eyed anemones . . . it is like an arbor when they close me in." She now had an editor who would listen, the love of her husband and daughter, her mother's altruism at a safe distance, support from friends in London, and nearly three weeks in an NHS bed to recover. The Saturday after she left hospital, she wrote "Tulips":

> I didn't want any flowers, I only wanted
> To lie with my hands turned up and be utterly empty.
> How free it is, you have no idea how free—
> The peacefulness is so big it dazes you,
> And it asks nothing, a name tag, a few trinkets.
> It is what the dead close on, finally; I imagine them
> Shutting their mouths on it, like a Communion tablet.

All the other flowers have disappeared and the red tulips remain, "too excitable" against the whiteness of the sheets and walls. Seeing that the letters are banal and the journal intense makes "Tulips" more mysterious still: we have all there is to have, and we still can't see quite how she's done it. But she knew she had: the *New Yorker* took the poem and she sent it to Theodore Roethke, whom she'd met earlier in the year and imitated in "Poem for a Birthday," the climax of *The Colossus*. She would also draw on the hospital atmosphere for "Three Women," her short verse play. Knopf soon accepted *The Colossus* for publication in America—she was no longer simply the poet's wife.

Plath and Hughes decided to move to Devon, where they found a thatched cottage with no central heating called Court Green in the village of North Tawton. The idea was to escape from Ted's fame in London, to be close to nature, to save money on rent by buying, and to have space for separate studies and their many babies (another was due in January). They placed an ad in the *Evening Standard* to sublet Chalcot Square, and tore up the check of the "chill busybody man" who got there first in favor of another couple, "the boy a young Canadian poet, the girl a German-Russian whom we identified with, as they were too slow and polite to speak up . . . the couple are coming to supper this week."

In September they moved and began furnishing their fourth home in as many years. It turned cold, another record-breaking winter, and it was months until they could afford carpets. "I am dying for a Bendix!" Sylvia wrote to her mother, complaining about the washing, and her mother found money for an American machine. (She also made her mother send over American vitamins, American bras, American cake mix.) Ted carpentered Frieda a doll crib for a Christmas present, and Sylvia painted it with hearts and flowers. The "repulsive shelter craze" made her wonder to her mother "if there was any point in trying to bring up children in such a mad self-destructive world" but Nick was born anyway, in January, with the Hughes "handsome male head with a back brain-shelf." She began reviewing for Karl Miller at the *New Statesman*, won the Guinness Poetry Award for "Insomniac" and a $2,000 Saxton grant for *The Bell Jar*, which she planned to dedicate to her analyst. "I would love to have the dedication to R.B.," Beuscher replied. "I have often thought, if I 'cure' no one else in my whole career, you are enough." In a letter to her London publisher, she defended the novel from "the libel issue": "Buddy Willard is based on a real boy—but I think indistinguishable from all the blond, blue-eyed boys who have ever gone to Yale. There are millions, and hundreds who become doctors. And who have affairs with people." She attended the local church, crossly—the Trinity was "a man's notion, substituting the holy ghost where the mother should be"—and befriended her midwife, Winifred Davies. "I find myself liking baby talk," she told Marcia Brown, her closest friend from her college days, "but I miss the other things—notions, ideas, I don't know what." In spring, the bank bloomed yellow with daffodils.

But in early July, she picked up the phone to a woman's voice: "Can I see you?" Ted said he had no idea who it was. "I was pretty sure who it was," Sylvia wrote to Beuscher.

A girl who works in an ad agency in London, very sophisticated, and who, with her second poet-husband, took over the lease on our London flat. We'd had them down for a weekend, and I'd walked in on them (Ted & she) tête-à-tête in the kitchen & Ted had shot me a look of pure hate. She smiled & stared at me curiously the rest of the weekend.

After a sleepless night, he took the train to London for a "holiday." Ted told Sylvia he "loved her and the children, would come back and hadn't touched another woman since we were married. I have discontinued the phone, for I can't stand waiting, every minute, to hear that girl breathing at the end of it, my voice at her fingertips, my life & happiness on her plate." Sylvia's idea of herself and the life she was living was shattered.

> I am simply not cool & sophisticated. My marriage is the center of my being, I have given everything without reserve . . . I write, not in compensation, out of sorrow, but from an overflow, a surplus, of joy . . . I feel ugly and a fool, when I have felt so beautiful & capable of being a wonderful happy mother and wife and writing novels for fun & money. I am just sick. What can I do?

In her next letter to Beuscher, nine days later, things already seemed different. "What has this Weavy Asshole (her name is actually Assia Wevill) got that I haven't . . . I mean I was not schooled with love for two years by my French lover for nothing . . . I'm damned if I am going to be a wife-mother every minute of the day." With the blow came exhilaration, and electroshock *The Bell Jar*–era imagery: "It broke a tight circuit wide open, a destructive circuit, a deadening circuit & let in a lot of pain, air and real elation. I feel very elated." What sort of life was she living anyway?

Her next two letters were to two men she would make passes at, the critic Al Alvarez and the poet Richard Murphy.

*

In 2018, Frieda auctioned a number of her parents' possessions at Bonhams. (She held a second sale three years later, including the photo from the Platinum Summer.) In Mayfair, I held Sylvia's beloved Rombauer, the binding missing from overuse, the recipes annotated in her unjoined-up, childishly angular handwriting. I wondered what the underlined "Shrimp Wiggle" was, but wasn't about to make it myself. But I had cooked like Sylvia, or rather my mother had, coming across a recipe in the *Guardian Weekend* magazine for the Plath family tomato soup cake with vanilla frosting, and bringing it out as a surprise with candles for my twenty-eighth birthday. (Sylvia to Aurelia in September 1961: "How many ounces are there in an American tomato soup can you use for tomato soup cake? I didn't think to question, but our cans seem to be bigger than yours, as my cake was a bit 'wet.'" It's true: in America soup mostly comes concentrated, in smaller cans.)

My idea of marriage was a Plath–Hughes one: meeting at Oxford, honeymooning in Venice, sharing a study, writing a book each, painting our living room French gray, babies in view. I had "love set you going," the first words of *Ariel*, engraved inside my wedding ring. I wanted that fusional marriage yet I lost myself in it; it broke down when our fantasies for each other clashed instead of harmonized. He imagined me pushing a pram in red lipstick, while I worried that I wouldn't be able to keep myself showered. I imagined negotiating for time to write and only managing a sentence before he came home from the park with the stroller: neither baby nor book. The idea of a shared life, a place I could live, where I would be believed in and valued, crumbled. After twelve years together, my marriage was over in less than a year of raising the questions. I was thirty-four, stunned and exultant. I wanted to understand why it ended, what had changed, and I asked and asked—of friends, in therapy, when high, when sober, of serious books, of stupid ones—and it was six years later, chatting to Frances, that something was offered that finally made sense. I'd met Frances during my post-divorce party-going phase: we were at Oxford at the same time but hadn't met then. She is a writer too, a fine one, of poetry and fiction, and her faith in me has brought so much to my writing, and to my life. We took long walks through the parts of northeast England she loved; we cooked together; we talked on the phone for hours about Tolstoy and D. H. Lawrence and Adrienne Rich and Jane Austen. On the phone that day, I was talking about the latest email I'd got from my ex-husband. "You've never seemed to miss him," she said. "It's your idea of marriage that suffered, I think." My husband had moved away, married again and had children. I was happy he had the life he wanted, and while we're in touch every so often, he's not a part of my life and that seems right. I had struggled because I believed in a certain sort of marriage and found myself unequal to it. But now I think anyone would find themselves unequal to such an ideal—Sylvia certainly had.

During my divorce, I remember thinking: am I victim or beneficiary? Sylvia's late poems suggest: always both. The speaker of "Lesbos," "The Jailer," "Daddy," and "Lady Lazarus" couldn't be more of a victim, but she expresses herself as if no one has told *her* that. The *Ariel* voice makes something glorious of a woman's always abject—divorced or not—position in the world. "Don't talk to me about the world needing cheerful stuff!" Sylvia wrote to her mother ten days after Ted left the marital home. "What the person out of Belsen—physical or psychological—wants is nobody saying the birdies still go tweet-tweet but the full knowledge that somebody else has been there & knows the worst, just what it is like." Another Sylvia emerges in late 1962, one that would no longer paint hearts on furniture: a badass nearly divorced Sylvia. It makes more sense of the odd junk-shop feel to Bonhams in 2018: a schoolgirlish green and navy tartan skirt had been put on a mannequin with a bright blue paisley 1960s top; a Victorian upholstered chair sat next to a glass and cane coffee table. But now it's clear: the schoolgirl skirt and the Victorian chair belonged to her marriage, and the silken paisley and cane coffee table to her new life.

Sylvia considered some sort of open marriage, but felt she couldn't stand it: "What I don't want to be is an unfucked wife." Ted came back from London and told her "this is a prison, I am an institution, the children should never have been born." His attitude was like that of the hawk in his poems: "I kill where I please, it is all mine. He was furious I didn't commit suicide, he said he was sure I would!" She was scared she'd become a martyr like her mother; she hated the evenings and could only sleep with the help of pills, which wore off at 5 a.m.—her Devon midwife suggested making coffee then, and working on her writing until Nick woke at 6 a.m. The lowest point came when she found Ted's poems about Assia, "describing their orgasms, her ivory body, her smell, her beauty, saying in a world of beauties he married a hag, talking about 'now I have hacked the octopus off my ring finger.' Many are fine poems." It was torture, she told Beuscher:

I am just frantic . . . I still love Ted . . . I am drowning, just gasping for air . . . I have no one . . . How can I tell the babies their father has left them . . . How and where, O God do I begin? . . . Frieda just lies wrapped in a blanket all day sucking her thumb. What can I do? I'm getting some kittens. I love you & need you.

At the end of this letter I was in tears, and had to stop reading. Plath received a reply from Beuscher before she posted the letter and added a PS: "Much better. The divorce like a clean knife. I am ripe for it now. Thank you, thank you."

The day Ted left, she wrote "The Applicant": "Will you marry it?" the salesman asks. "It is waterproof, shatterproof, proof/ Against fire and bombs through the roof." The next day, she wrote "Daddy": "I made a model of you,/A man in black with a Meinkampf look//And a love of the rack and the screw./And I said I do, I do." There is a recording from late 1962 of her reading both poems, her nasal Boston accent sneering cheerfully through the dramatic monologues: they are almost camp, the way she tells them, and funnier than they have a right to be. "Right now I hate men," she wrote to Beuscher. And to her mother: "I am up at 5 writing the best poems of my life, they will make my name." At around the same time, Ted wrote to his sister, Olwyn: "You're right, she'll have to grow up—it won't do her any harm."

In Devon, aged thirty with her husband gone, she rode horses and took up smoking. She learned how to keep the coal stove going all day—something Ted had never mastered. She did the paperwork, dug the garden, took the bins out. She had lost twenty pounds, but began cooking and eating again. "Ted may be a genius," she wrote to her mother, "but I'm an intelligence." She took up tarot, wondered about Spain to escape another winter. Women rallied around her: after a telegram from Aurelia, her midwife found a twenty-two-year-old trainee nurse to take care of the children while Sylvia wrote, with late poppies and cornflowers on her desk. Ruth Fainlight wrote supportively from Tangier, accepting the dedication of "Elm," and her family and friends in Massachusetts sent money and things for the children. But she refused to let her mother rescue her: "I must make a life as fast as I can," she wrote to her, "all my own." Prouty sent a check and suggested she go shopping. In Winkleigh, Sylvia went to the hairdresser, getting a more fashionable fringe cut in but keeping the long braid she curled around her crown. She went to Jaeger and bought a camel suit and sweater, a blue and black tweed skirt, a green cardigan, black sweater, and red wool skirt, with earrings, hair clasp, and bracelet made of pewter to match. She planned to raise the hems of all her old clothes.

On her thirtieth birthday itself, while the nurse watched the babies, she took a riding lesson with Miss Redwood. Riding over Dartmoor on a horse called Ariel had been a relief. That day, she wrote "Ariel," which would become the title poem of the collection that would make her name. Could the poem also be a manifesto of sorts, an encouraging note to self for this new life? She starts the ride still, "in darkness," but she is soon away:

> Something else
>
> Hauls me through air——
> Thighs, hair;
> Flakes from my heels.

White
Godiva, I unpeel——
Dead hands, dead stringencies.

And now I
Foam to wheat, a glitter of seas.
The child's cry

Melts in the wall.
And I
Am the arrow,

The dew that flies
Suicidal, at one with the drive
Into the red

Eye, the cauldron of morning.

I don't feel I will ever understand this poem, but that hasn't stopped me from loving it. It is broken yet coherent, austere and beautiful, sexy but scary, in the world and hidden from it, in motion and yet in one place. Heather Clark, in her modern biography of Plath, *Red Comet*, points out that it's one of the first poems about a mother who writes, moving over an imaginary landscape at her desk while the baby wails in the next room. In *The Bell Jar* Buddy Willard had repeated a saying of his mother's to Esther: "What a man wants is an arrow to the future, and what a woman is is the place the arrow shoots off from." But the woman, the poetess, is the arrow now, with sparks flying from her heels.

After her birthday, she made a trip to London—she had settled on moving back there, among friends, and found a flat on Fitzroy Road, where Yeats once lived. Alvarez had told her she was the first woman poet he'd "taken seriously since Emily Dickinson," and she visited him and read him her new poems. She also intended to go to a party that Ted might be at, with Assia. She was working on "Lady Lazarus." "O my enemy," Plath has Lazarus say, "Do I terrify?" She is expensive, a "pure gold baby":

> There is a charge
>
> For the eyeing of my scars, there is a charge
> For the hearing of my heart——
> It really goes.
>
> And there is a charge, a very large charge
> For a word or a touch
> Or a bit of blood
>
> Or a piece of my hair or my clothes.
> So, so Herr Doktor.
> So, Herr Enemy.

The Lazarene woman is a Jewish survivor of the Nazi slaughter, a sinner-survivor of Lucifer's fire, but mostly I like to think of Sylvia steeling herself against coming face to face with her rival, her ex, and all the gossipers, with the drumbeat of these fuck-you lines in her head: "Out of the ash/I rise with my red hair/And I eat men like air."

Soon she was back in London for good, furnishing Fitzroy

Road. "I have fresh white walls in the lounge, pine bookcases, rush matting which looks very fine with my straw Hong Kong chairs & the little glasstopped table, also straw & black iron," she told Aurelia. (This is the one I saw at the auction house.) "Now I am out of Ted's shadow everybody tells me their life story & warms up to me & the babies right away. Life is such fun." She was leaving the red of her previous life behind in favor of blue: "<u>Blue</u> is my new color, royal, midnight (not aqua!) Ted never liked blue, & I am a really blue-period person now." Frieda was slowly emerging from the shock; Nick was not yet a year old. She began filing for divorce and accepted Ted's offer of £1,000 a year for them to live on, low though she thought it was. *The Bell Jar* came out, under a pseudonym so as to protect the people she'd fictionalized in it, to acclaim. Ted visited once a week. "Everything has blown & bubbled & warped & split— accentuated by the light & heat suddenly going off for hours at unannounced intervals, frozen pipes, people getting drinking water in buckets & such stuff—that I am in a limbo between the old world & the very uncertain & rather grim new," she wrote to Marcia. (The next day, in "Balloons," she wrote of a child biting into "traveling/Globes of thin air" and being left with a "red/Shred in his little fist.") She was going back and forth to her sympathetic GP, who was prescribing a mixture of uppers, downers, and sleeping pills that could interact in unpredictable ways. Also on that day, Monday, February 4, 1963, she wrote to her analyst:

I feel a simple act of will would make the world steady & solidify. No one can save me but myself but I need help & my doctor is referring me to a woman psychiatrist. Living on my wits, my writing—even partially, is very hard at this time, it is so subjective & dependent on objectivity. I am, for the first time since my marriage, relating to people without Ted, but my own lack of center, of mature identity is a great torment. I am aware of a cowardice in myself, a wanting to give up. If I could study, read, enjoy people on my own Ted's leaving would be hard, but manageable. But there is this damned, self-induced freeze. I am suddenly in agony, desperate, thinking Yes, let him take over the house, the children, let me just die & be done with it. How can I get out of this ghastly defeatist cycle & grow up. I am only too aware that love and a husband are impossibles to me at this time, I am incapable of being myself & loving myself.

Now the babies are crying, and I must take them out to tea.

With love,
Sylvia

A week later, on Monday, February 11, the day she was supposed to enter an asylum again, Plath was found dead in the kitchen at Fitzroy Road. She had left milk and bread for her children, sealed the kitchen door, placed her cheek on a cloth on the opened oven door, and turned on the gas. She was thought to have died between 4 and 6 a.m., the time of day when her sleeping pills wore off. "Edge," written six days earlier, imagined a woman "perfected./Her dead//Body wears the smile of accomplishment." Ted Hughes, who was in bed with the poet Susan Alliston in the early morning of February 11, maintained that he and Sylvia had been "days" away from getting back together. "My love for her simply continues," he wrote to Aurelia in May 1963. The odd thing is that her last thoughts don't really contradict his: they could be reunited, but she would still have to find her way out of her old identity and into a new one. She would have to be born thrice. "I suppose suffering is the source of my understanding," she wrote to Prouty, "and perhaps one day I shall be a better novelist because of this." And perhaps a different sort of wife, who didn't think marriage was something she could only disappoint. I read this and I think: I shouldn't have collapsed myself into my marriage; I shouldn't have made my husband the arbiter of my worth as a writer, or a person, or anything else. I should have spoken up about the things that bothered me. Finding someone to marry so early protected me, in a sense. I didn't have any dubious sexual encounters in my twenties, I didn't get my heart trampled on, I didn't have to cope with anything on my own. By leaving my husband, I discovered, like Plath, that I hadn't grown up yet. I hadn't found a mature identity of my own and it has been unending, agonizing, confusing work over these past years to find one. But I have had the chance and support to do it, which Plath didn't.

I sometimes like to imagine that Sylvia Plath didn't die at all: she survived the winter of 1963 and she still lives in Fitzroy Road, having bought the whole building on the profits of *The Bell Jar* and *Double Exposure*, her 1964 novel about "a wife whose husband turns out to be a deserter & philanderer although she had thought he was wonderful and perfect." She wears a lot of Eileen Fisher and sits in an armchair at the edge of Faber parties, still wearing the double-dragoned necklace that was sold at auction, with the badass divorcée pewter bracelet on her wrist like an amulet. She is baffled by but interested in #MeToo. She still speaks Boston-nasally, but with rounded English vowels. She stopped writing novels years ago, and writes her poems slowly now she has the Pulitzer, and the Booker, and the Nobel. She is too grand to approach, but while she's combing her white hair and you're putting on your lipstick in the loos, you smile at her shyly in the mirror and she says: "What are you looking at?"

Toni

In 1989, Toni Morrison gave an interview to *Time* magazine. She had won the Pulitzer Prize for *Beloved,* but had not yet won the Nobel—which is to say she was the sort of famous that gets asked about social problems, but not the sort of famous that couldn't be needled. And Bonnie Angelo of *Time* magazine, who'd covered Kennedy's White House and Thatcher's Downing Street, didn't go easy on her. Toward the end of the interview, they came to the topic of single-parent households. Angelo contended that there was a "depressing" number of them, and a "crisis" in teenage pregnancies. Morrison didn't see the problem. Or rather she didn't think the problem was the young soon-to-be mothers, the problem was the rest of us. She raised a notion that's still extraordinary, something you don't hear said very often even more than thirty years later:

> They can be teachers. They can be brain surgeons. We
> have to help them become brain surgeons. That's my job.
> I want to take them all in my arms and say, "Your baby is
> beautiful and so are you and, honey, you can do it. And
> when you want to be a brain surgeon, call me—I will

take care of your baby." That's the attitude you have to have about human life.

Society doesn't want to pay for it. But why not hand money to teen moms? "The rich get it handed," Morrison said. "They inherit it."

Give cash to the poor, look after their babies when they want to go to medical school, and abolish the family in favor of the community. This is not what I imagined Toni Morrison stood for during the twenty years I knew about her but hadn't read her. She was one of the most famous living writers for half my life, and yet I underestimated her. I misinterpreted her regal bearing, thinking she was pious and conservative, not someone who'd give up her life for a single mom who wanted to be a brain surgeon.

Although *Beloved* was one of the first books I bought at sixteen with my Saturday job money, it remained on the shelf. In early 2020, during one of the book trading sessions among the staff of the literary magazine I worked at in London, where we always had advance copies we couldn't review, I acquired a special edition of *Beloved*, with somber dyed black edges. Climbing out of a depression then, crying in the bath less and less, I clung hard to reading, deciding I would read a book a week. There were other people who did this, I discovered on the internet. To keep myself on track I did something uncharacteristic: I made a spreadsheet. I would note down when I began each book, as well as basic information—title, author, date, length—about each one as well as a note on the gender and ethnicity of each author (as I would basically read only women if left to my own devices). I loved that spreadsheet. The rows stacked up, I greedily amassed data, adding my weird notes, finding ways to game even my own system by getting in a tiny book during a busy week, working out how many pages I needed to read a day, and letting certain books I really really wanted to read spill over into the following week. It should have been bloodless and robotic, but what happened is that every day I read Faulkner, DeLillo, Morrison, Steinbeck, Larsen, Baldwin, Salinger, Hemingway, Stein, and Bellow. (I'd accidentally started with *The Scarlet Letter*, and so had darted around in the American canon, following hunches and stray threads and undergraduate reading lists I found online. I didn't ask my friends, because then I would have to talk about the embarrassing spreadsheet.) I had an amazing time that year, much of it the first pandemic year. Of all the books that I knew about but had never read, I loved Faulkner and DeLillo, but the greatest discovery was Morrison.

"Shadows holding hands!" is the note I made in the spreadsheet row for *Beloved* in the week of January 26, 2020. And if I search within my emails I find I wrote about *Beloved* to friends. Each time I wrote about the book I struck notes of astonishment. "I also read *Beloved* for the first time," I wrote to Lidija, "and I couldn't believe how incredible that novel is: it's unfashionable, right, and so ubiquitous that no one tells you it's a masterpiece! Such a true novel." I remember cornering Paul at work, airing my first ideas about what I thought *Beloved* was doing. It was a novel searching for a form. Progress toward this would *have* to be halting, and the book would *have* to be sinuous, it would *have* to speak in different voices and styles, its narrative would *have* to be divided among the characters. It was too much for one person to carry. *Beloved* does what Woolf asked of the woman-authored novel, it finds a new form, and it even has the confidence to let you see its birth. Could *Beloved* be an example of *écriture féminine*? Paul smiled at me: he'd read *Beloved*, of course. Most everyone had. And he told me that there had been a course of lectures on women's writing when he had been at university that had culminated in *Beloved*. *Beloved* was what women's novels could, should, ought to be, and because of Morrison, are.

So this was the shape of one literary-critical argument I could mount, the sort of thing I could lean on in conversation with people who thought Morrison was wise and old-timey and lyrical instead of daring and contemporary and brutal. I didn't talk so often about the other things I liked about *Beloved*, and that I like more and more as I reread it. It is a story about formerly enslaved, currently traumatized people finding a way to build a life again. When you're trying to imagine how to arrange your life so that the things and people that seem most important to you are at the center of it, you often end up thinking about love. You are how you are able to love, to be loved, and sometimes how you are able to love is very little or not at all. One of the reasons I liked reading Morrison so much at this moment in my life was that she gave me a space to think things through. She herself thought fiction was "a haven, a place where it can happen, where you can react violently or sublimely, where it's all right to feel melancholy or frightened, or even to fail, or to be wrong, or to love somebody, or to wish something deeply, and not call it by some other name, not to be embarrassed by it. It's a place to feel profoundly." I was alone in many ways, but in my reading I had company for the big questions, fine company, who wanted nothing more of me—and did not force or require or implore—than my sustained attention.

Chloe Anthony Wofford was born in Lorain, Ohio, in 1931. Lorain, on the coast of Lake Erie, just west of Cleveland, was then a steel town, attracting migrants of many different races from across the US. (The mill was shuttered in 2017, but may yet reopen.) Her family had landed there during the Great Migration: Chloe's grandmother had brought her own girls out of Alabama when she thought young men were circling them. Chloe's father, George, worked at the plant, coming home one day to tell her he'd welded the perfect seam. (He signed it with his initials though he knew no one would ever see it.) He was wary of white people, turning visitors away at the door, while her mother, Ramah, would invite them in for tea. At twelve, Chloe became a Catholic (her mother was Episcopalian but she was close to a cousin who was Catholic) and took the name Anthony, which her friends shortened to Toni. She was on the high school debating team, the yearbook staff, and the drama club; she wanted to be a dancer when she grew up, like the first American prima ballerina, Maria Tallchief, who was from the Osage Nation. In her high school yearbook photo, Toni's hair is neatly curled under, not quite hitting her shoulders. She wears lipstick and there are gold hoops in her ears. In a documentary she participated in at the end of her life, her graying dreadlocks were purposefully arranged and her nails were painted in chic dark polish. And there are pictures of her in the 1970s with an Afro, leather jacket, and hoops again. Though it never looks like her image is overwhelmingly important to her (she let herself be photographed at her desk, dancing, hugging her boys), she nevertheless looks interested in the details, in elegance, in beauty.

To send Toni to college, her father took a second job, which was against union rules, and her mother handed out towels in an amusement park and sent her daughter the tips. Toni got a place at Howard in Washington, DC (where Zora had gone), to major in English. She acted there too, as Queen Elizabeth in *Richard III*, already displaying, in an enormous bifurcated hat, the majestic bearing I would come to misinterpret as stiff. She went on to graduate studies at Cornell, writing her thesis on Woolf and Faulkner, then to teach English in Texas, before returning to Howard in 1962. There she met a Jamaican-born architect, Harold Morrison, whom she would marry and have two boys with, and it was also where her novels quietly began. She joined a writing group on campus and started what would, many years later, and under different circumstances, become *The Bluest Eye*, her first book. She would never speak much about her marriage; the partnership didn't last long. The couple spent the summer of 1964 in Europe with their toddler son, but she returned to America separated, and pregnant. She decided to go back home to Lorain.

It is so much easier to see the shape of a life from its end. Harold Morrison went to Jamaica after the separation, and spent much of the rest of his life designing buildings there, becoming distinguished in his own right. If they hadn't split—though they did, so this is an idle thought—that could have been where Toni landed. One of the great American novelists lost to her native land! It seems impossible, which perhaps was one of the things she felt when she left him. When I try to imagine thirty-three-year-old Toni returned to the Midwest, pregnant while caring for a toddler, on her own now with no notion of what would come next, the imperious image I had of her softens. Yet even down on her luck, she maintained a bright backbone of confidence, the sort that Beauvoir possessed throughout her life too. She left the marriage feeling, I imagine, that she could cope. We know she didn't think being a single parent was a problem (though perhaps she had arrived at that opinion through experience, and didn't know it in 1964), and that her instinct would be to take her children back to her community. Needing work to support her family, she changed the address on her subscription to the *New York Review of Books* partly for the classified ads, and when three copies of the same issue turned up, each with a position vacant for a textbook editor in upstate New York in the back, she felt triply encouraged to apply. She got the job, and took her female-headed family to Syracuse.

A portrait of the artist as a young divorcée: lonely, tired, in a new place with few friends. The evenings are long and cold once the children are in bed, and she misses the community she grew up in. The songs she'd heard at home as a child; the ghost stories her mother had told her; the violin her grandfather had played. She takes out a story she began years before. She packs a pipe with tobacco, and smokes it while she's thinking, feeling, remembering. And then she begins to write.

Several novels later, Morrison was able to identify the conditions that brought her to writing fiction. She knew that her writing followed a period of depression, of loneliness, isolation, melancholia, such as the one after her divorce and one after her father's death. But she didn't see that sunken state as only depression. "It's an unbusy state, when I am more aware of myself than of others," she said in 1983. "It's not necessarily an unhappy feeling; it's just a different one." She was much more of a Wollstonecraft, who wrote herself out of a lull, than an Eliot, who wrote once she was loved and stable. "I would think I was at my nadir," she said, "but it was then that I was in a position to hear something." She could access another way of being: "Writing is discovery," she said in 1983, "it's talking deep within myself." She could explore her history and imagine her future. It "became the one thing I was doing that I had absolutely no intention of living without." Out of the ashes, she had a patch of freedom, and a method. She would always have it now, no matter if her books sold a few thousand copies, as *The Bluest Eye* did, or *Beloved*, which has sold millions.

Around the time she was making these evening discoveries, she moved to New York. The textbook publisher she worked at in Syracuse was closing regional offices, and so she was moved to the Random House building in the city. She lived in Queens, not wanting to forgo a garden, and made a life of her own. She didn't go to parties; she got up early as well as worked in the evenings; she snatched moments while she was folding socks, say, to work over her ideas for what would happen when she did sit down at her desk. Morrison once made a list of her responsibilities, in order to strike out the inessential. Being a mother and writing were the two things that only she could do, and so they were what she organized her life around. She put her desk at the heart of the house, not behind a locked door. "Shush I'm working," Joan Didion's daughter remembers her mother saying, and Didion is less than proud when she recalls this later. (I wonder what sort of parents would never have cause to say something similar? I certainly heard it from mine, who weren't writers at all.) "There was never a place I worked, or a time I worked, that my children did not interrupt me, no matter how trivial—because it was never trivial to them. The writing could never take precedence over them," Morrison recalled in 1987. "I would never tell a child, 'Leave me alone, I'm writing.' That doesn't mean anything to a child. What they deserve and need, in-house, is a mother. They do not need and cannot use a writer."

The Bluest Eye came out in 1970 with Holt, Rinehart and Winston, but attracted the attention of her colleagues on other floors of her office building in Manhattan. She switched publisher, and Robert Gottlieb at Knopf became her editor for the rest of her writing life. Jason Epstein, the president of the company, moved her from editing textbooks to commissioning books for a general audience. She used her list to publish Black writers, almost exclusively. "It's something Toni likes to do," Epstein told the *New York Times* in 1979, "and it can be useful." She coaxed Angela Davis and Muhammad Ali into writing their autobiographies; she brought out the daring fiction of Gayl Jones and Toni Cade Bambara.

It is nearly as common for editors to write books as it is to mourn the loss of the type of editor who would never write a book. Editing and writing are seen as distinct skills, and even antithetical ones. I have known editors who wanted to write fiction but could not escape the voice in their head perfecting every sentence before it is set down. I have known writers who understand editorial work as the primary way of introducing mistakes. Yet I have worked as an editor for the majority of my writing life, for more than eighteen years now. Editing at its best can feel like you are writing all the things you yourself don't have time for, and more beautifully than you could manage. Sometimes I've envied friends who are full-time writers, and longed to have days filled only with developing my own thoughts and setting them down. And then often I am so grateful to be part of a team, to have people to discuss things with, to ask advice of, and proud to see something I've worried over make it into print. I know that my experiences of being published have made me more understanding of those writers who don't enjoy being edited, even when they understand it's necessary. The best way I thought of it before reading about Morrison was to arrange the incompatibilities on a dial: there are editors who lean toward writing, and writers who lean toward editing, and I moved left and right across it.

The first thing to say, perhaps, about Toni Morrison's parallel careers as a writer, editor, and teacher in a university is that they were economically necessary. She was head of the household. A job brings regular income and, in the US, healthcare for you and your family. This is before you even touch the good that comes from being part of a community and influencing public discourse with what you publish or say in a lecture theater. Morrison saw what she did inside and outside the office as part of a single activity. "All of my work has to do with books. I teach books, write books, edit books, or talk about books. It is all one thing." And now that I have this thought—I add the caveat that Morrison is Morrison, and if anyone could do it all it was her—it helps me. Editing and writing: it is all books. It is all one life. She started writing, she would remind interviewers, because she wanted something to read. What she wanted to read didn't exist yet, so she wrote it.

When I told Sarah, one of my newer friends in New York,

someone I deeply admire for her feminist principles, that I was reading a lot of Toni Morrison, she said that *Conversations with Toni Morrison*, a University Press of Mississippi book edited by Danille Taylor-Guthrie, was a book she returned to time and again. One idea from that book that meant a lot to her was Toni's notion that Black women have the capacity to be both ship and safe harbor, because during slavery women both worked the fields alongside men and ran a household. Those two activities were never separate for enslaved Black women. "A grown-up—which I think is a good thing to be—is a person who does what she has to do without complaining, without pretending that it's some enormous, heroic enterprise," Toni said in 1981. "One doesn't have to make a choice between whether to dance or to cook—do both. And if *we* can't do it, then it can't be done!" It has sometimes seemed to me, never so acutely as in the period when I was trying to work out if I wanted to stay in an ever-more-traditional-seeming marriage or to jump into the unknown, that conventional womanhood is posited as a series of incompatibilities. One of the things that felt impossible to me was to have children and to write—I felt, or rather I feared, that I wouldn't be able to cope. It's not that Morrison doesn't see that writing and editing and parenting are in opposition, because they are, but rather that she decides to accept the oppositions and begin to sort of neutralize them by bringing them together. Do the elements that make up a life need to be in conflict? We need to do these things anyway, so why not see them as complementary, even compatible sometimes, and part of a full, broad, adult life.

About a week after the first draft of this book was completed, my father called on a sunny Saturday morning to say that my mother had stopped eating. I flew back to England from New York that evening, and for two weeks, I sat at her side with my family, often with my hand in hers. Mine bore the traces of a dusty pink gel manicure I had had with Lidija; my mother's was bonier now, her veins raised and visible, but her grip was strong. She curled her hand around mine, and if I tried to wriggle my fingers out she pursued them. She wanted to hold hands. My mother died three Saturdays later, her breath falling away jaggedly with my brother beside her. That morning she'd been holding my hand, if more loosely. One of the last things I did for her was wash her body, and put her in one last dress, with an abstract print of blue fans. I kissed her forehead, and smoothed her hands, my warm palm to hers.

As I was losing my mother, slowly and then definitively, I lost the sense that I could cope if I took on more, to be a daughter and a mother myself, an editor and a writer too. I lost my living evidence that women had always coped with things. Toni offers a solution to this problem: turn your parents and grandparents into ancestors, whom you can always have around you, encouraging you. Toni said she felt "endowed" by the "tenacity" of her female ancestors. I am still working out how to have my mother as an ancestor. I talk to her in my head; I address myself to the picture I brought home from her funeral, of her as a young mother with chubby baby me wrapped in her arms; I wear a diamond ring of hers. But sometimes—look at me, Mum! I say when I wear red lipstick like she did, or turn up for my yoga class—I manage it.

I feel more confident now that, like Toni, I can do more than one thing. I'm never not going to write: it's the way I live. But I can also see that I've learned to care for myself and others, by tending to my mother and my family while she was ill. I've come to a strange place: I can be happy in this life that I've made without a partner or a child, yet I can also see how my life could work with one or the other or both. One of my first feelings after my mother died was a sense that some margin between me and the world was gone; that the person I knew I could always turn to was no longer there. But grief shifts, changes, recedes, offers new ideas. Nearly three months after her death, I had a strong conviction that she wanted me to feel capable. It is my duty even to make good on her investment in me. She didn't put years of effort into my life for me to collapse when she couldn't be by my side any longer. The point was always for me to live on, and for her to become my ancestor.

The publication of *The Bluest Eye* in a run of 7,500 copies was met by good reviews. Morrison had started from something a friend had told her when they were children. She had prayed to God for blue eyes, and when her eyes hadn't turned blue, she no longer believed. It set Morrison thinking about where a Black girl had even got the idea of praying for blue eyes, and established the moral terrain of the novel. Stylistically, she staked out her own ground too. From its second sentence, you know *The Bluest Eye* will include the rape of a young girl by her father, and from the end of the first chapter, you notice a refrain depicting the perfect American family, which will recur throughout: both of these decisions show an experimental, confident, literary sensibility that makes sense when you recall that Morrison was thirty-nine when it was published. (I am thirty-nine as I write this; when I have worried out loud to friends that I am too old for writing, falling in love again, moving to New York, or any combination of the three, more than one has brought out this fact about Toni, unprompted. Toni has become an ancestor, the way Wollstonecraft was for Eliot, Eliot was for Woolf, Woolf for Plath, someone women use to encourage one another when our lives don't fit conventional shapes.)

The Bluest Eye is peopled with sex workers and cruel classmates; holy men and spoiled white children. It sometimes reminded me of the early parts of Ferrante's Neapolitan quartet, when Lenù and Lila are prowling the neighborhood to get their dolls back. In *The Bluest Eye*, dolls stand for the imposed standard of loveliness plaguing Pecola Breedlove and her sister—and so Pecola wants to dismember the dolls. "Adults, older girls, shops, magazines, newspapers, window signs—all the world had agreed that a blue-eyed, yellow-haired, pink-skinned doll was what every girl child treasured." Pecola demurs. "I could not love it. But I could examine it to see what it was that all the world said was loveable." This could almost be a statement of Morrison's project as it would unfold over the novels to come—she cannot love the racist world, but she could examine it.

Morrison's first novel was written because she wanted to read a story that didn't yet exist. She depicted Black life for Black readers, and that was part of the attraction for her. Her attitude to everyone else was: sure, you can come in, but these books are not for you. "Quiet as it's kept," *The Bluest Eye* begins—the phrase comes from the American South and means that there is a secret here—and those four words signal already that Morrison is not going to explain. But that is not to say, I don't think, that she would have disapproved of someone like me trying to write about her. It's true that she found publishing her novels to be a lonely experience because critics at the time didn't see the depth and breadth of the Black literature she was working with and against. But she also saw books written from within the African American community as equivalent to books written from Ireland or Russia or Japan, and noticed that no one required those writers to explain their communities to the rest of us. In 1983, she called out the author of a book on women writers for saying she didn't feel qualified to critique the work of Black women. "I think that's dishonest scholarship," she said. "I may be wrong but I think so, and I took the trouble to tell her that. I feel perfectly qualified to discuss Emily Dickinson, anybody for that matter, because I assume what Jane Austen and all those people have to say has something to do with life and being human in the world." As I read Morrison, it's the points of difference that pull me in. The things I learn have tempted me to write about her even though I'm not African American and have no lived experience of racism. I often feel reading her that she has solutions to things I'm struggling with, solutions I haven't heard before. I feel about Toni the way she feels about Austen.

For her second novel, Morrison wrote, there was an expectation that she should address the "'problem' of being a 'Negro' writer." This demand, she recognized, had a grand tradition—it had been asked of Zora, who also balked at it—but it also created a "no-win situation." She was not swayed, and *Sula*, one of my favorites, was the result. Sula and Nel grow up together in Medallion, Ohio. Sula goes to the city and Nel stays in Medallion, gets married and has children. Sula acquires a habit of freedom that women, then and now, recognize as destructive to the community. She "lived out her days exploring her own thoughts and emotions, giving them full reign." The attitude is deeply feminist, and even admirable, but it is also one that causes her to feel no remorse when she seduces Nel's husband. "I got me," Sula tells Nel. "My lonely is *mine*." The balance of rivalry and love in Sula and Nel's relationship makes me think of Lila and Lenù, Simone and Zaza, *The Bell Jar*'s Esther and her double, Joan. Morrison ends her story in a similar way to Ferrante: Sula dies and Nel is left with the thought that losing a husband is one thing, but losing a friend is another entirely:

> "We was girls together," she said as though explaining something. "Oh Lord, Sula," she cried, "girl, girl, girlgirlgirl."
> It was a fine cry—loud and long—but it had no bottom and it had no top, just circles and circles of sorrow.

Generations of readers have found it hard to like Sula, and to them Morrison has something to say. Whatever the inhabitants of Medallion "think about Sula, however strange she is to them, however different, they won't harm her. Medallion is a sustainable environment even for a woman who is very different. Nobody's going to lynch her or call the police. They call her bad names and try to protect themselves from her evil; that's all." Sula's not about to be canceled, exiled, or ostracized even when she behaves badly, and that is to the community's credit. In the preface to *Sula*, Morrison describes the circle of single and separated parents she relied on while living in Queens. "The things we traded! Time, food, money, clothes, laughter, memory—and daring." The character of Sula takes form under the sympathy she found in that community, and the courage it bred in Morrison: "In that atmosphere of 'What would you be doing or thinking if there was no gaze or hand to stop you?' I began to think about just what that kind of license would have been like for us black women forty years earlier." Medallion by way of Queens can both invent a Sula and contain her. The Black community, in both Morrison's life and her fiction, is a place where a woman who doesn't fit into the normal categories can thrive.

Morrison's next novel, *Song of Solomon*, was the one that changed her life. Written in the wake of her father's death, it imagined a young Black man's journey to find his roots, and describes the transformation that came from knowing them. It sold well and won the National Book Critics Circle Award; the success rubbed off on *Tar Baby*, a tragic romance across class lines. (One line I love from that novel, describing falling in love: "He unorphaned her completely.") In 1983, she left Random House, four novels down and about to start on a play. She would write full-time from her home alongside the Hudson River in Rockland County, New York.

In a later foreword to *Beloved*, Morrison describes sitting where the rocks meet the Hudson, close to her house, a few days after she'd left her editing job in the city. She was searching in her mind, perhaps as she had done most days of her working single motherhood, for the snag. The unreturned phone call. The item she forgot to pick up at the grocery store. The thing her son said to her when he came in tired from school. But there was nothing. "Then it slapped me: I was happy, free in a way I had never been, ever. It was the oddest sensation . . . It was a purer delight, a rogue anticipation with certainty. Enter *Beloved*."

It doesn't feel like much of a coincidence to me that Morrison wrote her best novel when she'd stepped away from her day job. But the feeling of freedom had an edge to it. Maybe there was an edge to George Eliot's sense of her own liberation when she left the *Westminster Review*; as perhaps for Sylvia Plath when she left her post teaching at Smith. Freedom can feel clear and light and it can also feel buzzy and slightly scary, and in gaining mine, I've seesawed between the two ranges of feeling, and at moments tipped into despair. Some of the first empty weekends after my divorce were vertiginous, with no one in them who needed me to cook, pair their socks, or go with them to the movies. Yet I could spend Sunday morning in bed with a novel or eat cereal for dinner or walk around naked. It is not always clear how to use freedom. In leaving her editorial responsibilities behind, Toni opened up a space for herself to fill—at last one not forced on her by sadness.

If Morrison was newly liberated, so were the characters in *Beloved*. The novel chronicles the work of getting free. All the characters in *Beloved* are officially free when the story begins, but before them is the more difficult task: to say what they did to get free. Part of the deep pleasure of the novel is watching the characters find ways of saying the impossible. They prepare the way, but they also just ask. Sometimes they stay silent; sometimes they know something they shouldn't and the storyteller is oh so relieved to drop her burden because the tale is known. There is pleasure too in watching Morrison—the writer not editor—revel in her freedom, roaming around in her own repertoire and finding the only shape her fifth novel could take, one that's intricate and obvious and new and old at once.

"Enter *Beloved*," Morrison says in her Foreword—and in her version, it happened exactly like that. Just as the novel decides a ghost can walk flesh and blood back into its family home, the novel I can hold in my hands was built from an apparition. Morrison describes looking out at the rock-edged river from her porch, and Beloved was suddenly there. "She walked out of the water, climbed the rocks, and leaned against the gazebo. Nice hat." From these two moments by the Hudson, Morrison could begin.

Beloved is a ghost story. Sethe, Baby Suggs, her mother-in-law, and Denver, her daughter, all know that their house at 124 Bluestone Road in Cincinnati, Ohio (a free state in the 1870s where slavery is illegal), is haunted by a baby ghost. The ghost of Sethe's daughter who died when she was two years old. At the beginning of the story, both Sethe's sons flee, scared off by a broken mirror and tiny handprints in the flour, so the house is unmanned in several senses. Denver wants to talk to her ghost-sister, and end the haunting. But when she calls her, all that happens is that the sideboard moves. Morrison often tells you the plot before the story has begun—the sort of thing more associated with a self-conscious writer such as Muriel Spark, who opens *The Prime of Miss Jean Brodie* by telling you the fate of every girl dazzled by their teacher—and she'll use the same technique in the two novels that come after *Beloved*. *Beloved*'s premise was found while Morrison was editing *The Black Book* in 1974, a compendium of newspaper clippings, pictures, and ephemera about Black culture and life. In it she learned of the 1856 murder trial of Margaret Garner, who had killed her baby rather than have the child returned to slavery. *Beloved* is powered not by plot but by a mystery: who's the grown stranger who one day walks into 124 and stays? (I admit the mystery has lost some of its hold now that the novel is so well known.)

Before the stranger arrives, an old friend turns up at Sethe's door. Sethe knows Paul D from her time at Sweet Home in Kentucky, when she was enslaved to Mr. Garner. Paul D is the last of the Sweet Home men, and he brings stories of that place with him, rising up out of Morrison's prose and into Sethe's and Paul D's mouths. Denver is amazed to meet someone who knew her daddy. Sethe is wondering whether this man who now shares her bed is someone she can relax into loving. In the new life, you have to learn to love again, or perhaps for the first time. Under slavery, love was suppressed—women were raped by their owners and the enslaved in general were treated as animals and bred. To love one particular person, for no other reason than they appealed to you, was daring, even dangerous. Paul D shouts at the baby ghost and then comes up with the notion that he, Sethe, and Denver should go to carnival and spend every cent of the two dollars he has with him. They drink lemonade and watch One-Ton Lady; they nod and swap smiles and pleasantries with the neighbors that don't come by the haunted house. They don't quite behave as a family yet, not just yet. "They were not holding hands, but their shadows were."

I used to find Morrison ubiquitous but there are some, then and now, who find her gushy. It's the lyricism they can't stand. How can a novel about rape, murder, and a racially motivated system of dehumanization such as slavery actually be about love? Isn't that just what we want to hear? That the insults of slavery could be survived and triumphed over? For these people, it certainly didn't help that Oprah endorsed Morrison so heavily, both on her televised book club, and in the movie of *Beloved* she produced and starred in. Morrison seems, in this view, like the sort of writer that America would have had to invent if she hadn't existed. You can explore the darkest sides of the history of the United States safely with her.

Morrison can seem sentimental—I get it, I see it, most of those enslaved died and left no trace at all, not even a baby ghost—but in reading her, I find that these cute moments, like the lovers' shadows holding hands, can be followed by strange, unassimilable, and even violent ones. Which is to say that the more challenging side of the system Morrison explores isn't obscured or glossed over: it is just not the whole of Black people's lives in that period. Even if you focus on the loving moments, the violent ones do not evaporate. I think people forget this when they think about Morrison, as a Nobel Prize winner, as one of the towering figures of American literature in the late twentieth century. Over and over again Morrison's novels are banned, because a parent opens *The Bluest Eye* expecting a history lesson and discovers it's about incest, or that the story of *Beloved* is set off by Sethe and Paul D fucking.

Beloved walks out of the water and into the narrative, under her straw hat. She is taken into 124 and is immediately besotted with Sethe. Beloved loves to eat sweet things and ask Sethe for stories: "Tell me your diamonds," she says, smiling, because she wants to know more about Sethe's life as the employee of someone who gave her crystal earrings as a present. The stories that had been too painful to air before the stranger arrived are now told, because Beloved delights in them. Paul D's memories start to spill out too. He has things to say that change Sethe's story; he carries parts of the narrative she didn't know about, details she is not sure she can hear and stay sane. If what Paul D says is true and her husband witnessed her rape by two boys who also drank from her milk-heavy breasts, how can she go on? How can she let the appalling memory get worse still? Paul D and Sethe understand that they can't yet tell all. Neither can write—they can't put their shame in a letter and slide it under Angel Clare's door as Tess does—and so all their remembering has to be spoken out loud if it is to survive. Morrison knew there could be no contemporary, firsthand sources for stories like those of Baby Suggs, Paul D, and Sethe (Denver has learned to read and write, because in Ohio it is legal for Black children to learn). Morrison fills the gaps in the archives with her own, historically informed, imaginings, and she is liable to hand her narration to a speaker. The oral quality of her novels is political. "Black people have a story, and that story has to be heard," Morrison said in 1983, the year she left editing. "There was an articulate literature before there was print. There were griots. They memorized it. People heard it. It is important that there is sound in my books—that you can hear it, that I can hear it . . . What you hear is what you remember. That oral quality is deliberate." It is both a trace of the way African Americans were treated in the US, and proof of Black vitality. (Morrison says more specifically that the sound comes from avoiding adverbs, and I think it is also there in the grammatical compression of a sentence like "tell me your diamonds.")

To Sethe and Denver, Beloved starts out a sweetheart, but to Paul D, she "shines." He knows what that means; he traveled the country relying on the kindness of female strangers. He spends his nights on a pallet in the shed to avoid Beloved, but she finds him, demanding not to be told stories but for him to touch her. Beloved has not a little of Sula in her when she makes this request; the part of Sula that is demonic and unassimilable. When Paul D says Beloved shouldn't treat the people who've been so welcoming to her this way, she reasons that Sethe's love for her isn't strong enough for her to care. They continue to sleep together in the shed, but it is not the betrayal that changes the plot, it is the telling of a story.

A neighbor shows Paul D a newspaper clipping, which he can't read but understands concerns Sethe. He has to ask her to explain. For the majority of the time they were at Sweet Home, their master was Mr. Garner, who was relatively enlightened. Under his regime, Sethe married, making her own choice of Halle, Baby Suggs's son. Denver, Beloved, and their brothers were born to parents who wanted them, and who behaved as their parents. When Mr. Garner died, a distant nephew, School-teacher, inherited, and it was under his rule that Sethe was raped, Halle killed, and Paul D put in an iron bit. Sethe escaped Sweet Home with all her children, crossing north from Kentucky into Ohio, but Schoolteacher pursued his property across state lines, and found them at 124. She had killed Beloved herself, instead of giving up her daughter. Paul cannot understand her story, her motivations. "Your love is too thick," he tells her. "Too thick?" she replies. "Love is or it ain't. Thin love ain't love at all." Paul D protests, and leaves. It is dangerous for Sethe to tell her story; it is better when someone already understands—someone who was there, like Beloved.

When Sethe finally works out who Beloved is, she is elated. Then the novel does an extraordinary thing and bears out its own promise. It lets its women speak, it imagines what those women sound like, and it gives the novel over to them, each in turn. (Plath tried something like this too, in *Three Women*.)

"Beloved, she my daughter," Sethe says, marveling that she can speak freely because she feels fully, deeply understood by her returned daughter. "Beloved is my sister," Denver says, thrilled by the idea that her sister has come back so that they can wait for their father together. "I am Beloved and she is mine," Beloved says of Sethe, expressing an infant's need to have her name said out loud, and echoing *Song of Solomon*. And then the women finally talk to each other, each repeating "she is mine" and each meaning something different. The story is theirs to carry together, and they've found their own language for it. I've not seen any of the movies of *Beloved*, and perhaps there is a visual way of marking this breakthrough, but really what happens in *Beloved* could only happen in a book—it's about language. Sethe, Beloved, and Denver break through; Morrison breaks through. *Beloved* is optimistic about what language can offer a vitiated world. Finding a way to tell your story in your own words is something in itself. Perhaps that's more important to me than what the book has to say about love, but then Morrison's characters find words because they want to be known by someone they love. Sethe's attempts to explain what she did to Paul D, and her responses to Beloved's demands to hear family stories lead her to break through. (It is a disconcerting thing that the dead are so often addressed in or by books, unless you see it, as I sometimes do, that books are a great way to hang with people you can't be with: I don't feel as much when I go to Beauvoir's grave in Montparnasse as I do when I read *The Second Sex*.)

Morrison's first drafts were written in the language of commerce, of daily life, perhaps even of advertising. And then once that shape was in place, she would rewrite and rewrite and rewrite, to bring the sentences closer to creating the effects that she wanted. (Much of her teaching was reminding her students that you do not destroy what you've written by working over it, you discover, rather, what you are writing in the process of rewriting.) So perhaps there is a metaphor there too, in the difficulties the novel must overcome to tell its own story: this is what Morrison knows of the effort to tell a story. The women's breakthrough isn't the end of the story (though it might be its climax), but instead it marks a change in Sethe's relationship with Beloved, and with Paul D, and eventually the wider community too. Something is understood, and then something can begin to shift.

Having got what she wanted, Beloved's sweetness begins to turn sour. She claws at her throat, curls up on the floor. Denver hears her mother telling her unassuageable daughter that she had murdered out of love. Nothing Sethe can do is enough, because Beloved cannot be brought back into the realm of the living. And it is not even clear if Sethe wants 124 to grow calmer. (The domestic space in *Beloved* is emoting from the first.) The bad-but-best mother in her is not sure she wants to be forgiven, not sure if what she tells her daughter over and over again is what she believes. "The best thing she was, was her children," is another thing she thinks is true, and yet if all mothers believed that, there would be no way out for any of them.

Denver turns to the women in Cincinnati for help, who see, as Sethe doesn't, that fair doesn't always mean right. Love, for some of them, is considered a serious handicap. But they save Sethe anyway, and with the ghost exorcised, the story can change again. Denver plans on studying at Oberlin. The last we see of her, a young man is calling her name, and her face in response looks like a turned-up gas jet. Paul D learns the ghost has gone, but that Sethe has been reduced by the battle. "There are too many things to feel about this woman," he thinks, and tells her "you your best thing, Sethe. You are." Their actual hands can touch now, not just their shadows.

The last suggestion the book makes is that one purpose of remembering (or, in the novel's own, quite pretty, coinage, rememorying) is forgetting. I suppose this is a psychoanalytic function of a kind, in that Sethe has returned to the murder in order to resituate it, and even incorporate it with the life she will live now with Paul D. *Beloved* does have a plot—a stranger comes to town, causes havoc, goes away—but like other novels it has been compared to (Harold Bloom suggests *As I Lay Dying* and *Mrs. Dalloway*) the novel is animated by questions and problems, relationships and difficulties of articulation. As the book comes to rest, it feels like something has been worked through.

For Morrison, *Beloved* was the first of three novels. *Beloved*, set in 1870s Cincinnati, was about mother love. *Jazz*, set in 1920s Harlem, took another anecdote from life and explored the sort of love that causes a young woman to think she should die for it. *Paradise*, set in rural Oklahoma in the 1960s, imagines the difficulties a Black-founded town might encounter as the world around it tries to modernize. (In this *Paradise* continues a conversation started in *Their Eyes Were Watching God*, when Janie is unhappily married to the all-Black town's mayor. Morrison didn't read Hurston until she'd already written, but she felt buoyed by the fact that people saw similarities in their work, as if there was already a tradition there.) *Jazz* and *Paradise* are distinct, unusual novels in themselves, and the relationship between them, perhaps like that between Beloved, Denver, and Sethe, is intriguing—but really it is enough to have written *Beloved*. Morrison was given the Nobel Prize for Literature in 1992 and the Presidential Medal of Freedom by Barack Obama in 2012. She died in the summer of 2019, when she was eighty-eight.

I could have seen, or could see, none of the writers of this book in the flesh—they are the ghosts I choose to live with—but if things had been different, I would perhaps have been able to see Morrison speak, to hear that voice for real and not simply on the page or on YouTube. I could torture myself with thoughts like these, of how belated I've been not just in discovering Toni Morrison, but in so many areas of my life. It is mysterious to me why it takes so long to articulate my feelings. I don't know why it takes years of waste, noodling and thinking and ignoring and reading, in order to write. It's exasperating to me that I spend time building obstacles to the things that are obviously good for me. (I did not sleep through the night for years after my divorce until I finally took the advice I'd heard a million times: wear yourself out in the day with exercise.) But I have to accept the mystery, stop getting frustrated with myself for not knowing then what I do now, and marvel that I did in the end find the things I needed to know, or that they, somehow, found me. Morrison always made good use of magic and of patience, and she must have been teaching me something with that, even when she didn't appear to be.

Elena

At the beginning of April 2022, halfway through my second reading of Elena Ferrante's Neapolitan novels, I discovered I was missing the final book, *The Story of the Lost Child*. I'd reviewed it when it had come out in September 2015, the first review I'd written after my marriage had broken down, and so I'd had an early copy. I must have lent it to someone who was as desperate as I was then to know how the story of Lila and Lenù, friends (if that's not too easy a way of putting it) since childhood, ended. I was scared to keep reading without knowing I had the final volume to hand—you can be reading a Ferrante novel and then look up and the sky has gone dark. And this second reading had been the same as the last: I read while walking along the street, while eating, while waiting for my computer to restart. If I needed to pee, I would wait until the story let me (or I just took the book with me).

I went to a bookstore on the way back to my office on Broadway from a coffee with a writer, and the woman at the counter said that lending books was as good as giving them away, and I agreed—though I actually think that is the best destiny for books, to be passed around and read rather than jealously guarded on shelves. I didn't say that though. I didn't tell her that it didn't occur to me to mind that I had to buy a new one; in fact I couldn't even remember to whom I'd lent my copy in London in order to ask for it back. I paid, I refused a bag, she tucked a branded bookmark into the front cover with the receipt. When back out on the sidewalk I opened the book, and noticed the dates on the colophon. The book had first appeared in 2015 in English, as I remembered. The edition I was buying in the spring of 2022 was the twenty-fifth printing.

There are so many ways of measuring time from the spring I left my husband to the spring that I'm writing this book on the dining table in the apartment I share with Lidija in Brooklyn—seven years by the Gregorian calendar, countless coffee spoons, a nephew born and gone to nursery, Trump and Brexit and Covid—but I like the idea of it being twenty-five printings of Ferrante. Why not measure it in the millions of women who went out, like me, to get themselves a copy of *The Story of the Lost Child*? Maybe among them there were those, also like me, for whom the reading of Ferrante would be bound up with a chaotic, glorious, fearful, terrible, liberating moment in their own lives. When you break up with someone, people often re-assure you that you'll feel better again someday, and they suggest when—next summer, or when you fall in love again, or half the time of the relationship just ended, I even heard a formula that had a six-month minimum plus a month for every year you were together—and I clung to all of those predictions. They came and they went. No one said it would take seven years, and yet here I am, more better than not, scarred but standing. I tried not to waste time but I didn't know how to do it faster. And sometimes seven years doesn't even feel that long ago, especially when reading Ferrante again.

*

It felt as if everyone was reading Ferrante in the summer of 2015. Truly everyone. And we all wanted to talk about it. I felt guilty that I would be the one reviewing it, getting to have my say, when we were all reading it, all having our own experiences. One of the appealing things about Ferrante was that the reading took place with others. It opened up conversations about the shapes a woman's life should and could take. I'd left my marriage with an inkling that there were more possibilities than the ones I'd allowed myself, and I was desperate for conversations about those shapes, and searching for the people to have them with. The people who liked Ferrante were good people for these discussions.

When I separated from my husband, I lived in the flat we'd bought together while he lived elsewhere, first with a friend and then in a place that we paid for out of our joint account. I tried to fill it with a life of my own, but I could only manage it in fits and starts. Ferrante inspired one of my first attempts. I invited friends over to talk about her: a former correspondent in Rome for a national newspaper, a political historian, a philosopher, an editor on the magazine I worked at, a publicist for a publisher. I made salad and ordered pizza, which I laid out in boxes on the floor; I mixed cocktails with the bottles of Campari and Martini Rosso I kept around then for late-night Americanos. From old emails, I can see it was August, and I remember the sash windows were open and we smoked inside. We smoked inside my former marital home and we talked about Ferrante. Not everyone knew each other, and so we did talk about the books: the addictions we had to them, the Lilas and Lenùs we knew and which one we feared we were, things we were starting to read about Milanese feminism and the Years of Lead in Italy. The next morning, I took a photo of the coffee table in the living room: an iMac, five tarot cards—the World, Justice, the Fool, Judgment, and Death—laid out in a row, an empty packet of Marlboro menthols, a torn brown paper bag of flat white peaches, an empty plastic box of Ferrero Rocher with gold wrappers crumpled beside it, my eyeglasses, several bottles of wine and an abandoned glass of white, kitchen roll, a hairband, an empty pizza box, and the now lost proof copy of *The Story of the Lost Child*, facedown. In the email chain the morning after, I told everyone that clearing up felt like dismantling a dream.

I loved that evening. When everyone left I wrote an email to the man I was in love with then, the one who had gone to Wollstonecraft's grave with me. "It was just fucking amazing," I wrote to him. "At so many points I looked around the room and was so in love and awe. I want to write something glorious that captures this moment but I'm not at all sure I can do it. I was the quietest. I just put my Dictaphone on. There was so much talk about dissolving the boundaries of the self and I kept thinking of Badiou and what he says about love accommodating the viewpoint of the other and I just thought yes!" It was a time when I was reaching out, beyond what I knew, crudely sometimes, childishly, hopefully, and trying to make a life I could be proud of, that would make sense to me. On evenings like that, my life did make sense to me. It was like a light turning on: yes, this is it, this is me, I have what I need. I didn't yet know if I could make any of this stay, if I could make shapes and structures, friendships and partnerships that would hold. I didn't even know if you could keep this sort of energy; I'd never really felt it before. It seems to me now, twenty-five printings later, that I was forcing something into being as much as channeling it—I needed things to be different and I needed accomplices. I was falling in love in so many ways.

When I came to write my essay about Ferrante, in that empty flat, I didn't need to close the study door and negotiate with my husband about the time I was coming to bed. I let myself write all over the house. I wrote at the kitchen table, and I typed sitting on the floor with my laptop on the seat of a chair. I took breaks where I played music loud and danced until I'd shaken the previous paragraph off. And I began with the idea that the Ferrante books were something I was living rather than something I was reading, listing all my friends and their reactions:

S. said she had got back in touch with an estranged friend to give her the first volume in the series; K. felt that, impossibly, embarrassingly even, the books captured how she'd gone about finding an intellectual identity for herself. And we couldn't stop talking about the experience of reading them: S. read under sodium-orange streetlight while smoking a cigarette outside a pub, unable to break off to go in to the friends waiting inside; E. had a week of violent dreams after she finished the first volume; A. had sleepless night after sleepless night to finish them, and walked to work the next morning her head still full of Naples; B.—a man—couldn't go on reading as he started to feel bad about being a man. I got so confused about what was real and what was not while reading Ferrante on a train that I kept on forgetting that I hadn't missed my station.

I wanted my friends there with me in my writing, so I put them there, right at the beginning. Like Beauvoir, I wanted to be free, but I didn't want to be alone. And I wanted what Ferrante was saying about life to get through to me too. I wasn't sure then, I remember clearly, what she meant to say to us about dissolving boundaries. Did she mean that Lila, one of the main characters, was going mad when she felt that? What were the boundaries? Was I dissolving boundaries in what I was trying to do in my life? What was I trying to do?

One of the freeing, and also frustrating, things about Ferrante is that she doesn't make public appearances, or tell us much more about herself than she was born in Naples. "Elena Ferrante" is a made-up name. As she got more famous, she gave interviews by email, and told us more about how she came to write, which books meant something to her, what she was trying to say, and why she wouldn't come out of the shadows. In 2015, all we had were her books and these interviews, but no one I knew was complaining that this wasn't enough. We felt we knew her in all the important ways you can know a person: she is for the workers, not the bosses; she is against convention; she values women's experience; she reads widely and deeply but prefers writing like a pane of glass. As a reader, I was relieved not to have to contend with context, gossip, noise, but just to look at what she'd written. This choice of hers reminds us that we can do things the way we want to—that if someone tells us that this is the way things are done, we are still nevertheless allowed to say that we don't want to do them that way. It reminds us that some privacy is needed when you are making something new. The position she takes shows us that we too can be judged on what we say or what we do—we don't need to take on what other people assume about us. We could tell all this from the novels before the Neapolitan quartet, which had the "dense expansiveness of a dream, or a nightmare, about them," I wrote in 2015.

I loved what Ferrante said about her women. They "don't submit," Ferrante said in 2006. "Instead they fight, and they cope. They don't win, but they simply come to an agreement with their own expectations and find new equilibriums." There is a moment of such accommodation in *The Days of Abandonment*. Olga is stuck in the house with her two small children. One of them is sick and the other is the nurse:

> The child had on his forehead three coins and in fact he was sleeping, breathing heavily.
>
> "The coins are cool," Ilaria explained. "They make the headache and fever go away."
>
> Every so often she removed one and put it in a glass of water, then dried it and placed it again on her brother's forehead.
>
> "When he wakes up he has to take an aspirin," I said.

I loved this moment of care, twisted as it is, from *The Days of Abandonment*. Ferrante's early novels are sometimes like parables, offering new ways of living, new solutions. Things fall apart, but the reader never loses hope that the strange experimental period is the prelude to some sort of new balance. I wanted to believe that this is what I was doing in my own life, even when it felt chaotic, and I was buying fresh packs of cotton knickers instead of washing the ones I owned.

Ferrante explained more about the beginnings of the Neapolitan quartet in a collection of essays, *In the Margins* (2022). She described moving past the early novels with the help of Adriana Cavarero, the Milan Women's Bookstore Collective, and Gertrude Stein, all of whom had ideas to offer about the ways writing can incorporate one life in another's. In Cavarero, she finds the sentence: "I tell you my story in order to make you tell it to me," and in Stein's *Autobiography of Alice B. Toklas*, she finds a passage in Toklas's voice calling Gertrude a genius: "I felt like laughing, a laugh of sympathy." One of the problems of writing as a woman, as Ferrante sees it, is having to repurpose traditions that have been invented by men. As the draft Ferrante is calling *My Necessary Friend* becomes *My Brilliant Friend*, and eventually the Neapolitan quartet, Ferrante decides to put the fight on the page:

> A possible answer seemed to me Stein's: adapting and at the same time deforming. Maintain distance: yes, but only to then get as close as possible. Avoid the pure outburst? Yes, but then burst out. Aim at consistency? Yes, but then be inconsistent. Make a polished, highly polished, draft, until the words no longer encounter friction with the meanings? Yes, but then leave it rough. Overload the genres with conventional expectations? Yes, but in order to disappoint them. That is, inhabit the forms and then deform everything that doesn't contain us entirely, that can't in any way contain us.

The scuffles are happening on the level of sentence, structure, and style as well as in the lives of Lila and Lenù who, even within the confines of mid-century Italian society, are finding ways to live that feel most true to them. Some boundaries must dissolve because women are living in a world that is not made for them. Defiance, Ferrante suggests, may be necessary. The tidy, obedient, nice, pleasing life women are especially encouraged to live will not produce geniuses like Gertrude Stein or Raffaella Cerullo. Beauvoir says this too in *The Second Sex*: don't do your prescribed reading, women, read something that attracts you instead; go for a walk toward the ocean you've never seen instead of diligent loops around the park; you don't have to stay married to anyone you don't want to stay married to—make your life into a shape that makes most sense to you, to you first of all.

Ferrante was taking moments of rupture as her subject, but she wasn't a guide. She didn't know how my life would turn out. Reading the Neapolitan quartet seven years after this crisis in my life, I can see that in focusing so closely on these moments, Ferrante is saying that change is a constant, it is all there is, and it's not always for the better. Sit still and the boundaries will dissolve; run toward change and the boundaries will also dissolve. I was tiptoeing toward this when I tried to write about it in 2015:

Lila is at a party on New Year's Eve on a roof terrace surrounded by everyone in the neighborhood; she looks around at the laughing, dancing, talking figures with a "sense of repulsion" and suddenly can't not see "how poorly made we are . . . how insufficient." The simple horrors of living in a mafia-dominated neighborhood (the next things Lila hears are gunshots) are as nothing compared to the terror of normal life. Lila sees people as constantly on the edge of breaking, of bursting their boundaries. A copper pot explodes while she is washing up; she tells Lenù that it scares her more than anything. The "cracked and crumpled" copper—like the "cracked tin kettle" in *Madame Bovary* that exemplifies Rodolphe's weariness at hearing Emma say "I love you"—comes to stand for worn-out forms. "I knew—perhaps I hoped—that no form could ever contain Lila," Lenù writes, "and that sooner or later she would break everything again." In the first three novels, a specific event disrupts things; in the Neapolitan quartet, Lila is the kindling force.

"While I'm slicing salami I think how much blood there is in a person's body. If you put too much stuff in things, they break. Or they catch fire and burn," she tells Lenù later on, after marrying the neighborhood grocer. She goes on to hope her marriage will burn. The shapes that patriarchy, capitalism, tradition have forced our lives into are too readily accepted; when we see clearly, we understand that they can't be tolerated. Lila feels that life is taking a shape which accords with her sense of things only when she leaves her husband for her lover, Nino, and even then only for a moment: "She had the impression that she had left a soft space, inhabited by forms without definition, and was finally heading toward a structure that was capable of containing her fully, all of her, without her cracking or the figures around her cracking." All Ferrante's women and men are struggling with the old forms.

As I read the books again, I tried to pay attention to the things that caused boundaries to break. Very often it was an eruption of anger: I think of Lila on her wedding night, furious that her new husband had capitulated to the Solara family's control, yet knowing that her anger would be punished with violence and rape. It can also be caused by a loss of money, of standing in the neighborhood, of a foothold in the world. I think this is partly what Lila notices on the rooftop: that whatever alternative she tries to build to the Solaras' domination, they will always find a way underneath, around, behind it. She can't be in their power, and yet it is not clear what other structure there could be.

There are many old forms hanging by a thread in the Neapolitan quartet, and one not insignificant one is marriage. Lila marries for shelter from poverty and domination, but finds herself beaten and trapped; Lenù marries into the class above her own, but cannot truly love the decent man she married. If not marriage, then what? One of the answers Ferrante seems to propose is that female friendship should be the pillar of women's lives. In 2015, I believed that too, as I have believed since I was a child, and still believe. My friends are the pillars I have leaned on again and again and again in the last seven years. One passage of Ferrante's I picked out has stayed with me for years. Lenù has a feminist awakening and wants to write about Lila:

> I sometimes imagined what my life and Lila's would have been if we had both taken the test for admission to middle school and then high school, if together we had studied to get our degree, elbow to elbow, allied, a perfect couple, the sum of intellectual energies, of the pleasures of understanding and the imagination. We would have written together, we would have been authors together, we would have drawn power from each other, we would have fought shoulder to shoulder because what was ours

was inimitably ours. The solitude of women's minds is regrettable, I said to myself, it's a waste to be separated from each other, without procedures, without tradition. Then I felt as if my thoughts were cut off in the middle, absorbing and yet defective, with an urgent need for verification, for development, yet without conviction, without faith in themselves.

My divorce was finalized just after Valentine's Day in 2016, our flat was sold, and my ex-husband moved to another country. The work of dismantling the old forms was completed, but what about the new? The man I was in love with then was gone from England too, and I'd lost confidence in myself as a wife, a girlfriend, a lover. I didn't know what other relationship I wanted to be in, and let myself do futureless things, just to see. A one-night stand that left me only with a love bite; a date with a woman there that proved to me I was straight. But there was a spark from the Ferrante evening that hadn't gone out, and I kept talking with two of those women, over cheap drinks and crisps in Soho, over feverish text message threads, over flat whites in bookshop cafés. We thought there would be a certain power in doing things our own way, together. I needed to do something like this, to prove to myself that I hadn't blown up my life for nothing. My need was emotional, and commanding, not that I understood it well then. I wanted to give myself definition, and I wanted to work with my friends, spilling over from these discussions about life to making something together and back again into those discussions. We wondered about a magazine before settling on reprinting the books we wanted to read but couldn't find for one reason or other—mostly books that had been written during the 1960s and 1970s, in the wake of the challenges to capitalism, the class structure, the racist legacy of imperialism, the position of women, the system of government provoked by the uprisings and rebellions of 1968. We named ourselves after a line in a Sylvia Plath poem, and we gave each other necklaces with a shiny silver disc, like friendship bracelets. At the launch party, I read out the passage from Ferrante about what a waste it was for women's minds to be separate, and I thought I was taking her advice in bringing a small press into being. If marriage couldn't hold me, what about other structures? This one was so beautiful.

On rereading Ferrante in 2022, I looked again at that passage about women's minds. It is something that Lenù thinks toward the end of the third book. She is not in contact with Lila; she has two children with the husband she knows she doesn't love. But she has gained support for her writing from the women in the family she's married into, her mother-in-law and her sister-in-law. It is through them that she heard about Italian feminism of the 1970s, which was particularly impatient with the structures of society. Spit on Hegel, Carla Lonzi wrote, spit on Marx, spit on Freud, on marriage, on Nazism and socialism, on war and the class struggle. Lenù wants to write something too about "the invention of woman by men" and starts to see links between the ancient and the modern, the Bible and Tolstoy and Duchamp's Rrose Sélavy and it is in the middle of this, which feels to me like the swirl of excitement you have when you are on the cusp of writing something, when sentences are almost involuntarily unfurling in your head, that she begins to miss Lila, and the connection they shared. Once she has this thought, that the separation of their minds is a waste, she pauses: "Then the wish to telephone her returned, to tell her: Listen to what I'm thinking about, please let's talk about it together? But the opportunity was gone, lost decades ago. I had to learn to be satisfied with myself."

I had completely missed that on my first reading, and I had quoted the passage many times, not just at the birth of the press. I had not paid attention to the fact that the Neapolitan quartet is full of breaks, periods of silence, arguments. A lot of the critical discussion of the books focused ecstatically on the qualities of female friendship, of what women can do together, but anyone who has been in a female friendship knows that they can be fueled by much darker forces, and that feminism itself can be a dark force. Of course this was always already in Ferrante. I think of one of the first major reversals in Lila and Lenù's friendship, when Lila has left her marriage and is working herself sick in the meat processing factory. Lila's partner calls Lenù for help and she uses her status as a published novelist and the fiancée of a well-known family to fix things: she takes Lila to a fancy doctor to investigate a heart murmur, she writes about the factory's working conditions in a national newspaper, she hires a lawyer to get Lila properly paid, she babysits Lila's son. A heroine! But has she fixed things? The neighborhood can't be fixed that easily, or with those methods. Lenù wonders what she was trying to achieve: "To change my origins? To change, along with myself, others too?" Has she "acted badly? Should I have left Lila in trouble?" She did what she could, used the new tools at her disposal, and she did make something happen. But what she thought she was doing and the effect it had were different things. A bad feeling lingers.

After three years, I left the press in the winter of 2020. I'd wanted so much from it, things someone can't ask from a small publishing venture. In going back to Ferrante, I found that so much of the excitement about the creation of it was imprinted into the novels, and the fact that the venture hadn't lasted in its original form made me so sad. But I hadn't noticed in 2015 that Ferrante knew this too, somehow. She also understands that not all structures last, and offers solace. After all, these four novels are being written because Lila has disappeared, and she does not come back. The fact that something ended doesn't make it a failure—a lesson, it seems, I must learn over and over again. A lesson I have to learn if I want to make anything new out of the material of my own life.

One of the shapes I didn't see clearly on my first reading of the Neapolitan novels was its structure. It's hard to see how something is made over the course of four novels, and the first thing that got in the way was the confounding matter of Ferrante's style. In 2015, I wrote:

> Ferrante has said that she wants a sentence, especially an opening one, to have "a cold surface and, visible underneath it, a magma of unbearable heat." It's a style that doesn't seem like one. The coldness comes from a concern with what is being said—the magma, perhaps— as opposed to how it is being said. Ferrante told the *Paris Review* of the polishing that went into the short, earlier novels; by contrast, she says that she often didn't even reread the novels in the quartet as she wrote them. "The greater the attention to the sentence," she said, "the more laboriously the story flows." There is a gossipy ease in the

style of Ferrante's Neapolitan quartet, a transparency, an aliveness above all. That first summer on Ischia, Lenù writes letter after letter to Lila, and gets only one back, at the end of August. It may as well be the platonic letter. "The voice set in the writing overwhelmed me, enthralled me even more than when we talked face to face: it was completely cleansed of the dross of speech, of the confusion of the oral; it had the vivid orderliness that I imagined would belong to conversation if one were so fortunate as to be born from the head of Zeus and not from the Grecos, the Cerullos." (Lenù later finds out that Lila had drafted the letter many times before sending it.) Ferrante's tone, too, is a sort of cleansed conversational one, capable of ragged flights of excitement as well as striking, aphoristic moments, often in the same passage.

I don't read Italian, but one of the editors of the 2015 essay asked me to buy a copy of the fourth Ferrante book in its original language, so that I could at least see if the sentences had a similar structure. I did, and they do. But even having an idea of the plot this time didn't break the spell. The omnivorous readerly speed stops you from seeing the larger shape. But since I first read the books, they have been adapted in ways that do allow you to see the structure. I gave the Neapolitan novels to Melanie, and when she was pregnant with her second child, we went together to watch the theatrical adaptation over two long evenings at the National Theater in London. It's hard to watch a story you feel lives inside you come to life, as something is always lost, and I came away from that first evening skeptical still. But on the second, covering the third and fourth books, I could see the book rising from its soapy twists into something bigger and more elegant. Lila and Lenù are able in the end to come together for a moment, to learn from each other, to make art and life interact. The structure that in the book is always threatening to break turns out to be capacious actually, stately and patient.

I hope that life is like that too, and that it is our perspective, here in the middle of it, which leads us to worry and plot and call lawyers and doctors and newspaper editors. While Lenù was contemplating the idea of calling Lila, her childhood love Nino literally walks into her apartment and back into her life, and with him, eventually, comes Lila. Perhaps another element of Ferrante's art is that it seems so much like life as you read, so random and surprising and impossible to predict, when in fact she is leading you safely home. You can see by the end something that was clearly visible from the beginning, if only you were looking for it. In 2015, I glimpsed this, I think, by the end of the quartet. When Lenù writes and lets

Lila's voice in—as Lenù let the violent husband's voice in, as she lets her mother's voice in, as she lets her children, her sister-in-law, her husband speak—she admits that the boundaries between people can never be maintained, that porousness is one of the conditions of life. And that it might not be one of the saddest parts of the human condition: that even, or especially, you might gain more by letting in a voice you find dazzling than you lose. Lenù goes on to write, in a brief frenzy reminiscent of the writing of her first book, a short novelistic memoir about her relationship with Lila, called Friendship. It becomes a bestseller, and a fixture of school syllabi. But it's not what we're reading. What we're reading is Lenù's attempt, over months of writing, to give Lila "a form whose boundaries won't dissolve, and defeat her, and calm her, and so in turn calm myself." In novels, art always wins over life: "I loved Lila. I wanted her to last. But I wanted it to be I who made her last." As Ferrante shows, the battle is never cleanly won.

Lila's restless, animating, dazzling power in the book, almost to make the book happen, isn't supernatural or diabolical or perhaps even literary. It's one result of her struggle with herself. She is trying to understand why Marcello Solara wants to dance with her when she is told he's a fascist, and her political awakening comes out of that discovery; she is trying to work out the reason she feels so obliterated in her marriage when she takes scissors to a photograph of herself in her wedding dress and makes an abstract collage out of it. The trouble comes from unease with herself. One of the questions of the book is: who is the genius? Is it Lila, who can synthesize different ideas to make original and dazzling wholes? Is it Lenù, who can fix so much life and feeling on the page? The question is unanswerable, and maybe beside the point altogether, because it is the dynamic between them that produces so much of the movement and excitement of the book. It is a question that Lila and Lenù are naturally obsessed by, but as I reread it this time, I felt less able to judge. Sometimes, because all I know about Ferrante is that she was born in Naples, I've imagined that the Neapolitan quartet is her autobiography. I like it that way, and it's a reading her anonymity can allow. But it's not a sophisticated reading, and having watched the play, the TV show, and going back to read the novels twenty-five printings later, I've wondered more often about the decisions Ferrante made to show us all the different possible shapes a woman's life could take. I can see more clearly too that hers is a chronicle, specifically, of the second half of the Italian twentieth century and of what might and might not have been possible for the women who lived there. Those of us trying to make a new life in the twenty-first century have a lot to learn, and we are so good at forgetting.

In the first volume, *My Brilliant Friend*, Lila and Lenù acquire some money when they ask the neighborhood ogre, Don Achille, what he has done with their dolls. Don Achille sighs wearily at the accusation he has taken them, made boldly by these girls on his doorstep, and pulls out his wallet. But they don't spend money on new dolls, they buy themselves a book. The book is *Little Women*. At once *Little Women* is their shared entertainment, their prized possession, the only book of their own they've ever had, but it is also part of their first plan for escaping the neighborhood. Together, they could write something like Louisa May Alcott did and sell their stories, a thousand times over. They would have power and prestige and their own means. *Little Women* takes four young women and shows us the twists and turns of their growing up, the routes both that are open to them and that they open up for themselves. Amy, Meg, Beth, and Jo are in some ways one character; a prismatic array of possibilities for women in late nineteenth-century America. Teach, write, die, travel, have babies. Jo and Amy even share a love of Laurie, like Lila and Lenù for Nino. And at the heart of both books is a *Künstlerroman*, nestled within the *Bildungsroman*—the story of all these women growing up is also the story of one of them learning to write, or more than that, discovering the possibilities that writing offers. Not the money, the independence, and the status, but the particular place between the private and the public where she can work with something that has happened in life—Lenù's feminist volume comes out of her listlessness at becoming a wife and mother—and allow it to be shared and discussed. When Lenù has left the marriage that has disappointed her and is bouncing between her lover, her children, and the public who want to discuss her arguments in bookshops across France, Italy, and Germany, she is thrilled at the contact with other women, and then disgusted at herself for parading as a feminist while Nino is forcing her to live as his mistress, unable to leave his wife. Back on the page is where she can make sense of it, in that uncertain space between what she can do in the world and what she feels. The page is where you go if you can't continue a conversation in person, for whatever reason. The blank page, which is always there, and has in fact never left you.

There are still people in my life with whom I went through the fire of 2015. When I spoke to some of them about my rereading of Ferrante, and the sadness I had about the things I started then but that didn't work out, they could see things I couldn't see. I had a life of my own now, one said, as a feminist critic living in New York. Others reminded me that everything I made is still there. And that the experience, the ashes at my feet, would allow me to go into something new again, something that suited me better.

I've been wondering while writing this chapter how successful I have been in making a new life. I don't know how to judge that success, or even if that's the right way of thinking about it. I left a marriage seven years ago and I'm single as I write this: I don't know if I'll have children, I don't know if I can write the novel I want to write one day, I don't know that I'll find love again. In the process of trying to build a life that I like, I have tried things, and they haven't always worked. I've found that any commitment to freedom I've made is equally haunted by the accompanying compromises: living alone meant that there was no one to hear the little triumphs of the day, no one with whom to discuss the news in the evening, no one to ask if they too think the salad dressing needs more salt. When things get on top of me, I'm afraid to be alone. It looks unlikely I'll become a mother, and there are days where that seems OK, and others when it doesn't. So I notice these things, accept them, shift what I can.

When I lived with Željka in London, we developed shared traditions that responded to the way we wanted our lives to look now: "boyfriend text" was an apology before asking if we needed more dishwasher tabs or olive oil; "school dinners" was the request for food that just needed to be transferred from freezer to oven and eaten in front of the TV, no judgment. Then again in New York, I have my traditions with Lidija: we have spent hours talking about our lives over morning coffee, while one of her black cats (the other one is shy) winds between us to be fussed over. These are some of the happiest living arrangements I have known, and I wouldn't have known them if I had stayed married. Perhaps it no longer makes sense to think of myself as on a quest to get free: in fact, all I've made are choices to lean my life one way—toward singledom, toward childlessness—and those choices have had consequences both glorious and deeply sad, sometimes both at the same time. (And it's not as if my friends who have chosen partnership and children don't often feel the same way about their choices.)

There are moments when I feel I am living out the promise of my own liberation, when I can look myself in the eye. But it doesn't feel like a process of refinement, and it still feels messy and incomplete. I look to Lenù and Lila for hints as to how to live, but like them, I feel nervous about declaring myself liberated. It is almost a cliché: any number of books, films, or TV shows explore women's liberation only to land them at the end with a man and a baby. What I didn't know before, and what reading these women's lives and works has brought me, is that there are many ways of doing good work and living a happy life, and that it is more unusual for that to happen within the conventional set-up than you might imagine. The examples I've chosen sometimes make me despair but often I think, well, she did, so at least I could try. I never thought I could be Simone de Beauvoir, but I've always known she existed, and at times when I've been utterly lost, clinging desperately to the crumbling fragments of my life, that knowledge has been enough.

I remember seeing on Twitter someone scoff at the way I portrayed myself in my essay about Plath—what idiot would marry in pink because Plath did?—and to be honest, I know what she means. Did caring so much about Plath and her writing lead me to a helpful place? I had such an idealized notion of what it was to be married to another writer, but I didn't have Plath's confidence in herself, and so I never valued what I was able to do in my own writing. If I don't think of these women as heroines anymore, maybe I can think of them as friends? Lenù doesn't always even like Lila, and she doesn't always take her advice. But she is always there. On the morning of my mother's funeral, my family and I were driven from our home to the crematorium behind the hearse, and for twenty nearly silent minutes, I watched the pale reed coffin and overspilling flowers—blue hydrangeas, pink roses, and lilac stocks—I'd chosen to adorn it. I thought it looked beautiful (I'd wanted the spray to be wild and pretty and heart-lifting, and it was) but I could not deny that I was going to an event I have never wanted to go to. Here was the truth: my mother would no longer be there, for any of my life to come. My mother was dead. Nothing would be able to compensate for this: not writing, not reading, not friends, not lovers, not the rest of my family. I was at the threshold I had no desire to cross.

But when I got out of the limousine at the crematorium my friends were there, waiting for me. Devika, Melanie, Frances, and Željka standing together in the car park on a sunny Saturday morning in June. My heart lifted as I saw them: I was going to be OK, because they were there. (Always, always go to the funeral.) I waved, as if I were the princess or the movie star they made me feel like, and they returned to me the kisses I blew them. My writers were there for me too. I didn't want to write a eulogy for my mother just then, so I gave a reading. I did try, but I couldn't think past the last paragraph of *Middlemarch*. I had been to funerals in lofty churches and with eloquent speeches given by famous writers. And I always knew, no matter what she had meant to me, my mother would never be celebrated like that. Her life didn't make the obituary pages; she does not have a gravestone. But I could see all the tiny ways she had changed me and those around me, with her own unhistoric acts. That was good enough for Eliot, and good enough for me.

Surely the best lesson these women writers, my friends and

teachers, have for me isn't that I should copy them, but rather that I shouldn't. Their example exists not in order that I might slavishly follow it but so that I might develop the confidence to let go of them and become the author of my own life. I know that the decisions I make might have consequences I don't intend, and all I can do is promise myself that I can and will deal with those consequences when they happen. The ultimate freedom might be to take the wreckage of your life and write your own story with it. That's one thing that Mary, George, Zora, Virginia, Simone, Sylvia, Toni, and Elena all offered themselves, and it is something I can offer myself. You can too.

Notes on Sources

For all the classic novels I've cited, I don't think it matters very much what edition they're in. I most often buy the one that strikes me as the prettiest, but secondhand is usually best, not least for the previous reader's annotations.

I read Mary Wollstonecraft's *Collected Letters* in the Penguin edition edited by Janet Todd, one of the preeminent scholars of early women's writing, but I was charmed by Ralph Wardle's *Godwin and Mary*, published by the University of Kansas Press, which interleaves her letters with his. There is also a Penguin Classics edition where they appear together, of Mary's *A Short Residence in Sweden* and Godwin's *Memoirs of the Author of "The Rights of Woman,"* edited and introduced by Richard Holmes, the great scholar of the Romantic period. There are many modern biographies of Mary: the one by Claire Tomalin, *The Life and Death of Mary Wollstonecraft*, is addictive and a good place to start reading more about her.

George Eliot: The Last Victorian, by Kathryn Hughes, is the modern biography of Eliot, but I preferred to read Jenny Uglow's short one, *George Eliot*, written for Virago in its heyday. *The Journals of George Eliot* have been edited by Margaret Harris and Judith Johnson for Cambridge University Press, and

Gordon S. Haight's *Selections from George Eliot's Letters* pulled nine volumes of life's work into one enchanting book, for Yale University Press. *Selected Essays, Poems and Other Writings* have been edited by A. S. Byatt for Penguin, which I picked up secondhand online. The edition of *The Mill on the Floss* given to me by my mother is the Oxford World's Classics one, with an introduction by Dinah Birch and Ford Madox Brown's *The Irish Girl* on the cover. It came out in 1996.

Valerie Boyd's *Wrapped in Rainbows: The Life of Zora Neale Hurston*, published by Scribner, is not only the best modern biography but also fun to read. Zora's letters have been arranged by Carla Kaplan into a pseudo-biography called *Zora Neale Hurston: A Life in Letters*, but she was never very open in her correspondence. All of Zora's published work is available in the Library of America, edited by Cheryl Wall into two volumes: *Folklore, Memoirs, and Other Writings* and *Novels and Stories*.

Hermione Lee's *Virginia Woolf* is the best biography of a writer I've read. It should be the model for literary biography: it is arranged chronologically by theme, so the chapter on her childhood also analyzes Woolf's writing about her childhood across her life as well as telling you what Virginia's childhood was like. Her diary is available in a one-volume version edited by Leonard Woolf, published by Mariner Books, as well as the full five volumes, published by Harcourt Brace. Her essays on writers and writing are collected in lots of different editions, but my favorites are the two volumes of *The Common Reader*, available easily secondhand.

The great majority of Simone de Beauvoir's work has been translated into English well—look out for translations by

Patrick O'Brian, who also wrote *Master and Commander*—apart from *The Second Sex*. Toril Moi explained the reasons at length in "The Adulteress Wife" in the *London Review of Books*, in 2010. If you can't read it in French, I prefer the old translation by H. M. Parshley, which at least is the one most readers from the 1950s until 2010 will have read, but you'll have to find it secondhand. Apart from *Memoirs of a Dutiful Daughter*, the other volumes of autobiography are out of print, although Fitzcarraldo Editions reissued *A Very Easy Death*, her short book about her mother's dying, in 2023. The Beauvoir Series at the University of Illinois Press has brought many of her writings into new translations with scholarly apparatus: the *Feminist Writings*, *Wartime Diary*, and both volumes of *Diary of a Philosophy Student* are my favorites of the seven produced so far. To get a sense of what Beauvoir's writing was like in English, it's fun to read her idiosyncratic, mistake-filled letters to Nelson Algren, *A Transatlantic Love Affair*, available from the New Press. *She Came to Stay* (translated by Roger Senhouse and Yvonne Moyse), *The Mandarins* (translated by Leonard M. Friedman), *The Woman Destroyed* (translated by Patrick O'Brian) are fairly easy to find, but other novels such as *Les Belles Images* (translated by Patrick O'Brian) and *When Things of the Spirit Come First* (translated by Patrick O'Brian) are the sort of things you come across when idly browsing. *Inseparable* is available from Ecco in a translation by Sandra Smith. I also love *America Day by Day*, her account of her trip to the United States in 1947, available in a translation by Carol Cosman from the University of California Press, but like many of Simone's books, it is probably fifty pages too long.

There are many biographies of Sylvia Plath but *Red Comet:*

The Short Life and Blazing Art of Sylvia Plath, by Heather Clark, is the most recent, and both scholarly, readable, and unhysterical. The chapters on Plath's last weeks and days are excellent: both moving and illuminating. *The Unabridged Journals of Sylvia Plath, 1959–1962*, edited by Karen V. Kukil, are available from Anchor, and *The Letters of Sylvia Plath*, in two volumes edited by Kukil and Peter K. Steinberg, are available from Harper. Her *Collected Poems* are published by Harper Perennial, edited by Ted Hughes: I'm waiting for another edition of the poems, as much of Plath's juvenilia, including "Mad Girl's Love Song," one of my favorites, is missing from the current edition. But I do recommend *Ariel: The Restored Edition*, put together by Sylvia and Ted's daughter, Frieda, and *The Bell Jar* and her short stories, *Johnny Panic and the Bible of Dreams*, are also available from Harper Perennial. Jacqueline Rose's book *The Haunting of Sylvia Plath* is wonderful (make sure you read the footnotes), as is Janet Malcolm's *The Silent Woman: Sylvia Plath and Ted Hughes*. Robert Lowell's appreciation of Plath, "Two Poets," appeared in the May 12, 1966, edition of the *New York Review of Books*.

There's not yet a biography of Toni Morrison, but I used Hilton Als's profile, "Toni Morrison and the Ghosts in the House," from the October 27, 2003, edition of the *New Yorker*, as well as what she said about herself in the several books of collected interviews: I relied on *Conversations with Toni Morrison*, edited by Danille Taylor-Guthrie for the University Press of Mississippi. If you can, get the editions of the novels from Vintage with her forewords, which are invaluable and illuminating. Her speeches and rare essays are collected in *The Source of Self-Regard*; her sole book of criticism, *Playing in the Dark: Whiteness and the Literary Imagination*, is a glimpse of what she was like as a teacher.

Elena Ferrante's fiction is available from Europa Editions, translated by Ann Goldstein. Her various interviews are collected in *Frantumaglia*, and a lecture series she gave as *In the Margins*, also with Europa. If we're lucky, she'll write much more.